SULLY

*and the growth of
centralized government in France
1598–1610*

DAVID BUISSERET

*Lecturer in History,
University of the West Indies*

EYRE & SPOTTISWOODE · LONDON

First published 1968
© *David Buisseret 1968*
Printed in Great Britain for
Eyre & Spottiswoode (Publishers) Ltd
11 New Fetter Lane, EC4
by Cox & Wyman Ltd
Fakenham, Norfolk

Distributed in the U.S.A. by
Barnes & Noble, Inc.

SULLY

Engraving of Sully, probably from the painting by Ambroise
Dubois (*BN Estampes*). The verses below lament his exile from
power after 1610.

To my parents

Contents

List of Plates

Charts, Tables and Maps

Preface

In describing the birth and development of this book I hope to be able not only to acknowledge the help received from many people, but also to explain the nature and limitations of the work. *Sully* as a subject was first suggested to me by Patrick Bury, Fellow of my former college, Corpus Christi, Cambridge; his help, and that of John Roach and other Fellows, was invaluable, as were the college's research grants. At first my intention was to develop a doctoral thesis limited to Sully's economic thought and action; this topic, which now forms part of chapter IX, was worked out under the direction of Professor Wilson of Jesus College, Cambridge. After a year of his tutelage I went to Paris to work under the supervision of Professor Roland Mousnier of the Sorbonne. There it became clear that the material existed for a much fuller treatment of Sully's life and work, and Mousnier, who had just supervised a thesis by Bernard Barbiche of the *École des Chartes* on Sully's financial work, gave me every help in undertaking this.

Aided by a grant from the British Institute in Paris, and by repeated grants from the French government, I was able for the next eighteen months to work on 'Sully and the development of a national administration in France, 1598–1610'. At the end of that time my college elected me to a research fellowship, which meant that for the next three years I was able to work out each of the chapters, often in article form, much more fully than would otherwise have been possible. For the three financial chapters I owe much to many conversations with Bernard Barbiche; we are now working together on a new edition of Sully's memoirs for the Société de l'Histoire de France under the direction of Professor Michel François. The chapters on the communications and the fortifications and buildings involved the study of new kinds of material, ranging from maps to lock-sites; in this specialized field I received much help and

encouragement from Roger-Armand Weigert, Keeper of Prints
and Drawings at the Bibliothèque Nationale, from R. P. François de Dainville, from General Nicolas, former commandant of
the French army school of engineering, and from the staff of the
map room at the Bibliothèque Nationale. I also received a most
timely research-grant from the Twenty-Seven Foundation to
help with this work. For the chapter on Sully's life in retirement I was able to consult the present owner of the château of
Villebon, M. de La Raudière. The book as a whole has become,
I hope, less pedantic, thanks to the repeated criticisms of John
Bright-Holmes, my publisher; and less ungrammatical, thanks
to the efforts of my colleague John Ingledew of the Department
of English at Mona. Finally the trials of my wife should not be
forgotten; apart from typing out the final version, and correct-
ing many obscurities, she has clambered with me over more
fortifications and other sites than we care to recall.

I am afraid that some readers will miss the familiar anecdotes
concerning Sully's life, stories taken from his memoirs and reproduced, for instance, in the *Sully* of Henri Carré (Paris, 1932)
or in the *Sully-le-Grand* of Marie-Madeleine Martin (Paris, 1959).
While some of these tales may be substantially true, it is nearly
always impossible to verify them, and so they will not be
included here. My aim has been to get away from anecdote and
to concentrate on the sources; what the work therefore lacks in
picturesqueness I hope it will gain in accuracy. Other readers will
miss the mention of 'proletarian' revolts, of the class struggle and
of the state as the instrument of the possessing classes. I have not
attempted to describe affairs in these terms, because I do not
believe that these concepts help to explain the emergence of the
French state. To over-simplify, it seems to me that the development of centralized government in France was primarily the
result of foreign pressures, and that domestic discontents played
little part in the process at this period.

The footnotes have been pared to a minimum, but the list of
sources is correspondingly more developed, in the French
fashion. Quotations have normally been translated, and so have
commonly-anglicized place names, like Picardy or Orleans. I
have tried in the plates to use unfamiliar material, indicating

in the footnotes where more accessible reproductions may be found.

The work has been finished in Jamaica, far from the great libraries of Europe. All the same, it has been possible to verify most of my references, thanks to the liberal acquisitions-policy of the University Library, and to fellowships granted to me by the Newberry Library of Chicago.

University of the West Indies,   DAVID BUISSERET
Mona campus, Kingston, Jamaica
October 1966

Key to Abbreviations

AC   Archives Communales
AD   Archives Départementales
AM   Archives Municipales
AN   Archives Nationales
Arch. Aff. Étr.   Archives du Minisètre des Affaires Étrangères
BM   British Museum: add. mss. Additional MSS
BN   Bibliothèque Nationale: ms. fr. Manuscrits français nouv. acq. franç. Nouvelles acquisitions françaises
Bib. Institut   Bibliothèque de l'Institut de France
Valois   Noël Valois (ed.) *Inventaire des arrêts du conseil d'État* (*règne de Henri IV*) (2 vols, Paris, 1886 and 1893)

ERRATA

Line 5 read: Ministère; line 10 begins a new reference at nouv. acq. franç.; line 15 read: *d'État.*

SULLY

Introduction – the sources

The chief narrative source for the work of Sully – and indeed for the history of Henri IV's reign as a whole – are his memoirs, rather oddly entitled the *Sages et Royales Œconomies d'Estat*,[1] which is normally shortened to the '*Économies Royales*'. The most accessible edition of this work is still that published by Michaud and Poujoulat in 1837,[2] which follows the editio princeps of 1662 except for some very minor omissions. A paraphrase of the *Économies Royales* was published in 1747 by the abbé de l'Écluse des Loges,[3] and this is the version most commonly seen for sale and in libraries. From the critical standpoint it is valueless, although it played a great part in establishing Sully's legendary reputation.

The editio princeps is based on the manuscript of the *Économies Royales*, which consists of ten volumes,[4] each one freely annotated by Sully with such instructions as 'after this chapter 32 the attached document must be printed and numbered chapter 33'.[5] These autograph corrections by Sully, which are generally followed in the printed version, make it clear that he was responsible for the work, even though it is written in the second person, supposedly by his secretaries

---

[1] For a discussion of Sully's use of allegorical language in this title, see the contribution of Jacques Pannier to *Un bon Français: Sully*, ed. G. Hanotaux, etc. (Paris, 1941), 102–5.

[2] in the *Nouvelle collection des mémoires pour servir à l'histoire de France . . .*, 2nd series, vols II and III (Paris, 1836–9).

[3] under the title *Mémoires de . . . Sully* (3 vols, London, 1747).

[4] BN ms. fr. 10305–10314; these volumes were extensively used by Christian Pfister in an excellent series of articles on 'Les *Économies Royales* de Sully . . .', *Revue Historique*, liv (1894), 300–24; lv (1894), 67–82 and 291–302 and lvi (1894), 39–48 and 304–39.

[5] BN ms. fr. 10306, fo. 119r°.

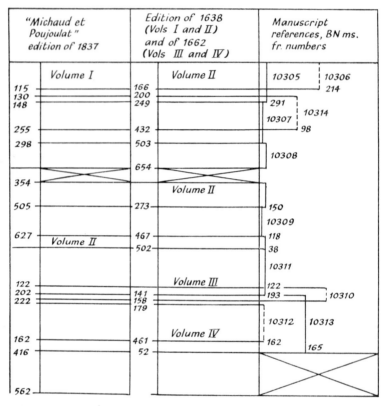

"Michaud et Poujoulat" edition of 1837		Edition of 1638 (Vols I and II) and of 1662 (Vols III and IV)		Manuscript references, BN ms. fr. numbers		
	Volume I		Volume II	10305	10306	
115 130 148		166 200 249		291 10307	214 10314 98	
255		432				
298		503 654		10308		
354			Volume II			
505		273		150 10309		
627	Volume II	467 502		118 38 10311		
122 202 222		141 158 179	Volume III	122 193	10310	
162 416		461 52	Volume IV	10312 162	10313 165	
562						

TABLE 1   THE RELATIONSHIP BETWEEN THE VARIOUS VERSIONS OF THE *ÉCONOMIES ROYALES*

addressing him. Table 1 illustrates the relationship between these manuscripts and the two main editions; it will be noticed both that some of the manuscripts overlap (in which case the originals are shown by a continuous line and the fair copies by a dotted line), and that the editions contain a good deal of additional material, mostly at the end of the last volume in each case.

In composing the *Économies Royales* Sully drew on several memoirs which he had drawn up at various stages of his career, on his capacious memory and on the numerous official documents which, as was customary, he had retained.[1] The first version was drafted after his dismissal in 1611 and before 1617. However, during the years which followed, moved as he was by current events and the apparent distortions of historians, he thought of a good many additions and amendments. These were incorporated in the first (incomplete) edition of 1638, and in the complete edition of 1662;[2] then, too, he omitted several passages of the manuscript, and it is these which we shall consider first.

Two were printed by the historian Christian Pfister in the late nineteenth century: the account of Rosny's[3] childhood used here in chapter II, and the political discourse of the 'sieur de Sigongne', which is discussed in chapter IX and which Sully had left out 'so as not to annoy anybody' – as he himself wrote. Pfister also mentioned an 'estat abrégé d'artillerie qu'il faut avoir devant Sedan' (for the campaign of 1606) which is used in chapter VIII. The other unpublished items of most interest in the manuscript are an 'estat de la faulte du fonds du domaine' and a 'memoire pour les gabelles de France'.[4]

The passages printed in the editio princeps but not found in the manuscript are more numerous; most concern the Grand Design, that supposed plan for a general European political settlement. Pfister has shown that many of these were added without much attempt at coherence or accuracy, but with the aim of misleading later generations over the bellicose intentions of Henry IV at the time of his death. Most of the other additions are 'éloges' or 'observations' of limited interest, although there is also a fictional account of Rosny's part in Henri IV's

---

[1] Richelieu began to put an end to this practice; see G. d'Avenel, *Richelieu et la monarchie absolue* (4 vols, Paris, 1884), ii, 328, note 3, and the interesting discussion of the question by James E. King, *Science and rationalism in the government of Louis XIV* (Baltimore, 1949), 148–9.

[2] For details of the early editions see Michel Riousse, 'Note sur les éditions des Économies Royales de Sully' (typewritten: Bibliothèque de l'Arsenal, Paris, Ms. 14021/26).

[3] *Revue Historique*, liv (1894), 311–12. 'Sully' took his title from the duchy he acquired in 1606 and I have used it when possible as being more familiar; however, in dealing with some events before that date it has seemed more convenient to give him his then correct title of ('baron' and then 'marquis') 'de Rosny'.

[4] BN ms. fr. 10311, respectively, fo. 90 and fo. 48.

conversion in 1593 and of his supposed embassy to Queen
Elizabeth of England in 1601.[1]

Even when the manuscript is faithfully reproduced in the
edition falsehood has sometimes crept in. Thus Sully has
claimed a part which he never played in the negotiating of the
truce of 1589 between the kings of France (Henri III) and of
Navarre (the future Henri IV), and has insinuated that the
royal mistress and prospective queen Gabrielle d'Estrées was
poisoned in 1598 by the Italian financier Zamet – a terrible and
unfounded charge.[2]

All the same, work on a new edition of the *Économies Royales*[3]
does not reveal many more such fabrications. Often it is possible
to compare authentic documents with those reproduced in the
Économies Royales, and to check on Sully's various estimates by
referring to administrative sources. Such comparisons generally
establish the accuracy of the *Économies Royales*, at any rate for
administrative history. Taking as an example the authentic
letters written by the king to Sully, of which it is possible to trace
about sixty,[4] we find that in each case the version of the
Économies Royales agrees with the original.[5] Other letters give the
same result; for example, the circular to the provincial financial
agencies printed in the *Économies Royales*, which corresponds
exactly with the copy of the Caen office,[6] or the letters to the
king and to the *chambre des comptes*, which both correspond again
with the originals in the Bibliothèque Nationale at Paris.[7] In
each case the only weakness in the version of the *Économies
Royales* is the date, which the secretaries got wrong because, as
'they' explained,[8] it was sometimes missing from their copies of

---

[1] *Revue Historique*, respectively, liv (1894), 313, and lvi (1894), 323–6.

[2] *Revue Historique*, liv (1894), 320–3.

[3] Which I have undertaken in collaboration with Bernard Barbiche,
conservateur at the Archives Nationales.

[4] Published among the *Lettres Missives de Henri IV* . . ., ed. Berger de
Xivrey and J. Guadet (9 vols, Paris, 1843–76).

[5] Except, as the editor remarks, for changes like 'mon amy' instead of
'mon cousin' in the king's address. Op. cit., vi, 347.

[6] Respectively, *Économies Royales*, ii, 257–8, and 'Lettres inédites de
Sully...', ed. Lucien Romier, *Bulletin Historique et Philologique* (1909), 569–70.

[7] Respectively, *Économies Royales*, ii, 243, and BN Dupuy 194, fo. 158;
and *Économies Royales*, ii, 177–8, and BN nouv. acq. franç. 239, fo. 105.

[8] *Économies Royales*, ii, 266.

letters. This also led to the printing of the same letter twice in different parts of the work,[1] but it is not a serious failing.

Sully's style, as Marbault, secretary to Duplessis-Mornay, acidly remarked,[2] was 'fortunately inimitable', and many of his falsehoods and fantasies announce themselves by the way in which he uses his own convoluted syntax in passages attributed to others, who might have been expected to write more elegantly. Again, some inventions may be detected by the elaborate preambles which he puts into the mouths of his secretaries who, when they wish to introduce a suspect document, often describe how they found it while rummaging about in an old drawer, or in some other unlikely place.[3] Others, again, may be traced by the way in which dates and places are omitted from the endings of suspect 'letters'.[4] While bearing these cautions in mind, then, we shall make limited use of the *Économies Royales*, comforted to some extent by the knowledge that the matter of administrative history was that which Sully saw least reason to falsify.

At the beginning of this century the historian Jean-Henri Mariéjol was able to remark with justice that 'souvent il n'y a d'autres documents que les *Économies Royales* pour contrôler les Économies Royales'.[5] This situation has been improved by the acquisition in 1955 of the 'Papiers de Sully' by the Archives Nationales in Paris. These papers consist of about fifty volumes, mostly of accounts, but also containing reports and a few letters. They had lain more or less unread at Sully-sur-Loire from Sully's death in 1641 until 1940, when a German shell – one of those 'braves cataclysmes' which Marc Bloch thought so helpful to historians – hit their sanctuary and necessitated their removal. After lying for some time in a New York warehouse they were finally recovered by the Archives Nationales, and are of course often used in this book. The Archives Nationales also

[1] For example, *Économies Royales*, i, 286a and 386b, 541b and 616a, and ii, 258b and 486b.
[2] He was one of Sully's most severe contemporary critics; his *Remarques sur les mémoires . . . de Sully* are printed after the *Économies Royales* in the edition of Michaud and Poujoulat. See p. 84b.
[3] *Revue Historique*, lvi (1894), 327–8.
[4] For instance, *Économies Royales*, i, 531a, ii, 65–6, 149–54, 212–18, etc.
[5] *Henri IV et Louis XIII* (vol. vi in the *Histoire de France*, ed. E. Lavisse, Paris, 1905), 52.

contain most of the *arrêts du conseil* for the reign; these were the legislative rulings of the councils,[1] and must form the backbone of any administrative history of the central government, even though their series is far from complete.[2]

In the 'Minutier Central' at the Archives Nationales are found the legal documents – deeds of conveyance, contracts, wills and so forth – from the hundred or so *études*, or lawyers' offices, of Paris. Each *étude* provides as a rule several large bundles of documents each year for the transactions witnessed by the *notaire* in charge of it; only about one-tenth of the collection has so far been catalogued, but for our subject there exist the printed *Actes de Sully* . . .[3] comprising the legal transactions which concern him from the *étude* of Simon Fournyer for the period 1600–10. No doubt other *études* contain more of these very informative documents,[4] but we have at least a good idea of their nature from this publication.

The other types of documents at the Archives Nationales of which considerable use has been made in this book are the registers of the various corporate bodies; the 'plumitifs' of the Paris *bureau des finances, cour des aides* and *chambre des comptes*.[5] The accounts of the proceedings of the equivalent provincial courts can often be found in the appropriate Archives Départementales. Thus I have consulted the registers of the *parlements* of Brittany, Burgundy, Guyenne and Normandy, of the estates of Brittany, Burgundy, Languedoc and Provence, and of the *bureaux des finances* at Bordeaux, Bourges, Caen, Châlons-sur-Marne, Poitiers and Rouen.[6] Unfortunately very little survives of the

[1] In contrast to the royal *édits, ordonnances* and *déclarations* they did not have to be verified by the sovereign courts (Gaston Zeller, *Les institutions de la France au XVIᵉ siècle* (Paris, 1948), 202).

[2] To the AN E 1A – series Noël Valois added *arrêts* from the BN and elsewhere in composing his *Inventaire des arrêts du conseil d'État (règne de Henri IV)* (2 vols, Paris, 1886 and 1893). The *Inventaire* is hereafter abbreviated to 'Valois'.

[3] Ed. François de Mallevouë (*Collection de documents inédits sur l'histoire de France*, Paris, 1911).

[4] There are, for example, artillery contracts in *étude* XIX (*liasses* 341 and 342) and *étude* CV (*liasses* 306 and 307).

[5] see chapter I for an explanation of these terms.

[6] Full reference-numbers for these documents will be found in the list of manuscript sources.

correspondence between these bodies and the central government; as the historian Armand Rébillon wrote concerning that of the Brittany estates, 'nothing survives of it and nothing can take its place'.[1] Such letters as do survive are mostly in the local provincial archives (see the list of sources, section B4).

There is no corpus of letters written by Sully as there is for so many other great French ministers, but most of the few letters of his which survive are at the Bibliothèque Nationale, in the 'Département des manuscrits'. There too is the splendid collection of 'Manuscrits français'; its origins are too diverse for detailed description, but, as will be seen from the list of sources, section B1, most of the documents from it used in this book came from the Parisian ecclesiastical establishments dissolved during the Revolution. Some use has also been made of the smaller collections of the Bibliothèque Nationale, collections often assembled by the ministers and *savants* whose names they bear, such as Clairambault, Colbert and Dupuy. The 'Département des manuscrits' also houses the 'fichier Charavay', an alphabetical card-index of documents which have come up for public sale; this is useful for obtaining details of material still in private hands, even if its entries are often tantalizingly brief.[2]

The Départements 'des estampes' and 'des cartes et plans' at the Bibliothèque Nationale have also provided much information for chapter VII, on the buildings and fortifications. But the best collection of maps and plans of this period is found in the British Museum,[3] whose older manuscript collections contain other useful material on seventeenth century France. Finally the lesser libraries of Paris should not be forgotten; much useful information has been derived from those of the Institut de France and of the Ministère des Affaires Étrangères.

---

[1] *Les sources de l'histoire des états de Bretagne* (Rennes, 1932), 49. See also the comments of Georges Pagès in his 'Essai sur l'évolution des institutions administratives en France . . . (1500–1700)', *Revue d'histoire moderne*, vii (1932), 8–57 and 113–37.

[2] Like those of the records of sales sometimes published in the *Bulletins de la Société de l'histoire du Protestantisme français*.

[3] BM add. mss 21, 117; see chapter VII.

CHAPTER I

The kingdom of France 1560–1600

Between 1560 and 1600 there was a lull in the process by which the Ile-de-France, centre of the French kings' domain, was gathering the rest of the provinces around her. Brittany had been finally secured in 1532, and by the Treaty of Cateau-Cambrésis (1559) a start had been made on the consolidation of the north-eastern frontier by the acquisition of Calais, Metz, Toul and Verdun. However, Paris remained very exposed to the east, with Artois and Flanders part of the (Spanish) Southern Netherlands, and Lorraine independent under its dukes. Farther south Franche-Comté was also under Spanish domination, and Lyons open to the attacks of the duke of Savoy from the north, while Roussillon on the Spanish border had yet to be absorbed. In the north-east and east the Somme, Meuse and Saône marked a frontier which was still a region rather than a line, although an attempt both at closer definition of the frontier and at its fortification was to be made under Henri IV (see map 1).

Under the French king were at least fifteen million subjects, as compared with the eight million of the king of Spain or the five million of Elizabethan England. Already for a century or so Paris had been the acknowledged capital of the realm: the seat of its kings and the centre of its religious, judicial and educational system.[1] As a city it was notoriously dirty and lacking any general plan; the Louvre already boasted Pierre Lescot's section of the *cour carrée*, the Châtelet had long guarded the splendid Sainte Chapelle, and Notre Dame was only the largest

---

[1] A recent and suggestive piece of work on 'Paris, capitale politique (*c.* 1200 à 1789)', is the chapter contributed by Roland Mousnier to *Paris, fonctions d'une capitale* (*Colloques, cahiers de civilisation*, Paris, 1961).

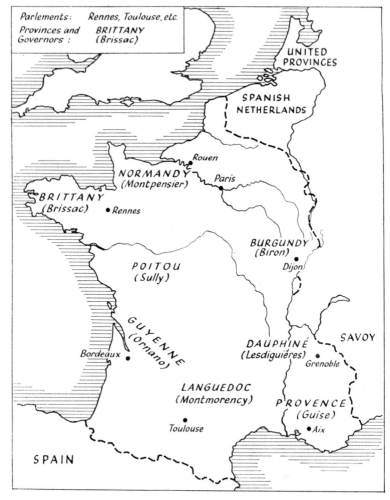

MAP 1 FRANCE AND HER NEIGHBOURS, *c.* 1600

of many fine churches and abbeys, but there had been little attempt to link these up with adequate paved streets, and no attempt at urban planning of the kind that was going on in contemporary Rome. It was Henri IV who began the architectural development of Paris as a capital.

In 1559 the monarchy had suffered a grievous blow when Henri II's passion for tournaments led to his death in a joust and to his succession by the weakly children of his wife Catherine de Medici. François II survived only one year, during which the Catholic Guise family insinuated itself into the highest councils, to the dismay of that Protestant party which was rapidly developing among the nobility and upper *bourgeoisie*, and which was led by Antony of Navarre. Charles IX succeeded in 1560 to a situation of hopeless hostility between these parties, which were openly at war by 1562. The next twelve years saw intermittent fighting broken by inconclusive truces; the Huguenots suffered heavy blows like the defeat at Jarnac (1569) where Sully's father was captured, and the Massacre of Saint Bartholomew (1572), but they remained strong enough to prevent the numerically superior Catholic groups from wiping them out.

The struggle continued after Henri III had succeeded Charles IX in 1574. Two years later the Catholics formed the so-called Holy League (*Sainte Ligue*) which the king for a while headed, but which he later left so as to be able to play the different groups off against each other. Further confused fighting followed, putting an end to the far-sighted plans for reform worked out by Henri III, who might have been a great king in a more peaceful age.[1] Henri de Navarre, son of Antony, began to emerge as leader of the Protestants; from about 1580 he showed great talent as a soldier, rallying to his banner exasperated moderates as well as fiery young Protestants like Sully. On the death of Charles IX Henri de Navarre had been second in line for the throne (at any rate by the acknowledged Salic Law of inheritance by the male line); with the death of the duke of Anjou in 1584 he became presumptive heir. Thus when Henri III was assassinated in 1589 it became a straight fight between his rightful successor and those League leaders who would not acknowledge him.

The leader of the League party was Charles, duc de Mayenne, and for four years the struggle raged throughout the kingdom. In 1589 Henri IV won a great victory over superior forces at

[1] See the interesting thesis of Aline Karcher-Vallée, summarized in *École Nationale des Chartes, positions des thèses . . . 1960*.

Arques (near Dieppe), but failed in his subsequent attempt to capture Paris, the League stronghold. The next year the king again won at Ivry (Sully was at both these battles), but once more failed in his attempt to starve Paris out; the city was relieved early in 1592 by the Spanish general, Parma, directed there from his campaigns in the Netherlands. To offset the help given to the League by Spain, Henri recruited forces from England, Germany and Switzerland. But what ensured his ultimate success was his abjuration of Protestantism (1593). After that the League, always weakened by its diverse social composition – wild Parisian democrats rubbing shoulders with the noblest lords – fell apart. In March 1594 Henri entered Paris in triumph and without resistance; although further provincial revolts had to be quelled, from this time the outcome was clear.

The long struggle had profound effects on the theory of kingship; it temporarily halted the development of absolutist ideas, so strong under François I. In their attempts to justify their resistance to Charles IX and Henri III the Huguenots produced two masterly treatises on the right of resistance to a tyrant. In the *Franco-Gallia* of 1573 an historical argument was used, based on the idea that Charles and his predecessors were imposing an alien Roman system on a Frankish people. It was contended that the Gauls had released the Franks from such Latin tyranny, and had substituted for it the sovereign power of the estates. The other main Huguenot line was developed in the more philosophical (and immediately less influential) *Vindiciae contra tyrannos* of 1579. Here scriptural and classical examples were cited to demonstrate in convincing fashion the right of subjects to resist tyrants. This hostility to the developing royal absolutism was by no means silenced under Henri IV, as the writings of Louis Turquet de Mayerne show.[1] All the same, the success of his rule opened the way to a revival of absolutist theories, best expounded a generation later by Le Bret (*De la Souveraineté du Roi*, 1632).

[1] See Roland Mousnier, 'L'opposition politique bourgeoise à la fin du XVIᵉ siècle et au début du XVIIᵉ siècle', *Revue Historique*, ccxiii (1955), 1–20.

Henri de Navarre had struggled to the throne through twenty years of civil wars, leading numerous daring exploits in any one of which France might have lost her future king.[1] His early years had been neither courtly nor sheltered; in his native Béarn he had been brought up roughly by his spendthrift father Antony and his brilliant and cultivated mother Jeanne, daughter of François I's saintly sister Margaret and that coarse ruffian Henri de Navarre (1553–1617). He never lost his love for strenuous exercise, including not only hunting but also long bouts of tennis. His was a passionate, zestful nature not only on the field of battle, where he would sometimes risk his life for a minor tactical advantage, but also in private life; his addiction to voluptuous pleasures indeed bordered on the psychotic. Thus his court was something of a bear-garden in which manners were far from refined and in which there was little sign of the development of elaborate ceremonies in the Spanish style. And yet this scruffy, odoriferous squire from the Pyrenees once in power showed himself to have a masterly grasp of the problems of his day. The nine great volumes of his correspondence[2] are full of far-sighted projects concerning the pacification of the Protestants, the encouragement of all kinds of industries, the planning of Paris as a great capital, the rational development of the armed forces, and so on. Moreover he saw to it personally that many of these projects were carried out; when he was assassinated in May 1610 France lost one of her greatest kings.

The administrative machine which he inherited was crude but effective. To write his letters and deal with his correspondence he had the four secretaries of state (*secrétaires d'État*), whose office had been increasing in importance and enlarging its functions since the mid-sixteenth century.[3] For affairs impinging on the judicial system – as most did – he had the chancellor, who was *ex officio* patron of all the French *parlements* and who held the seal without which no administrative decree

---

[1] These early years are best described by Pierre de Vaissière, *Henri IV* (Paris, 1925).
[2] Cited here as *Lettres Missives*.
[3] Their functions are well described in N. M. Sutherland, *The French secretaries of State in the age of Catherine de Medici* (London, 1962); there is no equivalent work for the reign of Henri IV.

was valid. During the reign there were three chancellors; Hurault de Cheverny, who died in 1599, Pomponne de Bellièvre who succeeded him until 1605, and then Brûlart de Sillery who held the office until 1613. The other most important high officer was the *surintendant des finances*, who between 1600 and 1611 was Sully.

The king would call his highest council (the *conseil des affaires*) together most mornings and discuss with them pressing problems of all kinds. The chancellor would be there, as would Sully, and probably also Villeroy, the most eminent of the secretaries of state and the one in practice responsible for foreign affairs. The tendency was for weak monarchs to have large and unruly councils; as one might expect Henri IV kept his small, leaving routine business to be dealt with by the *conseil d'État et des finances* (financial affairs) and the *conseil des parties* (judicial affairs). Both these lesser councils, to which members of the *conseil des affaires* often also belonged, had during the sixteenth century hived off from the central 'king's council' much as the *parlements* had done in medieval times.

By the later sixteenth century there were eight *parlements*; the central one at Paris and provincial ones in Toulouse, Grenoble, Bordeaux, Dijon, Rouen, Aix and Rennes. These were all primarily judicial bodies, each with its several chambers in which different types of cases were heard. Under François I they had attempted to extend their competence into the political field, but had been rebuffed. However, they retained their function of registering and so authorizing all legislation to be applied to the area for which they were responsible, and this led to many conflicts with the monarchy under Henri IV, especially in *parlements* headed by a strong *premier président*. Financial edicts had also to be approved by the appropriate *cour des aides*; there were separate ones at Paris, Montpellier and Rouen while at Grenoble and Bordeaux they formed part of the *parlements*. In the jurisdiction of each *parlement* also functioned a *chambre des comptes* – sometimes independently and sometimes as a part of the *parlement* – whose task it was to check and approve the accounts of financial officials.

These officials had been organized by Henri III in 1577 into about fifteen *bureaux des finances*; for the central government they provided the chief provincial administrative organ, acting through the four or five *élections* which each one contained.[1] The early *intendants* are elusive figures, members usually of the Paris *parlement* who since the mid-sixteenth century had been used by the central government to go out into the provinces for short and well-defined missions; to check a town's finances, for example, or to re-establish justice in a devastated region. Sully somewhat increased their use, but even in the mid-1640s, after Richelieu's expansion of their activities, they were far from the power they were to attain in the 1690s, when one sat permanently in every provincial centre and controlled the most diverse local affairs.

The *parlements* were judicial bodies in permanent session; the equivalent (if there was one) to the English Parliament was the system of estates, united from time to time in the estates-general (1560, 1576, 1588 and 1614). In each of the six great, formerly independent, provinces – Brittany, Normandy, Burgundy, Dauphiné, Provence and Languedoc – and in some minor ones as well, the local estates met once a year, usually for a fortnight, to discuss local affairs and send a *cahier* of grievances to the king. They also approved the coming year's taxes to be levied by their officials and paid over to the royal treasury; normally the royal demand was put by a special envoy who addressed the opening session of the estates and hoped to be granted at least two-thirds of the sum he requested. The independence of *pays d'états* ('regions [having] estates') varied according to the circumstances of their absorption by the French crown and to the prevalence of regional sentiment, which was normally strongest in the regions farthest from Paris. The Brittany estates were notoriously stubborn, while those of Normandy were relatively weak and were indeed abolished without much resistance by Mazarin. The estates of Burgundy, mindful of the province's great ducal past, held out more strongly than might have been expected in a body relatively close to the centre of royal power. In Dauphiné provincial aspirations were hampered by continual quarrels between the estates and the *parlement*, as a result of which

[1] A recent work on these officials is Jean-Paul Charmeil, *Les trésoriers de France à l'époque de la Fronde* (Paris, 1964).

Richelieu was able to suppress the former. The estates of Provence and of Languedoc remained strongly independent down to the end of the *ancien régime*.

Most towns had mayors and councils with whom the central administration had also to contend; they sent *députés en cour* to wherever the king was staying, to deal with their town's affairs. In Paris the most celebrated *prévôt des marchands* at this time was François Miron (mayor, 1604–6), who had many a brush with the royal authority. The autonomy of the towns had grown during the civil wars, when they were often used as centres by the rival factions. In each provincial centre, often in opposition to the municipal and religious authorities, was also a royal governor. These had been more important when the kingdom was being conquered than they were by 1600; except in time of foreign war or domestic revolt their role was largely honorific, and their chief standing duty that of superintending the fortifications. However, some strong governors stand out; at Bordeaux the duc d'Ornano provided a focus for local discontent against fiscal oppression, and at Grenoble the duc de Lesdiguières was almost an independent potentate in a region which he had conquered from the Savoyards but which remained under their menace.

The governors were almost all nobles of ancient lineage, members of that *noblesse d'épée* which was losing its former simple function, as warfare became less and less an affair of small bodies of cavalry under a local leader, and more and more a business, involving both a high degree of discipline for manœuvres of all kinds of arms and some scientific knowledge for the artillery and engineers. The *noblesse d'épée*, after the civil wars, seemed to have lost its traditional function without finding a new role. The *noblesse de robe*, on the other hand, whose members were successful lawyers and merchants, found itself very much at home in the new conditions of peace and an expanding trade and administration. Once again we find the *bourgeoisie* of the greater towns eating into the lands of adjacent *seigneurs* and peasants, as part of a process which can be detected around Paris in the fifteenth century and was to gain momentum during the seventeenth. The two *noblesses* remained distinct in attitude and interests throughout our period, and indeed, according to some accounts, until the mid-eighteenth century. The other privileged class, the clergy, had been hard hit by the wars, when their revenues had often gone unpaid, but French Catholicism was about to undergo a revival under Saint François de Sales and Saint Vincent de Paul which would colour the whole century.[1]

Beneath the nobilities and the clergy lay the mass of 'the people', mostly peasants but including the artisans of the towns. In the later sixteenth century the peasantry and minor nobility, goaded by the exactions of Leaguers and Protestants alike, had often taken up arms in revolts with evocative names like those of the Gautiers of Normandy, the Tard-Avisés of Limousin and the Croquants of Périgord.[2] Usually they acted in self-defence, but occasionally they turned on the towns, which they regarded as the source of their torments. Some joined regular bands, like the one headed by the Breton 'capitaine Guillery', who established his robbers' nest in southern Brittany and terrorized adjacent roads in Poitou and Anjou until a full-scale military operation dislodged him in 1604.[3]

However, the condition of the French peasantry in time of peace was far from miserable; the advent of rural capitalism was long retarded except in regions near great towns, and at the time of Henri IV most peasants were small landowners. Their urban counterparts, the artisans, had suffered much from the inflation of the sixteenth century, and from their subjection to domineering and exclusive guilds; the seventeenth century saw if anything an extension of these *jurandes* as a means of royal control.

Cutting across the traditional social groups were the Protestants, strongest in the Midi and forming a real state within a state after the edict of Nantes (1598), which allowed them separate fortified towns (*places de sûreté*), three universities (La Rochelle, Nîmes and Montauban) and the holding of periodical

[1] On this revival, see the (posthumous) article of Lucien Febvre, 'Aspects méconnus d'un renouveau religieux en France entre 1590 et 1620', *Annales*, xiii (1958), 639–50.

[2] There is an interesting study of this latter revolt by J. Nouaillac, 'Henri IV et les Croquants du Limousin,' *Bulletin historique et philologique* (1912), 321–50.

[3] See the remarkable account of this in *Le Mercure François*, published at Paris in 1611 by Jean Richer, 289–92.

national Synods. The members of the Faith (as they said) or of the *'religion prétendue réformée'* (as their opponents said) were an unstable element in the constitutional structure, always ready to conspire with Swiss or German sympathizers, and likely enough, if provoked, to come out in open revolt, as indeed they did under Marie de Medici, before Richelieu crushed them. Under Henri IV Sully, as the leading Protestant, played a crucial role in keeping them contented.

They were very numerous at Lyons, which occupied the first place in France as a trading centre because of its links with Italy. Henri II had severely shaken the economy of Lyons by disavowing large debts contracted there for his wars (1557),[1] and the silk trade, at its height in the mid-sixteenth century, had greatly shrunk, as had trade in general in south-eastern France. In other parts, however, the war does not seem to have been as harmful to the economy as was once thought; some Atlantic seaports prospered throughout the sixteenth century and the Seine valley seems never to have suffered severely.[2] France was, all the same, in a very weak monetary position, dependent for her silver on such currency as might move north from Spain, either in the course of trade or as support for French rebels.[3] She was subject throughout the century to a considerable inflation which perhaps doubled prices between 1550 and 1600.

Atlantic silver between 1560 and the end of the century allowed Philip II of Spain to mount a series of great attacks against the revolted northern Netherlands; indeed, the intensity of his campaigns seems to have varied directly with the quantity of his shipments.[4] Spain's relations with France consisted of underhand assistance to the League and then the intervention of Parma in 1592. Philip II suffered bankruptcy for the second

---

[1] See Roger Doucet, 'Le grand parti de Lyon au XVIe siècle', *Revue Historique*, clxxi (1933), 473–513, and clxxii (1933), 1–41.

[2] See respectively, Étienne Trocmé and Marcel Delafosse, *Le commerce rochelais de la fin du XVe siècle au début du XVIIe siècle* (Paris, 1952), and J. U. Nef, 'Comparison of industrial growth in France and England, 1540–1640', *Journal of political economy*, xliv (1936), 289–317, 505–33 and 643–66.

[3] F. C. Spooner, *L'économie mondiale et les frappes monétaires en France (1493–1680)* (Paris, 1956), 182.

[4] This is interestingly demonstrated by Pierre Chaunu in 'Séville et la "Belgique", 1555–1648', *Revue du Nord*, xlii (1960), 259–92.

time in 1596, and this was no doubt one reason for his conclusion of the treaty of Vervins with France in 1598. Thereafter open intervention was replaced by veiled hostility; Spain encouraged plots against Henri IV, and France subsidized the United Provinces in their increasingly successful revolt. The Dutch were just entering on their great age. In the armies of Maurice of Nassau the bellicose nobility of Protestant Europe was trained in the latest techniques of drill and scientific warfare, while Dutch ships penetrated the Portuguese monopoly in the East and surprised Spaniards in the New World as well as in the Mediterranean. With France the United Provinces could not but have close political and technical relations, even if Henri IV was jealous of the success of the Dutch East India Company, and dismayed when the Dutch made a truce with the Spaniards in 1609.

With the Southern Netherlands relations were less cordial. There the archduke and duchess Albert and Isabella ruled for the Spanish king, and so were necessarily involved in his opposition to Henri IV. Strained relations over the trade embargo of 1604 gave no hint of the *rapprochement* after Henri IV's death, when Rubens, as the representative of the Catholic Netherlands, would come to Paris and exalt the court of Marie de Medici in a series of magnificent paintings which survive at the Louvre.

Relations with England were ambiguous. Elizabeth had helped Henri de Navarre in his years of struggle, but James I was more Hispanophile and indeed concluded a treaty with Spain in 1604. Moreover, French merchants constantly complained of English pirates, whom English monarchs either could not or would not restrain. Ireland the French knew chiefly from the many refugees who fled from the English campaign of 1601; sometimes they were welcomed in France, but more often they were packed off home by the first available ship.[1] France's traditional relationship with Scotland had lapsed during the civil wars and was not to be revived until the days of the wandering Stuarts.

[1] See my short article, 'The Irish at Paris in 1605', in *Irish Historical Studies*, xiv (1964), 58–60.

In Germany there were numerous Protestant princes who were well represented at the French court.[1] In 1552 Henri II had allied with several of them against the Emperor (treaty of Chambord), and during the 1590s Henri IV had received much support from Maurice of Hesse. The princes were in general too prone to encourage the aspirations of dissentient French Protestant nobles like the duc de Bouillon, instead of uniting, as Henri IV wished them to do, in aid of the Dutch against the Spaniards. In fact the Germans resisted his pressure until 1610, when the treaty of Halle was signed in preparation for the war that was cut short by the king's assassination. To the south Protestant members of the Swiss confederation were friendly towards France; their troops had helped the king during his early years, and had to be paid off as best Sully could once the realm was at peace.[2]

The great enemy of the Protestant Swiss, and especially of the Genevese, was the duke of Savoy, whose territory straddled the Alps from the Mediterranean to Bresse, the province lying immediately to the north of Lyons. The duke, Charles-Emmanuel, pursued no fixed policy but tended at this period to ally himself with Spain; the duc de Lesdiguières, governor of Dauphiné, had several times to repel his incursions during the civil wars, and in 1588 the Savoyards had succeeded in seizing the marquisate of Saluzzo. In Italy proper the French maintained their traditional understanding with Venice, the first power to recognize Henri IV in 1589, and after the marriage of Henri IV to Marie de Medici in 1601 they had a close link with her uncle, the grand duke of Tuscany.[3] The papacy under Clement VIII (pope, 1592–1605) had recognized the king somewhat reluctantly after his abjuration, but under Paul V (pope, 1605–21) became increasingly friendly. French influence in Italy was much enhanced by the success in 1607 of the cardinal de Joyeuse in bringing to an end the dangerous quarrel between Venice and the papacy, which had begun in 1605 over a

[1] See Léonce Anquez, *Henri IV et l'Allemagne* (Paris, 1887).

[2] On relations with the Swiss, see E. Rott, *Henri IV, les Suisses et la Haute-Italie* (Paris, 1882).

[3] On Italian affairs, see F. Robiou, 'La politique de Henri IV en Italie', *Revue des Questions Historiques*, xxi (1877), 5–34.

traditional question of jurisdiction. Italy was of the greatest importance to general French strategy because it formed the Spaniards' main link with northern Europe, either on a line running from the Neapolitan kingdom (under a Spanish viceroy) up through central Italy and the Milanese to the Alpine passes, or directly north from Genoa, a Spanish satellite. Under Henri IV the rival powers manœuvred in northern Italy to secure control of the passes, the Spanish count Fuentès adopting a dangerously aggressive policy in his attempts to win control of the Grisons, but war did not break out there until the time of Richelieu.

In the Mediterranean in general French interests had suffered from the dislocations of the wars. The 'Bastion', a fortified position near Tunis in north Africa, had been lost in 1585 and after that French shipping (mostly from Marseilles) was open to the attacks of Barbary corsairs and other pirates – chiefly English and Dutch. Relations with Constantinople had been close in the early sixteenth century, and it was one of Henri IV's objects to re-establish French influence there in the face of Dutch and English competition. The sultans' enmity with Spain made this a relatively easy task, even if the French policy of simultaneous alliance with pope and sultan raised other difficulties. Largely because of her internal conflicts France had played little part in the expansion of Europe into the world, and in spite of isolated ventures she remained backward as a colonial power until the later seventeenth century. It was indeed these internal conflicts which had disrupted her steady development between the reign of Henri II and that of Henri IV; at this period she has established peace at home, and is ready to lay the foundations for what will become known as the *grand siècle*.

CHAPTER II

Sully's career to 1611

Maximilien de Béthune, the future duc de Sully, was born on 12 or 13 December 1560[1] at Rosny, near Mantes-la-Jolie, where his parents lived in a small manor among the woods above the Seine. His father, François de Béthune, was descended from the counts of Flanders, and Sully in later years liked to boast that 'tho' there were many richer in France . . . yet there were few of better House or Bloud, being descended of a King of France'.[2] His mother, Charlotte Dauvet, was of less exalted extraction, being the daughter of a *président* of the Paris *chambre des comptes*.[3]

Both his parents were Huguenots, and some time after Maximilien's birth his father left Rosny to join the Protestant rebels fighting Charles IX. François, however, was captured by the League at Jarnac (1569), when Maximilien was nine; all his possessions were declared confiscated, though he was allowed to return to Rosny and to live there in confinement under the guard of six archers. Maximilien must have been grieved by his father's capture, and by his mother's death

[1] According to the *Économies Royales*, i, 209a, and L. Dussieux, *Étude biographique sur Sully* (Paris, 1887), 1. On the other hand Sully himself apparently told the English ambassador, Sir George Carew, that he was born on 6 January 1560; see the latter's *Relation of the state of France, with the characters of Henri IV and the principal persons of that court*, written in 1609 and published as an appendix to *An historical view of the negotiations between the courts of England, France and Brussels, 1592–1617*, ed. Thomas Birch (London, 1749), 484. A further possibility is 13 December 1559, the date given by André Duchesne, *Histoire généalogique de la maison de Béthune* (Paris, 1639); he is followed by Henri Carré, *Sully, sa vie et son œuvre* (Paris, 1932), 1, and Marie-Madeleine Martin, *Sully-le-Grand* (Paris, 1959), 22.

[2] See the letter from Sir Henry Neville, English ambassador to Paris, to Robert Cecil, 29 January 1599, printed in *Memorials of affairs of state in the reigns of queen Elizabeth and king James I* . . . (3 vols, London, 1725), i, 149.

[3] For a succinct account of his ancestry, see H. Thomas, *Rosny-sur-Seine* (Paris, 1889), chapter II.

shortly afterwards, but he seems to have spent a happy enough childhood, playing with his three brothers, one older (Louis) and two younger (Salomon and Philippe) and sometimes walking with his tutor along the banks of the Seine and on its

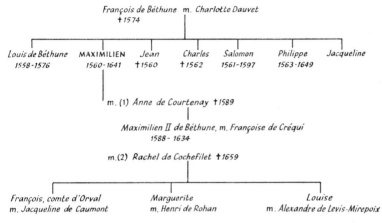

GENEALOGY OF THE FAMILY OF SULLY

islands, where he learned about the different kinds of plants and animals. He was inclined to pose precocious questions about politics and geography; how was it, for instance, that almost all peoples tended towards monarchy even though monarchs are not necessarily wise, and what the seas, rivers, mountains and towns marked on his father's maps were like. When he was about ten he also began to be trained in military horsemanship; sometimes, too, he was allowed an outing to Paris where he particularly enjoyed the antics of some Italian comedians.[1]

In 1572 his father sent him to the capital to continue his studies. But the year was badly chosen for a young Huguenot; one evening in August, hearing a great din outside his lodgings, he sent his tutors out to see what was going on. It was the beginning of the Massacre of Saint Bartholomew, and neither of his two Protestant tutors was ever seen again. Maximilien

[1] This paragraph is based on a passage from the manuscript of Sully's memoirs, omitted from the edition but printed by Pfister, 'Les Économies Royales de Sully', *Revue Historique*, liv (1894), 311–12.

himself was now in great peril, for his host was unwilling to allow
him to stay, at the risk of having the house sacked. So he put on
his scholar's gown and, tucking a Catholic prayer-book under
his arm, ventured out, hoping to reach some friends. After being
stopped and interrogated several times, with Huguenots being
slaughtered all round him, he reached the Collège de Bourgogne,
where his friend the principal concealed him in a small room
until the atrocities had ceased.

Although he escaped unharmed, as did his father who was not
in Paris at the time, Maximilien's attitude towards Catholicism
must have been coloured by this experience for the rest of his
life. He stayed on at Paris to work for a year or so more, but then
returned to Rosny, where his military training began in earnest.[1]
Thus, two years after his father died of pleurisy in 1574, he was
able to leave home to fight for the king of Navarre, whose court
he may have attended in Paris. None of his brothers came with
him; Louis was drowned in 1576,[2] but Salomon and Philippe
fought for the Catholic cause, and Maximilien was thus able to
pass with impunity through Catholic territory, using his
brothers' passports – and occasionally their names. He sometimes met his brothers in the intervals in the fighting, and sometimes too had to inquire anxiously after their safety following a
Huguenot victory.[3] They rallied to Henri IV on the death of
Henri III in 1589; Salomon died of an illness contracted at the
siege of Amiens in 1597[4], and Philippe lived on until 1649,
becoming a notable ambassador at Rome and holding other
important posts.

[1] Sully often emphasizes that he studied 'scientific' subjects like geography and mathematics, and he is a good example of the young noble
whose education attempted to fit him for changed conditions. In his
article on 'The education of the aristocracy in the Renaissance', *Journal of
Modern History*, xxii (1950), 1–20, J. H. Hexter argued that such examples
were common, and we could certainly find many more among Sully's
Protestant contemporaries; nobles like the young Turenne, whose education is described in his *Mémoires*, ed. Baguenault de Puchesse (Paris, 1901),
5, or Philippe Duplessis-Mornay, whose early years are extensively described in the work of M.-J. Gaufrès, *Philippe Mornay de Bauves, ou l'éducation
d'un gentilhomme protestant au XVIᵉ siècle* (Paris, 1868).

[2] Duchesne, *Histoire généalogique*, 437.

[3] *Économies Royales*, i, 63.

[4] Duchesne, *Histoire généalogique*, 474.

In 1583 Maximilien, now baron de Rosny, married Anne de Courtenay (plate 1), who before her death in 1589 gave birth to a son, Maximilien, who was to be a source of great sorrow to his father. In May 1592 Sully married again, and this time his wife, Rachel de Cochefilet, survived him, bearing him nine children, of whom one son and two daughters survived infancy. Rachel was a devoted and capable wife who did what she could to alleviate the sorrows of her husband's later years.

After joining the king of Navarre in 1576 Rosny spent the next decade fighting in his master's battles and skirmishes, mostly in the Midi. He had many narrow escapes from death and himself behaved with the licence and barbarity appropriate to his profession. Slowly he rose in the estimation of the king, and in 1580 was well enough regarded to be appointed 'chambellan et l'un des conseillers d'estat'[1], and to be sent on a mission to Paris to the court of Henri III.[2] After the latter's death Rosny was prominent in Henri IV's battles for the realm, playing his part both at Arques (1589) and at Ivry (1590).[3]

During the early 1590s Henri IV was engaged in a series of manœuvres and sieges (of Paris, Chartres, Noyon, Rouen, for instance) in which Rosny often fought as a gunner and as an engineer. He was also increasingly employed in administration and in negotiation. Thomas Edmondes, the English agent, writing to his master William Cecil, Lord Burghley on 20 June 1593 from Mantes, speaks of 'Monsieur de Rhosny, of his [the king's] counsell . . .';[4] he probably became a *conseiller d'État* shortly after 1589.[5] Certainly by 1593 he was employed in some responsible capacity close to the king, for an *arrêt* of 1598 orders him to be paid 3,600 *livres* as the remainder of his salary for that year, as well as 3,000 *livres* for a loan made to the king during the same period.[6] In November 1593 he signed the royal reply to a

[1] According to Duchesne, *Histoire généalogique*, 441; Sully's brevet as *chambellan du roi de Navarre* is preserved in AN K 101 pièce 1.
[2] *Économies Royales*, i, 52, and *Lettres Missives*, ii, 216–17.
[3] P.-V. Palma-Cayet, *Chronologie novenaire*, ed. Michaud et Poujoulat in the *Nouvelle collection des mémoires pour servir a l'histoire de France*, 2nd series, xii (Paris, 1837), 218–19.
[4] *Edmondes Papers* . . ., ed. G. G. Butler (London, 1913), 134.
[5] Valois, lxxiii.
[6] Valois, n° 4591.

petition from some Protestant envoys,[1] and towards the end of that year began his negotiations with Villars, the governor of Rouen, who was holding out there for the League. These negotiations had already baffled several envoys, but Rosny conducted them with great skill and they ended with the capitulation of the town in March 1594.[2]

Early in 1594 appear the first *arrêts* for which he was *rapporteur*,[3] and which consequently establish beyond doubt Rosny's presence in the *conseil d'État*. The increasing favour in which he was held is shown by the grant of 15,000 *livres*, declared payable to him in September 1594, as well as by royal confirmation of a gift of land on which the Place Royale would later be built.[4] About the beginning of 1595, to judge by the list of *rapporteurs*, he seems to have left the council, and is thus not mentioned among certain commissioners appointed from it in January 1595 to investigate the running of various revenue offices in the provinces.[5] According to the meticulous financial historian Albert Chamberland, it was in July 1596 that he entered the *conseil des finances*;[6] he seems to have spent much of the intervening time on his land at Moret-sur-Loing, near Fontainebleau.[7] Certainly he was in the *chambre des comptes* at Paris for the king's business on 1 August,[8] and was active in the preparation of a programme to be presented to the Assembly of Notables. This was a consultative body of dignitaries called by the king (as an alternative to the discredited estates-general) to advise him on the numerous problems of reconstruction. It met at Rouen in August 1596; Rosny had prepared a list of 'means of finding

[1] *Journal de L'Estoile pour le règne de Henri IV*, ed. Louis-Raymond Lefèvre, in the *Mémoires du passé pour servir au temps présent* (3 vols, Paris, 1948–60), i, 329.

[2] *Journal de L'Estoile*, i, 400, and *Économies Royales*, i, 137–9.

[3] The *rapporteur* was the council-member who brought the *arrêt* before the council.

[4] Valois, nº 1363, and 1686; see chapter VII on the construction of the Place Royale.

[5] Valois, nº 1899.

[6] See his article on 'Le conseil des finances en 1596 et 1597 et les *Économies Royales*', *Revue Henri IV*, i (1905–6), 259.

[7] *Économies Royales*, 191–9.

[8] AN P 2665, fo. 23rº.

money which may be proposed to the estates at Rouen' and he may well have addressed it.[1]

In September of that year he was commissioned with four others to tour the provinces in search of money. The regions of Orleans and Tours were allotted to him, and his efforts were much more successful than those of his colleagues, chiefly because he showed no scruple in seizing funds such as those destined for the payment of members of the courts.[2] Echoes of the discontent aroused by this arbitrary conduct reach us from several subsequent documents, for he had apparently ridiculed several members of the *cour des aides*, and had said that this was a useless institution whose work could as well be done by one or two honest gentlemen. Nothing came of the complaints against him, for, as the king remarked when dealing with a discontented official in May 1599, everybody knew that Rosny's commission had been granted 'to aid His Majesty in his direst need'.[3] Although there is no record of any of the other *commissaires* receiving a special reward, Rosny got 3,600 *livres* late in November for his work,[4] and it seems to have been this marauding expedition which finally established his reputation as a financier in the eyes of the king. After October 1596 we find him once again a frequent *rapporteur* in council, where he would remain prominent for the rest of the reign.

According to the *Économies Royales* it was at the end of 1596 that he first tried his hand at preparing the *états des finances*,[5] and although this claim was repeatedly challenged by the hostile Marbault,[6] secretary to the Huguenot leader Duplessis-Mornay, Marbault was misled by his belief that Rosny only entered the *conseil des finances* in April 1598. In fact, from late in

---

[1] For the list, see BN ms. fr. 18510, fo. 105r⁰; on the assembly, see Raymond Charlier-Meniolle, *L'assemblée des Notables tenue à Rouen en 1596* (Paris, 1911).

[2] On this 'tournée', see Albert Chamberland, 'La tournée de Sully et de Rybault dans les généralités en 1596', supplement to the *Revue Henri IV*, iii (1909).

[3] AN P 2666, fo. 257–8.

[4] Valois, n⁰ 3114.

[5] *Économies Royales*, i, 224 and 293. This term is explained in chapter III.

[6] *Remarques sur les mémoires . . . de Sully*, 35a, 37a and 45a.

1596 onward Rosny was at the centre of the financial administration, working with Nicolas de Harlay, sieur de Sancy, and
Charles de Saldaigne, sieur d'Incarville. The former had been
appointed head of the *conseil des finances* in 1594, and although
he was still in charge in April 1597, by January 1598 he had
fallen out of favour with the king.[1] Meanwhile Rosny had had
another chance to show his talents. In March 1597 the Spaniards
captured Amiens; this was a severe blow to the king, as the
town contained much military material[2] and was the gateway
to Paris. He at once led his forces to recover it, and during the
siege, which lasted from March until November 1597, Rosny
established himself at Paris, which he used as a base for squeez-
ing money out of the French towns and provinces by new taxes
and creation of offices.[3] On 22 August he wrote to the secretary
of state, Villeroy, asking him to find out from the king if he
(Rosny) might come and join in the fighting,[4] but, as the
Économies Royales relate, the king was finding him too useful as a
procurer of money to allow him to risk his life at the front.[5] All
contemporary writers are agreed that the supply and equipment of the army at this siege was admirable, and if Rosny
cannot be allowed credit for the field-hospital at Longpré-
lès-Amiens at least the general responsibility for supplies was
his.

Having recaptured Amiens late in September, the king returned to Paris for the end of the year. There Rosny had already
begun his researches into past financial abuses, if we may believe
a letter of December 1597 from the English agent Robert
Naunton (later Sir Robert Naunton, master of the court of
wards) to his master the earl of Essex, in which is mentioned the
plight of an 'old Financier . . . called to a rear-account by de

---

[1] *Lettres du cardinal de Florence sur Henri IV et sur la France, 1596–1598,*
ed. Raymond Ritter (Paris, 1955), 131 and 227.
[2] There is an interesting list of this in a letter of 6 March 1596 from
Paris, written by Sir Walter Mildmay to the earl of Essex; *Calendar of
manuscripts of the marquis of Salisbury at Hatfield House* (18 vols, London,
1883–1940), vii, 99.
[3] See the letter of which he was one of the signatories from Paris to the
king, 12 August 1597; BN ms. fr. 20051, fo. 367.
[4] Letter mentioned in the Fichier Charavay.
[5] *Économies Royales,* i, 251.

Rosny' in spite of his acquittance signed by the late king.[1] Early in 1598 Henri IV began preparing a journey into Brittany, where the duc de Mercoeur was leading the last centre of resistance within the realm. Rosny went with the king on this expedition, which was rapidly successful; he spent some time at Angers arranging financial settlements,[2] and at Rennes had a quarrel with the estates of Brittany – forerunner of many another such conflict – over the question of the extent to which the king should now recognize their liberties and privileges.[3] Mercoeur had a short but romantic life after his submission; called by Rudolph II to command the Imperial army against the Turks he conducted a brilliant campaign in Hungary during 1601, and then died at Nürnberg early in 1602 on his way back to France. His funeral oration was pronounced by Saint François de Sales. Back at Paris in June 1598 Rosny entered on a new phase in his career as the acknowledged head of the financial system. For France, too, a new phase was beginning with the edict of Nantes, proclaimed in April, which temporarily set the Protestants' fears at rest, and the treaty of Vervins with Spain, concluded in May 1598.

During the next twelve years Rosny was a member of the king's inner council, where he worked with Pomponne de Bellièvre, appointed chancellor in August 1599 and succeeded in 1605 by Nicolas Brûlart, sieur de Sillery (1544–1624), and with Nicolas de Neufville, sieur de Villeroy (1542–1617). Bellièvre was born in 1529, and served four monarchs with distinction as diplomat, counsellor and *surintendant des finances*. It was his misfortune that in his later years he should have found his influence in council contested by a younger man as dynamic as Rosny. The clash of their constitutional ideas was aggravated by their contrasting characters and the nature of their offices. While Rosny was impatient, ruthless and bellicose, Bellièvre was

[1] Letter printed in *An historical view*, ed. Thomas Birch, 84.
[2] See his letters of 12 and 21 March, respectively to Villeroy and to Montmorency, both from Angers; BN ms. fr. 15911, fo. 388, and BN ms. fr. 3548, fo. 73.
[3] For the king's letter announcing the arrival of Rosny at Rennes, see the *Lettres inédites de Henri IV*, ed. Auguste Galitzin (Paris, 1860), 265–6; for events there, see Louis-J.-M. de Carné, *Les états de Bretagne* . . . (Paris, 1868), 251–3.

reflective, concerned with justice and averse to violent action; as he said, 'one must act gently and after due thought'.[1] In his office of chancellor Bellièvre often received complaints from the members of the sovereign courts – of which he was *ex officio* protector – about Rosny's extortions and parsimony. In March 1603, for example, Guillaume Daffis, *premier président* of the Toulouse *parlement*, wrote to Bellièvre complaining that his *rentes* had been cut.[2] In September of that year we find the *bureau de l'hôtel de ville* of Paris asking the chancellor to use his weight in council against the unpopular intrusions of [Rosny's] new farmers of the *aides*,[3] and there were also frequent complaints about his creation of offices. While Bellièvre would thus often have to remonstrate with Rosny on behalf of numerous suppliants – who frequently had a good case – Rosny would often be required by the king to put pressure on the chancellor to approve various edicts, sometimes of doubtful justice.[4] Hence the continual conflicts between the two men, in which Rosny often behaved very intemperately; as Bellièvre wrote to Villeroy in December 1602 after one of these quarrels, 'he treated me like some petty clerk'.[5] It is painful to see the aged Bellièvre treated so harshly, but from Rosny's point of view his hectoring was a success; he was getting the upper hand in 1604, and the following year the seals were withdrawn from Bellièvre. He died in 1607.[6]

His successor as chancellor, Sillery, was the creature of the third force in council, Villeroy. Described by the English ambassador, Sir George Carew, as the 'dean in chapter of all the statesmen in Christendom',[7] Villeroy had served Henri III with Bellièvre and, when he became secretary of state in 1594, took up again an office which he had already held for twenty-one years and would now hold for a further twenty-two, until

[1] Quoted by J. Nouaillac, *Villeroy, secrétaire d'État et ministre de Charles IX, Henri III et Henri IV, 1543–1610* (Paris, 1909), 383.
[2] BN ms. fr. 15989, fo. 295.
[3] Bib. Institut, fonds Godefroy, 263, fo. 232.
[4] See for instance, *Économies Royales*, i, 329a, 413b and 539b.
[5] BN ms. fr. 15894, fo. 547.
[6] For the stages in this struggle, see Roland Mousnier, 'Sully et le conseil d'état et des finances', *Revue Historique*, cxcii (1941), 68–86.
[7] See his *Relation of the state of France*, 489.

1616. Like Bellièvre, he contrasted with Sully in being both a member of the *noblesse de robe* and a Catholic. It was the religious difference which led to most of the squabbles which they had, quarrels whose importance is somewhat overestimated in the *Économies Royales*.[1] For while both were beneficiaries of the system of government by a very small council, so that contemporaries could complain that things went ill because 'Rosny and Villeroy do everything by themselves',[2] each had his own sphere of influence, which for Villeroy was foreign relations. Moreover, his supposed Hispanophilia, as opposed to Rosny's fierce Protestantism, has been exaggerated.[3] The bitterness which Sully shows towards him in the *Économies Royales* probably arises from Villeroy's influence in securing his dismissal in 1611, for the correspondence between the two men during Henri IV's time is always perfectly correct, if not cordial.

It could hardly be otherwise when both were in daily conference with that great king, who liked to have their conflicting opinions but who would not have tolerated constant quarrelling. Henri IV seems to have had a particular liking for the Arsenal and to have visited Rosny very often after the latter, as *grand maître de l'artillerie*, had taken up residence there in 1599. The *Économies Royales* describe several of these visits,[4] confirmed by contemporary writers like Sir George Carew who described how the king 'walketh in his garden between the arsenal and the bastille', gloating over his arms and his money.[5] Although the king and Sully had many minor disputes, their 'froideurs' never lasted long, partly because of the volatile royal temperament

---

[1] In his article on 'Dix lettres inédites de Sully', *Revue des Questions Historiques*, li (1914), 136–45, J. Nouaillac showed that Sully did not in fact send Villeroy a letter of reprimand over the L'Hoste affair; Nouaillac's case is confirmed by two other letters, both from Sillery to Villeroy (BN ms. fr. 15578, fo. 213 of 26 April 1604, and fo. 222 of 1 May 1604), describing Sully's attitude as sympathetic, 'en aiant tousjours parlé de fort bonne façon'.

[2] Quoted by Nouaillac, *Villeroy*, 313.

[3] See Francis de Crue, *Les derniers desseins de Henri IV* (Paris, 1902), and the *Correspondance entre Henri IV et Béthune . . . 1602–1604*, ed. J. E. M. Lajeunie, *Mémoires et documents publiés par la société d'histoire et d'archéologie de Genève*, xxxviii (1952), 189–474; 437, note 1.

[4] *Économies Royales*, i, 552b, 560a, 600a, etc.

[5] See his *Relation of the state of France*, 436.

and partly on account of Rosny's general trustworthiness and
favoured position as the leading Protestant.

The king ran his private affairs a good deal less efficiently
than his kingdom, and had often to call on Rosny to pay his
gambling debts and to placate his wife and mistresses. The
accounts of this in the *Économies Royales* have seemed to many
critics to border on the fantastic, but they can often be confirmed. The many letters in which the king calls on Rosny for
gambling money find their corresponding entries in the
accounts, where the minister's disapproving hand has often
inserted the words 'pour jouer'.[1] The accounts also show payments to a remarkable number of mistresses, payments which
Sully often made very unwillingly, to judge by a letter of Sir
Ralph Winwood, the English ambassador, to Robert Cecil in
May 1601. There Winwood describes how 'Monsieur de
Rhosny doth storm, that his miserable, sparing and cruell
exactions upon the People . . . should be squandered in this
manner' [upon a new mistress].[2] Rosny's role was not confined
to grumbling at the dissipation in this way of his hard-won
treasure. He had many direct dealings with the queen and the
mistresses, all of whose children, indiscriminately mixed, were
reared together in the king's unlikely household. That he was
used as an intermediary with the mistresses emerges from a
letter of 1608 from the king to the marquise de Verneuil, in
which he says that *he* told 'M de Seully' to give her that horrid
message forbidding her to bring her son when she came to see
him because it upset the queen, and that it is consequently no
good taking it out on Sully.[3] The latter indeed often acted as
mediator between king and queen, sometimes giving her
suggestions for humble letters to patch up her relations with her
royal spouse. One of these – preserved in the original – advises
her to write to the king and tell him that she wishes, out of her
extreme affection for him, to love and honour all that he loves,
and so to do as she has been bidden and receive 'madame de
Verneuil' amiably.[4] On occasion too the king used Rosny to

[1] See for example, BN ms. fr. 4559, fo. 79–82.
[2] *Memorials of affairs of state*, i, 331.
[3] *Lettres Missives*, vii, 662.
[4] BN Dupuy 407, fo. 70.

refuse Marie de Medici costly objects which she coveted; thus in
1603, when she was negotiating for the purchase of the Sancy
diamond, 'the king gave underhand encouragement to M. de
Rosny to break off the deal'.[1] We may guess that interventions
of this kind did nothing to endear Rosny to the queen, and may
have contributed to his downfall when she became Regent in
1610; his general relationship with the king, in which he combined the functions of a Colbert with those of a *confident*, was
curious and indeed unique.

As the leading French Protestant, Rosny was a key man in the
king's attempt to reconcile the two religious parties. His own
Protestantism seems to have been sincere, although it is not true
that he filled the administration with subordinates of the same
faith. Even if he had not been personally a convinced Protestant,
it would have been politically undesirable that he should be
converted to Catholicism. For it was he who, by his presence in
the highest councils, gave the discontented Huguenots of the
Midi some degree of confidence in the king's religious and
political policy, which seemed to become more and more
hostile to them as the years went by. From the king's point of
view he was the great mediator, whether for persuading the
extremists not to hold inopportune assemblies,[2] or for addressing
such assemblies as did meet,[3] or for giving soft answers to
Protestants who came to see him in Paris about the alarming
affairs of their provinces.[4] He was also useful in writing admoni-
tory (and extremely smug) letters to the factious nobles of the
Faith, men like the duc de Bouillon, who was always intriguing
in the north-east, the prince de Condé and the duc de La
Trimouille – two incorrigible conspirators.[5] After 1599 Rosny

[1] See the letter of the representative of the duke of Mantua, writing back
to his master from Paris in October 1603, quoted by Germain Bapst,
Histoire des joyaux de la Couronne de France (Paris, 1889), 230–1.
[2] See for instance, his letter of May 1606 to the duc de La Force, BN
Périgord 6, fo. 44, and the *Économies Royales*, ii, 1576.
[3] At Châtellerault in 1605, for example; see below.
[4] See the 'Journal du voyage de M. Daniel Chamier à Paris en 1607',
Bulletin de la Société de l'histoire du Protestantisme français, ii (1853–4), 292–320
and 430–46.
[5] For these letters, see respectively Bib. Société de l'histoire du Protestantisme Français, Ms. 708, fo. 28, and Bib. Salins, Ms. 37, fo. 43; also
Économies Royales, i, 252–3.

D

spent most of his time in Paris, with occasional visits to Fontaine-bleau when the court moved there. In the summer he would sometimes make longer journeys.[1] Between early July and late September 1599 he visited various points along the Loire south of Orleans, in August and September of 1600 he was in or near Lyons, in May and June of 1602 in Poitou, in June and July of 1603 in England, again in Poitou in June and July of 1604, and in 1605 at Châtellerault for July and August.

No doubt his Loire visit of 1599 allowed him to talk with Protestant leaders like Duplessis-Mornay, established at Saumur, and to judge their reactions to the edict of Nantes, promulgated the previous year. In 1600 he was at Lyons for the organization of that year's campaign against the duke of Savoy, for he had been appointed *grand maître de l'artillerie* in November 1599. It was then that he moved from his 'logis pres les Enfans Rouges'[2] to the Arsenal, his administrative base for the rest of the reign. During the negotiations for the treaty of Lyons, which settled affairs after the Savoy war, Rosny showed notable realism in pressing for the renunciation of Saluces (Saluzzo, for which the war had nominally been fought), and for the acquisition instead of the rich territories of Bresse, Bugey, Valromey and Gex, just to the north of Lyons. This formed the terms of the eventual settle-ment, to the disgust of Villeroy, who no doubt agreed with the Protestants and nobles that it was 'a shameful and dishonour-able treaty';[3] not only was the king giving up a foothold on the 'Italian' side of the Alps, but he was actually proposing to make a profit from this concession.

The visit to Poitou in 1602, during which Rosny accompanied the king, was intended to calm the disaffection which had been developing in that region, where there were many Protestant gentlemen. On their return to Paris in mid-June the king decided to arrest the duc de Biron, who like his father before him was a great soldier but whose implication in various plots had become too clear to be ignored. Rosny had been appointed governor of the Bastille early in 1602, and so was responsible for

[1] The following account is based on the dating of his letters.
[2] Mentioned in the *Économies Royales*, ii, 101a.
[3] Quotation of Sir Ralph Winwood writing to Robert Cecil in February 1600; *Memorials of affairs of state*, i, 295.

the imprisonment of this dangerous captive. A letter in his hand to the king gives details of the precautions which he took, both in guarding Biron in the Bastille and in mobilizing the artillery in Paris and at Lyons, ready for any revolt in the province of Burgundy, of which Biron had been governor.[1] But there was no revolt, partly because Rosny as 'an administrative measure' had some time before withdrawn the guns from some of Biron's Burgundian fortresses, and the unfortunate Marshal was safely executed late in July 1602.

Elizabeth of England having died in April 1603 (New Style),[2] Rosny was sent over there early the following June, with a suite of 250,[3] to sound James I and conclude a treaty of friendship with him. Rosny had been picked for this task partly because of his Scottish acquaintances, of whom the most prominent was the Catholic archbishop of Glasgow, who was a Béthune.[4] James Beaton, as he was commonly called, had firmly opposed the reformers and had left Scotland with the French party – and with the plate and records of his cathedral – on the death of the Regent in 1560. Settling in Paris he acted as Scottish ambassador there until his death in 1603, acquiring such a reputation for saintliness and moderation that in 1598 James VI (who became James I of England) recognized him as the official ambassador for the new Scottish régime. Rosny's talks with James were a great success and before leaving for France early in July he had come to a provisional agreement for a treaty of alliance against Spain. In fact James seems thereafter to have repented of this, and by August of the following year had signed a treaty of peace

---

[1] BN ms. fr. 15581, fo. 35; no doubt this is the letter to which Sully refers in the *Économies Royales*, i, 99b.

[2] By the (Old Style) English calendar she died on 24 March; this was ten days behind the (New Style) corrected Gregorian calendar of 1582 which had early been adopted in France and which is used throughout this book.

[3] Partially enumerated in the *Calendar of manuscripts of the marquis of Salisbury*, xv, 125 and 160.

[4] Sully was in correspondence with the archbishop (see BN ms. fr. 6621, fo. 165, letter from Sully to him announcing the death of Queen Elizabeth), and unkind tongues claimed that he was in fact 'of the family of the Betons, though himself will not acknowledge it, but pretendeth to be descended from the lords of Bethun in Flanders'. Sir George Carew, *A Relation of the state of France*, 484.

with Spain. All the same, Rosny had earned general praise for his conduct of the negotiations and had shown that the sour guardian of the royal treasure could on occasion act the supple and accommodating courtier.[1] There survives a curious example of his diplomatic punctiliousness; Sir Lewis Lewkenor, master of ceremonies, wrote to Lord Cecil on 27 June from Dover that 'standing this night upon the pier with M. de Rhosny a packet of letters was delivered unto him . . . wherein among others was one of His Majesty's own hand to the French king with this superscription: "A mon trescher frere le Roy treschrestien", which did put him into such an exceeding passion [that he sent it back, for "Monsieur" to be inserted before "le Roy"].'[2] No doubt he remained interested in French relations with the English crown, for in November 1603 we find him writing to the French ambassador at London urging him to bring pressure to bear against those English pirates about whom French merchants were always complaining,[3] and about whose depredations he had himself spoken to James.

The next year he was again in Poitou during June, investigating further rumours of plots, for in December 1603 he had been appointed governor of the province. He took his duties seriously, going so far as to raise 4,000 men and four guns on one occasion, in order to root out some nests of robbers.[4] In October 1604 he and Sillery were the French commissioners for the treaty which again permitted trade with Spain, suspended as a recriminatory measure in February of that year to make the Spaniards raise their own embargo.[5] During July and August of 1605 Rosny was at Châtellerault, addressing the Protestant assembly there on behalf of the king. Although his reception by his fellow-

---

[1] The nature of Rosny's success is well summarized by Pfister, 'Les Économies Royales . . .', Revue Historique, lv (1894), 299. For a less favourable estimate, see William A. Shaw (ed.), Report on the manuscripts of Lord de L'Isle and Dudley (5 vols, London, 1925–62) iv, ix.

[2] Calendar of manuscripts of the marquis of Salisbury, xv, 152–6.

[3] BM Cotton, Caligula E X, fo. 181.

[4] See H. Boone, 'Le protestantisme à Saint-Hilaire-sur-Autise', Bulletin Philologique et Historique (1926–7), 68.

[5] On this negotiation, see J. de Sturler, 'Documents diplomatiques et administratifs relatifs aux différends commerciaux et maritimes survenus entre les Pays-Bas et la France, 1599–1607', Bulletin de la commission royale d'histoire de Belgique (1939).

Huguenots was far from cordial, for he did not seem to show them the favour they expected, he succeeded in carrying out his instructions for the discouragement of further assemblies, and satisfied his co-religionists by a four-year extension of their right to hold certain fortified towns ('*places de sûreté*').[1] Then he returned to Paris, whence he made fewer journeys into the provinces between 1606 and 1610.

In March 1606 he became a duke, his land at Sully being raised to the status of a *duché-pairie*; this was the last great honour Sully received before becoming a *maréchal de France* in 1634. These latter years of Henri IV's reign were mostly spent in peaceful consolidation of the realm, although after 1609 preparations for war with the Hapsburgs began to gather momentum. Throughout the reign Sully had been in favour of renewed French intervention in the north-east, partly because he hoped to recover certain lands there for his relations of the house of Espinoy. As Sir Ralph Winwood put it, in a letter of February 1601 to Robert Cecil, 'Your Honor doth remember that Monsieur de Rhosny hath a particular interest, that doth move him to this action of Flanders, which he would advance with the main of his power.'[2] He had been opposed to the Dutch truce of 1609 with the Spaniards, arguing that it would be better to wage a relentless war until a proper peace could be concluded. He therefore threw himself willingly into the preparations for war of 1609, especially as he hoped that the main campaign would take place in the north-east.[3] Originally planned with a limited end in view, the scope of these preparations was greatly enlarged after November 1609, when the prince de Condé fled to Brussels with his wife Charlotte, upon whom the king had for some time been casting lascivious eyes.[4]

[1] See Léonce Anquez, *Histoire des assemblées politiques des Réformés de France (1573–1622)* (Paris, 1859), for details on these towns (162–3) and on the Assembly (216–20).

[2] *Memorials of affairs of state*, i, 383; details of the 'interest' are well set out by J. Nouaillac (ed.), *Un envoyé hollandais à la cour de Henri IV: lettres inédites de François Aerssen à Jacques Valcke, 1599–1603* (Paris, 1908), 105, note 2.

[3] See the interesting documents quoted by J. L. Motley, *The life and death of John of Barneveld, advocate of Holland* (2 vols, London, 1874), i, 187–91.

[4] The change of plan is described by J.-H. Mariéjol, *Henri IV et Louis XIII*, 129–30, and more fully in Paul Henrard's *Henri IV et la princesse de Condé, 1609–1610* (Brussels, 1870).

In the *Économies Royales* there is an interesting account of the advice given to the king on this occasion by his various counsellors; Sully took the rather subtle view that nothing should be done, so that the archduke and -duchess Albert and Isabella would expel Condé and his wife, thinking them to be either stool-pigeons or embarrassing nonentities. His advice was not taken, but the *Économies Royales* version of the episode is interestingly confirmed by that of François de Bassompierre,[1] the future *maréchal de France* who was close to the king at this time.

The assassination of Henri IV in May 1610 meant that the military plans would not be carried out on the grand scale of their conception, and also meant that Sully's position became precarious, for the Regent Marie de Medici was a friend of Spain and no friend of his in the political field, quite apart from their personal relations.[2] She began to make payments of as much as 400,000 *livres* without his prior knowledge, so that we find him reduced to writing on a certain account 'je ne say que c'est de cest article' – 'what is this entry all about?' (see plate 3). Worse than this, she did not give him the support against the *grands* which he had received from the late king, who had known them all in his early days and appreciated the danger of their ambitions.

Sully had had many fierce quarrels with various princes and nobles, quarrels reported in eager detail by contemporary writers. The most celebrated were those with the duc d'Épernon and the marquis de Vitry in October 1598, and with the comte de Soissons in August 1603. On each of these occasions the king took his side unequivocally, going so far as to offer his services as a second if it came to blows with Vitry.[3] Sully for his part argued that he was doing the king's business – nearly always financial business which was encroaching on some noble privilege – and so was answerable only to the king and his council.[4] Under the

---

[1] See *Économies Royales*, ii, 308–9 and the *Journal de ma vie; mémoires du maréchal de Bassompierre*, ed. marquis de Chantérac (4 vols, Paris, 1870), i, 259–60.

[2] For an account of their relations at this time, see Berthold Zeller, *La minorité de Louis XIII: Marie de Médicis et Sully* (Paris, 1892).

[3] *Journal de L'Estoile*, i, 545–6.

[4] See the account of the quarrel with Épernon, BN ms. fr. 4740, fo. 99-102.

regency he no longer enjoyed this protection, so that in January 1611 Villeroy was able to concert the opposition of Condé, Soissons and the queen's Italian favourite Concini in order to secure his resignation.[1]

It has been claimed that Sully's influence was already waning in the lifetime of Henri IV, because the king was tiring of his overbearing nature and of his corruption.[2] But Sully was not corrupt by the standards of his time, and the two men had already patched up many a quarrel. Moreover, he was far too valuable as a financial and military organizer to be discarded just when a war was about to begin.

When he retired in 1611 he still had thirty years of active life in front of him; now, however, we shall pass on to his work while he was in office, leaving the account of the years of his retirement to chapter X.

[1] Zeller, *La minorité de Louis XIII*, 215.

[2] Crue, *Les derniers desseins de Henri IV*, 34; Marbault, *Remarques sur les mémoires de Sully*, 58a; and the *Mémoires du cardinal de Richelieu*, ed. Courcel, Delavaud and Lacour-Gayet (10 vols, Paris, 1908–31), i, 27–8.

CHAPTER III

Surintendant des finances
the working of the financial system

The civil wars may not have been as damaging as was once thought. In many regions the worst effects were averted by local pacts made between neighbouring hostile leaders; for example, the king himself had an agreement with the duc de Mayenne to spare the duchy of Nemours,[1] and in 1592 the royal governor in the Ile-de-France, the sieur d'O, agreed with the sieur d'Alincourt that they would have an eight-month truce in (large) specified areas, that the inhabitants could pass freely with their belongings during this period (partly to 'facilliter la cueillette des fruictz'), and that d'Alincourt would give passports to the royal collectors of *tailles*.[2] Such truces were common, and the latter provision illustrates the curious permanence of the financial structure. Even in a territory ravaged by conflicts war was waged less thoroughly than we nowadays should consider seemly, so that the enemies of the king often confined themselves to mulcting his treasurers, without preventing them from continuing to carry out their tasks even in disputed areas. In June 1590, for example, certain subordinate officials wrote to the Caen centre that some people in their division had not yet paid their taxes 'because we have not yet been able to discover if they belong to the League or not'.[3] Again, many *trésoriers de France* who had served Henri III continued in office under the League and then into the reign of Henri IV; there was a stability of personnel as well as a continuity of administrative routine.[4]

[1] 'Un traité inconnu entre Henri IV et Mayenne', ed. Eugène Thoison, *Bulletin Historique et Philologique* (1894), 452–63.

[2] BN ms. fr. 3982, fo. 37–8.

[3] *Lettres et chevauchées du bureau des finances de Caen sous Henri IV*, ed. Lucien Romier (Paris, 1910), 13.

[4] Charmeil, *Les trésoriers de France*, 29, gives two examples.

The fact that the old structure had largely survived made it possible for Rosny in 1598 to breathe new life into the system without radically changing it; we cannot do better than describe the organization with his own account of it as our guide.[1]

At Paris was the *conseil des finances*, which co-operated with Rosny in the general direction of financial affairs, but which became less and less important as the reign went on.[2] Immediately below Rosny, who after 1600 held the title of *surintendant des finances*,[3] came the three *intendants des finances*, Jean de Vienne, who died in 1608, Gilles de Maupeou and Isaac Arnauld. Their chief task was to communicate with the provincial centres, known since 1577 as the *bureaux des finances*.[4] Each of these lay in a town at the head of a generality, and was staffed by ten *trésoriers de France* with a *receveur-général*, the *trésoriers* serving alternately, five each year,[5] and the *receveur's* office being held by three men, one serving every three years.[6] Each generality contained a certain number of *élections*, in which the financial officers were the ten or so *élus*, who in their turn directed the *asséeurs* and *collecteurs* responsible for collecting the *tailles* in each *paroisse*.[7] The hierarchy therefore went like this:

---

[1] The 'Relation de monsieur de Sully sur les finances de France', a memoir found in many manuscript-collections of the seventeenth century (BN ms. fr. 23042, fo. 132–59, the copy used here; also BN ms. fr. 2408, 16626 and 17291, with BN Dupuy 89). A variant of this 'relation' was published by R. Doucet, 'Les finances de la France en 1614', *Revue d'histoire économique et sociale*, xviii (1930), 133–63; it should be supplemented by the *règlement des finances* printed by G. Boussinesq, *Revue Henri IV*, i (1905), 189–90.

[2] Valois, lxxv, note 7; see also Mousnier, 'Sully et le conseil d'État', *Revue Historique*, cxcii (1941), 68–86, for qualifications.

[3] See my article written in collaboration with Bernard Barbiche, 'Sully et la surintendance des finances', *Bibliothèque de l'École des Chartes*, cxxiii (1965), 538–43.

[4] The *bureaux* were officially suppressed by an edict of December 1598, but as it was not obeyed it has seemed to me more realistic to ignore it. They were officially reinstated in November 1608.

[5] Valois, n⁰ 8629.

[6] This cumbrous system was the result of (fiscally-inspired) multiplication of offices.

[7] In accordance with the edict of March 1600, analysed by J.-J. Clamageran, *Histoire de l'impôt en France* (3 vols, Paris, 1867–76), ii, 357–9.

conseil des finances
and *surintendant*   Paris
          |
    3 *intendants*
          |
10 *trésoriers de France*   15 generalities
3 *receveurs-généraux*
          |
    10 *élus*   150 *élections*
          |
asséeurs and *collecteurs*   22,600 *paroisses*

TABLE 2   THE GENERALITIES: SUB-DIVISIONS

Generality	élections	paroisses	average annual wage of the trésoriers* (livres)
Paris	20	1,970	5,699
Soissons	6	1,197	2,855
Amiens	6	1,260	2,877
Châlons	9	2,207	2,891
Orléans	12	1,237	4,505
Tours	14	1,563	2,754
Poitiers	9	1,600	2,855
Limoges	9	1,600	2,855
Bourges	9	532	2,830
Moulins	7	128	2,800
Riom	4	819	2,849
Lyons	3	720	2,966
Rouen	21	2,876	2,934
Caen	9	1,426	2,980
Bordeaux	15	3,508	2,805
	153	22,643	2,850 (average)

* The figures for the *trésoriers'* wages are taken from the 'Traités . . . relatifs au domaine et aux finances . . .', BN ms. fr. 11165, fo. 355–60; the other figures come from the 'Relation de monsieur de Sully . . .' The generalities have been left in the usual contemporary order (of seniority by age).

Table 2 shows how widely the subordinate units in a generality might vary in number; it also brings out the relative importance of the generalities of Paris and Rouen. It applies only to the *pays d'élections* and so leaves out the great provinces of Brittany, Burgundy, Dauphiné, Provence and Languedoc, which were *pays d'états* and so had a different system, which will be described separately.[1]

[1] It is of course true that there were *élections* in some *pays d'états* (Roger Doucet, *Les institutions de la France au XVIe siècle* (2 vols, Paris, 1948), i, 348), but the traditional distinction still seems to me valid, as will become clear in the course of this book.

For the direct taxes in the *pays d'élections* the *surintendant* drew up a *brevet des tailles* which, after being submitted to the king for approval, was broken down for an appropriate extract to be sent to each generality.[1] There the *trésoriers de France* split down their allocation among the *élections*, sharing the burden out according to the measure of prosperity they had observed during their visits of inspection (called *chevauchées*) the previous autumn.[2] Then they sent back to Paris – as Sully says, 'to the council, that is to say to the *surintendant des finances*' – the consolidated account of how they had divided the imposition specified in the *brevet*. This list was known as the *état de la valeur des finances*, and having received it Sully would then draw up the most important document of them all, the *état du roi*.

This gave for each generality the details of income and the way in which this revenue would be spent, some being paid to local *trésoriers* for specific funds (the artillery, fortifications and so on; see chapter IV), some going to pay for collection-expenses and some being remitted to the central treasury (the *épargne*). The drawing-up of this summary was for Sully the most exacting task of the financial year, involving the preparation and assembly (using symbols and numbers keyed to a main list) of about one hundred minor *états* which had then to be fitted into the master-plan.[3] All kinds of officials would share in deciding the allocations which would be made, of money to be spent in the various provinces for the fortifications, for instance, or for the navy, and the king himself took a leading part in these discussions.[4]

The *état du roi* covered the whole of France including the *pays d'états*. In these regions there were generally no *élus* and so there was no possibility of applying the procedure described above. There were, however, *bureaux des finances* whose treasurer levied monies under the direction of the provincial estates. In both

[1] The *arrêt* accompanying the *brevet* for 1608 is printed in the *Économies Royales*, ii, 268a; it is a faithful transcript of the original, AN 120 AP 25, fo. 21r⁰.
[2] Valois, n⁰ 6626, an *arrêt* regulating the functions of the *trésoriers de France*, gives details of this procedure.
[3] It is this task which Sully describes in the *Économies Royales*, ii, 298b.
[4] *Économies Royales*, i, 534 and 538.

pays d'élections and *pays d'états* were the tax-farms (*fermes*), whose contracts were often awarded at Paris by the *conseil* and whose revenue – a considerable proportion of the whole – was paid over either locally or to the *épargne*. It will be realized, however, that the farmers drew a heavy, if for us unassessable, profit from their offices, and this, combined with the fact that the collection-expenses for other taxes are hard to judge, means that the income of the *épargne* by no means represented the whole burden imposed on the people, which may sometimes have been half as much again as the sum collected for the king.[1]

When the *état du roi* was complete it was signed by the king and then distributed; appropriate extracts were sent to each generality,[2] and one copy went to the *trésorier de l'épargne*, the official responsible for receiving and paying out the monies of the central fund. He accepted the generalities' contributions when their *receveurs-généraux* had accumulated sums sizeable enough to justify the considerable escort which they had on their way to Paris; there was no fixed rule about this. Sully attached great importance, as we shall see, to the *état du roi* being followed in detail, and was able to check the provincial accounts when, one month after the end of the financial year, the *receveurs-généraux* sent in their *états de recette et dépense*, counter-signed by the *trésoriers de France* of the generality. Finally the *trésorier de l'épargne* combined all the provincial accounts into his own general *état au vrai*,[3] which was eventually verified and signed by Sully and some other member of the council. In this final account were also included the *finances extraordinaires*, including such unpredictable sources of income as the sale of offices and of timber (from royal estates), and unforeseeable expenditure like the king's private payments. The documentary cycle thus went like this:

[1] In the case of the *taille*, collection-expenses amounted to about one-quarter of the net income. See the 'Relation de monsieur de Sully' and Avenel, *Richelieu et la monarchie absolue*, ii, 344.

[2] That for Châlons of 1602 is the only one known to have survived; it is printed in the *Revue Henri IV*, iii (1909–12), 151–65, as part of an article by Albert Chamberland on 'Le budget de la généralité de Châlons en 1602'.

[3] See chapter IV for details of this process, and chapter V for a discussion of the *chambre des comptes*, to which the accounts were eventually submitted.

August	*Surintendant* sends out the **brevets des tailles** to the *trésoriers de France*, who draw up their **états de la valeur des finances**
October	and return them to Paris.
January	*Surintendant* uses these to draw up the **état du roi**. Taxes are collected and payments made in accordance with this, to which the **états au vrai** must correspond.

The general outline of the organization within which Sully worked had been developing over the past century, and in November 1594 a great *règlement* had laid down the principal procedures, described above, which would be followed during his *surintendance*. Albert Chamberland considered that Sully's immediate predecessors were remarkable men,[1] and it is certain that some, like Bellièvre, were capable and honest, and that in the *Économies Royales* Sully attacks them all with an unreasonable lack of discrimination.[2] However, without undertaking their individual biographies it is not possible to judge what would have been their capacity had they been, like Sully, able to direct the finances when France was at peace, and had they not all the time had to improvise desperate expedients to meet the demands of war.[3] The Rouen assembly and Paris *parlement* made many suggestions for reform – of the *conseil des finances*, for example, and of the method of levying *tailles* – which were later adopted by Sully.[4]

The vital links in the financial system were the *bureaux des finances*. Most of their records have perished, but from seven sets of registers which have survived – those of the *bureaux* at Bordeaux, Bourges, Caen, Châlons-sur-Marne, Paris, Poitiers and Rouen – together with the work of Jacques Permezel on the *bureau* at Lyons,[5] it is possible to gain some idea of the nature of Sully's dealings with them and of his influence on them. The

[1] 'Le conseil des finances', *Revue Henri IV*, i (1905), 275–84.
[2] See for example, *Économies Royales*, i, 82a and 99b.
[3] See Bib. Institut, fonds Godefroy, 144, fo. 9–14, 56–7 and 58–9, for three *procès-verbaux* of the *conseil des finances* of 1595; expenditure far outran income.
[4] See the *Mémoires de Sancy et de Villeroy, documents divers . . .*, ed. Auguste Poirson (Paris, 1868).
[5] *La politique financière de Sully dans la généralité de Lyon* (Lyon, 1935).

publication of Sully's letters to the *trésoriers* at Caen[1] has given a rather unfavourable impression of the general efficiency of the *bureaux*. But the one at Caen was unduly slack, and we meet with none of the scathing letters of the kind he found it necessary to send to Caen in the records of the *bureaux* of, for example, Bordeaux, Châlons or Paris. In most of the generalities the annual cycle of submission of accounts went through smoothly, with Sully carrying on a brisk but friendly correspondence about, for instance, the enclosed *arrêt* or *brevet des tailles*, or about some statistical information which he needed and which was often sent to him promptly. In general the *trésoriers de France* were both more honest and more efficient than has been thought.[2]

Sometimes, indeed, it was the *bureaux* which had to complain of the staff at Paris. In 1607 the *brevet des tailles* (due in September) did not reach Caen until the following January,[3] and in 1610 the same thing happened in the generality of Bordeaux.[4] The *état du roi* was generally dispatched on time in January or February but in the early days of Sully's administration it was sometimes late; in 1599, for example, it did not arrive at the Paris *bureau* until 15 March.[5] Again, monies might be designated for payment for a non-existent service; thus in 1607 the Brittany estates in session at Tréguier complained that sums were being levied 'under the heading of garrisons which do not exist'.[6] This may, of course, have been merely a fiscal expedient on Sully's part. The central organization was also sometimes inefficient in its awarding of leases for farms and of contracts for public works. Thus in March 1610 the *trésoriers* at Bordeaux wrote to Sully that the lease for the *traite foraine* of Bayonne was made under conditions which were too favourable for the

---

[1] Romier, 'Lettres inédites de Sully', *Bulletin Historique et Philologique* (1909), 541–94, completed by my own 'Lettres inédites de Sully aux trésoriers généraux de France à Caen (1599–1610)', *Annales de Normandie*, xiii (1963), 269–304.

[2] This is also the conclusion of Charmeil, *Les trésoriers de France*, 94.

[3] AD Calvados, series C (not yet inventoried), 'Délibérations et ordonnances du bureau des finances', 2 January 1608.

[4] AD Gironde, C 3875, fo. lr°.

[5] AN Z 1 F 135, fo. 42r°.

[6] BN ms. fr. 22315, fo. 81.

lessee, and that one of their number (Étienne de Pontac) had received several more favourable offers.[1] Albert Chamberland noticed several equally unprofitable leases from Paris in the generality of Châlons.[2]

A leading member of the *bureau* at Caen was Guillaume Novynce, sieur d'Aubigny, one of those *trésoriers* whom Sully, as Chamberland noticed, was in places using to undermine the position of the *bureaux*.[3] Aubigny had spent a good deal of time in Paris on the affairs of the generality,[4] no doubt meeting Sully there, and had in 1604 been appointed 'commissaire pour la recherche des malversations des finances' in Normandy.[5] His colleagues can hardly have relished his activities in this role, and in 1610, as we shall see, he again quarrelled with them over his operations as *lieutenant du grand voyer*. His equivalent in the generality of Châlons was Jean de Lon, sieur de Lorme – also, significantly enough, appointed a *lieutenant du grand voyer*. His action in 1602, when he accepted on his own behalf a commission for a domain inquiry there,[6] led his colleagues to pass a resolution of censure. This stated that for the future all commissions concerning the generality and addressed to any individual *trésorier* should be brought before the *bureau* for registration.[7] The aim of this measure was to 'avoid all jealousy, kindle peace and lead to a more fraternal life in the future'; also no doubt to safeguard the *bureau's* integrity against infiltrations of this kind.

A great many of Sully's celebrated investigations into the *trésoriers'* supposed malversations were carried out at Paris. He personally made extracts from certain accounts in the possession of the *chambre des comptes* at Paris; these accounts contained

[1] AD Gironde, C 3875, fo. 10–11; the *traite foraine* was a customs-tax.

[2] 'Recherches critiques sur les réformes financières en Champagne à l'époque de Henri IV et de Sully', *Travaux de l'Académie de Reims*, cxi (1901), 243–71.

[3] 'Recherches sur les réformes financières', 257.

[4] BN nouv. acq. franç., 240, fo. 10, and Romier (ed.), *Lettres et chevauchées*, 171.

[5] *Lettres Missives*, ix, 49 and 53; I have described Aubigny's activities more fully in 'A stage in the development of the *intendants*; the reign of Henri IV', *The Historical Journal* (1965), 32–3.

[6] AD Marne, C 2490, fo. 167v⁰.

[7] Loc. cit., fo. 201r⁰.

details of royal *dons* about which he reported directly to the
king. His work survives as a volume among the 'Papiers de
Sully'.[1] He also set members of his entourage to the checking of
old accounts in order to track down discrepancies. Thus when
Aubery Du Maurier entered Sully's service in 1607 (see pages
69–70) he was assigned to the auditing of the balances in the
états au vrai from 1599 onward;[2] his work also has survived
among the 'Papiers de Sully'.

There were general *arrêts* for the *trésoriers* to submit their
accounts from distant dates, and one of these, of February
1602, is particularly interesting because on it Sully has altered
the wording from '1598' to '1597', graphically demonstrating
his enthusiasm for pushing the investigations back in time.[3]
There were also special *arrêts* and letters-patent for various
generalities to submit accounts of particular funds; for the
Poitiers *bureau* in 1599 to send in the accounts of its *receveurs-
généraux* since 1594;[4] for the Bordeaux *bureau* in 1601 to present
copies of their *départements des tailles* since 1598;[5] for the *trésorier* of
the Brittany estates to account in 1609 for the years 1598–1608,[6]
and so on. In the latter generality Sully also used a local in-
vestigator during 1603 and 1604, a certain 'Bernard' whose
reports show that the Brittany *trésoriers'* 'pots de vin' (Sully's
phrase) came to 6,000 *écus* for each 90,000 *écus'* worth of *rentes*
leased out.[7]

Many of the abuses against which Sully struggled were less
flagrant. Although it was well understood that the *état du roi* was
meant to be a firm directive, officials did not hesitate to disobey
its instructions when they seemed inhumane. Thus in August
1603 the *trésoriers* at Bordeaux wrote to one of the *intendants des
finances* that they *had* to pay certain wages, such as those of the
'Regentz des Colleges de cette ville',[8] and in 1601 the Caen

[1] AN 120 AP 12; see AN P 2666, fo. 150v°, for an account of the work.
[2] See his 'Mémoires autographes', Bib. Poitiers, Ms. 298, fo. 26r°; the
work is found in AN 120 AP 29, fo. 143–8.
[3] Valois, n° 6857.
[4] BN ms. fr. 5319, fo. 71v°.
[5] AD Gironde, C 3873, fo. 40r°.
[6] Valois, n° 14553.
[7] AN 120 AP 37, fo. 81–2.
[8] AD Gironde, C 3874, fo. 32–4.

trésoriers sent Sully a letter of similar tone explaining that they had included the officers' wages in the *états des ventes de bois*, even though royal letters forbade it. For it was a 'chose de telle commisération' that they could not obey that order.[1] Sometimes this apparent faith in the benevolence of the administration took less touching forms, as in the case of those *élus* of Troyes who in 1608 wrote directly to Sully explaining that they would not levy any more taxes for the Châlons bridge, as it had been completed. The *surintendant* replied with a very sharp letter to the Châlons *bureau*, explaining the gravity of an action which contradicted His Majesty's *états*, and ordering the *trésoriers* to see to it that the *élus* understood this.[2] Sully's vigilance seems to have been having some effect, for although more than two million *livres* were paid out between 1598 and 1608 without the authorization of the *états du roi*, it is noticeable that the sums thus misapplied were diminishing towards 1608 in most of the generalities.[3]

The *trésoriers* generally seem to have kept a firm hand on their subordinate officers, and to have tried to make them obey Sully's instructions. Sometimes they would conduct their own investigations. In February 1610, for instance, the Bordeaux *bureau* wrote to one of its *receveurs des tailles* (the equivalent in the *élection* to the *receveur-général* of the generality) that he should stop the *élus'* wages and payments for expenses until they sent in an account of their distribution of the *taille* which had been requested from them; he himself ran the risk of suspension from his office if he disobeyed this order.[4] Often, however, the *trésoriers* were unable to control their subordinates. On 8 April 1604 the king wrote to the duc de Montpensier, governor of Normandy, for him to enforce the embargo on Spanish commerce which had been decreed the previous February.[5] The governor passed the order on to the *trésoriers*, who diligently instructed the appropriate officers within their generality,[6] but

[1] Romier (ed.), *Lettres et Chevauchées*, 126.
[2] AD Marne, C 2491, fo. 79.
[3] AN 120 AP 13, fo. 29–31, gives a list of such sums unduly employed.
[4] AD Gironde, C 3875, fo. 9v⁰.
[5] BN nouv. acq. franç., 239, fo. 69.
[6] for example, the *officiers des traites foraines;* see Romier (ed.), *Lettres et Chevauchées*, 173–4.

E

to so little effect that the royal injunctions had to be repeated on 29 April and again in June, July and August.[1] There is little reason to suppose that they were being better obeyed in October when the restrictions on trade with Spain were officially removed.

The *trésoriers* encountered other difficulties – mostly arising from inadequate communications – in their attempts to carry out Sully's instructions. These more practical problems are well illustrated by the case of the Bayonne pikes. In the *Économies Royales*[2] is printed a letter of 19 March 1603 from Villeroy to Rosny, describing how 4,500 pikes had been seized at Saint-Jean-de-Luz from a merchant of Dunkirk, who had bought them in France and was proposing to smuggle them to the Spanish Netherlands. On 26 March Rosny replied that the seizure had been well calculated and that

> the king has done even better to command that the pikes be confiscated and taken to his arsenal at Paris. I shall not forget to write to monsieur de Gramont [governor of Bayonne] about it and to the *trésoriers de France* so that they can see to it.[3]

Rosny then wrote to the governor of Bayonne, who after receiving the letter early in April got in touch with the *trésoriers* and ordered them to instruct the *officiers de la traite foraine* to send the pikes to Paris.[4] The route lay by sea to Rouen, however, and there was difficulty in paying the captain of the ship. On 1 September Rosny wrote to say that all necessary expenses might be taken from the *recette générale* of Bordeaux,[5] and on 25 October the Bordeaux *trésoriers* wrote to their colleagues at Rouen asking them to receive the pikes when they arrived.[6] Meanwhile Rosny had sent impatient letters on 2 October and 17 October, to know what was causing the delay; the *trésoriers* explained their difficulties to him in a letter of 27 October, and on 3 December were able to write that the pikes had at last

---

[1] BN nouv. acq. franç., 239, fo. 70, 72, 74 and 76.
[2] Op. cit., i, 418.
[3] BN ms. fr. 15578, fo. 32.
[4] AD Gironde, C 3874, fo. 20.
[5] Loc. cit., fo. 45v⁰.
[6] Loc. cit., fo. 48r⁰.

sailed.[1] Unfortunately this is as far as we can trace their progress. A letter of June 1604, from the *maîtres des ports, passages, et traictes de Guienne estably a Bayonne* describes how the man sent by Sully from Paris had taken charge of the pikes and sailed from Saint-Jean-de-Luz, adding, however, that they do not know 'what has happened since then to the ship or the pikes'.[2] Neither do we, but even the unfinished story serves as a good example of the material difficulties encountered both by the local men and by the administration in Paris which tried to help and direct them.

Perhaps the weakest point of the local organization was the disinclination of the *bureaux* effectively to supervise their *receveurs-généraux*. Few were as resolute as the *trésoriers* at Bordeaux, who in September 1603 wrote to their *receveur* to say that they had received a letter from Rosny telling them to hasten the sending of the monies for the second quarter, and adding on their own initiative that 'if you do not show more diligence than you have in the past, then we shall start bringing pressure to bear on you'.[3] More often the *bureaux* preferred to remain on good terms with the official who, after all, paid their wages; sometimes, too, there was the suspicion that they deliberately left funds with the *receveur*, as Sully said, 'pour en disposer apres a votre fantaisie'.[4] For the financial officials of the provinces formed a compact social group, having all the advantages and limitations of the corporate spirit. The Normandy estates thus complained in November 1593 that 'most of the *trésoriers* are related to the *receveurs*, which is why justice is not observed in the administration'.[5] No doubt this allegation was true, and its substance could probably have been extended to the rest of France.

As we have noticed above in the case of the *trésoriers* at Châlons, the *bureaux* were much concerned to strengthen their

---

[1] Loc. cit., fo. 55 and 60.
[2] BN ms. fr. 23198, fo. 211; to the king, Bayonne, 30 June 1604.
[3] AD Gironde, C 3874, fo. 47.
[4] BN nouv. acq. franç., 239, fo. 100.
[5] Article XX of the November 1593 *cahier*, in the *Cahiers des états de Normandie sous le règne de Henri IV*, ed. Ch. de Robillard de Beaurepaire (2 vols, Rouen, 1880–2), i, 14.

corporate character, going so far as to claim that they, who had been established by royal enactments during the sixteenth century, were among the sovereign courts, antique bodies in some sense independent of the royal authority.[1] Their solidarity made it difficult for Sully to apply effective sanctions to their members in cases of disobedience. He could, as in the case of the *trésoriers* at Limoges in December 1601,[2] threaten to suppress the generality altogether, but this was clearly a menace of limited use – the ultimate deterrent. Again, he could hint that if the *trésoriers* did not toe the line it might be necessary to install *chambres de justice* or to send *commissaires extraordinaires*, but this too was a weapon which lost its edge with frequent use. The best sanction at his disposal was the stoppage of wages, and this was used effectively in 1608 against those *élus* of Troyes who refused to levy taxes for a completed bridge; their salaries were stopped 'until they have made up for what they failed to impose for the construction of the bridge'.[3] It was also used against some *trésoriers* and *receveurs-généraux*. In June 1609 Sully wrote to Martin de Bragelongne, *receveur* in the generality of Caen, that he should stop the wages of the *trésoriers* in that *bureau* until they had sent in certain accounts.[4] In this case the *surintendant* was successful in his aim, but the weakness of his method is illustrated by the fact that later in the same year he had to call on the *trésoriers* themselves to stop the wages of a former *receveur*, who had not sent in his accounts to the council. Peter and Paul could not be expected indefinitely to rob each other at the behest of Paris, without coming to some collusive agreement. No doubt this was clear to Sully himself, who, being unable in a venal organization to select his own officers for the *bureaux*, was content to build up his own network of officials outside the *bureaux* for special purposes (particularly for *voirie* and artillery; see chapters VI and VIII), and to attempt the subversion of some *trésoriers* in the way we have noticed.

[1] For their family solidarity, see Édouard Éverat, *Le bureau des finances de Riom 1551–1790* (Riom, 1900), 84, and for their pretensions, Mousnier, 'Sully et le conseil d'État', *Revue Historique*, cxcii (1941), 76, note 1.

[2] AN 3B, fo. 461r°.

[3] Valois, n° 8629, with AD Marne, 2490, fo. 79r°.

[4] BN nouv. acq. franç., 239, fo. 116.

On occasion he also seems to have intervened in the appointment of officers. We know from a report drawn up by Raymond de Bonnefons, *ingénieur du roi* in Provence, that a certain Chahu was regarded as a better *trésorier de la marine* than his colleague Bionneau, who was suspected of favouring dishonest officials.[1] It is therefore interesting to find one of the *intendants des finances* coming into the *chambre des comptes* at Paris in June 1600 to point out that, the *chambre* having omitted because of Bionneau's opposition to register Chahu's appointment, 'the sieur de Rosny has been committed by king and council to establish Chahu in the possession of this office'.[2] The opposition to Bionneau seems still to have been strong three years later, to judge by an *arrêt* of 22 February 1603, which maintains Chahu in office since Bionneau has been 'referred to the Chambre Royale [*chambre de justice*]'.[3] It is not easy to discover more about this case, the only one providing clear evidence of Sully's interference in the appointment of financial officers.

But such intervention must have been rare, and the traditional view that Sully deliberately filled administrative posts with Protestants[4] is mistaken. In support of this contention are usually quoted the four Arnaulds,[5] Noël Regnouart, artillery secretary, the La Coustauderies, *commissaires ordinaires de l'artillerie*, and the engineer Jean Errard. To these we may add Gilles de Maupeou, who was *intendant des finances* with Isaac Arnauld and who was converted in 1600,[6] Jacques Alleaume the engineer and Benjamin Aubery, sieur Du Maurier. The latter had entered royal service as a courier in July 1607, after a chance encounter with the king in the new rue Dauphine; in October that year Sully sought him out and took him on as a

---

[1] AN 120 AP 48, fo. 69.
[2] AN P 2666, fo. 431.
[3] Valois, n° 7488.
[4] See for instance, a recent work, E. G. Léonard, *Le protestant français* (Paris, 1953), 50.
[5] Isaac, *intendant des finances*, Eustache-Louis, *trésorier des ponts et chaussées*, Pierre and Claude, both *conseillers d'état* and *trésoriers de France*. See the biographical dictionary of the brothers Haag, *La France Protestante . . .* (Paris, 1847–58).
[6] Jacques Pannier, *L'Église réformée de Paris sous Henri IV* (Paris, 1911), 193.

member of his staff, in spite of the libel which he had some years earlier published against the *surintendant des finances*. Thereafter he rose quickly in the favour of Sully, who saw to it that he was well rewarded and stood as godfather to his son (christened 'Maximilien') in 1608.[1] Du Maurier, thus launched by Sully, had a notable career after his master's dismissal, serving as ambassador to the United Provinces.

It is doubtful, however, if the existence of this number of Protestants in an administrative system as large as that directed by Sully need be ascribed to the latter's deliberate policy. The La Coustauderies were only two among about two hundred *commissaires ordinaires*, of whom the great bulk was no doubt Catholic. If two of the three *intendants des finances* were Protestants, none of the three *trésoriers de l'épargne*[2] seems to have been, and in the case of the latter office, as in that of many others, Sully's hands were anyway tied by the custom of venal transmission; even if he had wished to install Protestants he would have found it hard to do so. In many spheres outside his control the ratio of members of the Protestant faith to the rest was at least as high as in the personnel of the finances or the artillery. A large proportion of the Paris *parlement* was Protestant,[3] and this was the religion of most of the capital's great architects and artists.[4] In many other fields Protestants were outstanding; we need mention only the names of Barthélemy de Laffemas, of Olivier de Serres, the celebrated agricultural writer, and of Pierre Du Guast, sieur de Monts, Canadian pioneer.

Occasionally Sully seems actually to have discouraged the appointment of a member of his faith to a high office; thus the candidature of Théodore Turquet, sieur de Mayerne, as *premiere médicin du roi*, did not receive his support,[5] perhaps because Théodore's father did not share his constitutional views. Sir George Carew, the English ambassador, remarked

---

[1] For all these details, see Ms. 298 of Bib. Poitiers, on which H. Ouvré drew for his *Aubery Du Maurier* (Paris, 1853).

[2] The *trésoriers de l'épargne*, like the *intendants des finances*, were 'triennaux' – serving once every three years.

[3] John Viénot, *Histoire de la Réforme française* (2 vols, Paris, 1934), ii, 114.

[4] Pannier, *L'Église réformée de Paris*, 186.

[5] Pannier, op. cit., 185.

that 'touching the Protestants of France, they have no great aid or support from him, but he is as harsh and rough to them as to any others.'[1] This emerges well from a letter to the king written by Sully on the occasion of the death of a certain trusted officer; 'the Protestants,' Sully writes, 'may well approach you as a body and suggest several names [to replace him]. But it is important to have a man devoted to your service [and so I suggest either the sieur Maignan] . . . or if Your Majesty wishes to appoint a Catholic either young Bor or Le Boulay.'[2] His general aim, in short, was to recruit men of enterprise regardless of their religion, and it is thus inaccurate to speak of him as the predecessor of Herwarth in founding the *Banque Protestante*.[3] Even if he had had a free hand in appointing his functionaries, it is doubtful whether he would have used it for the benefit of members of the Protestant faith – this indeed was precisely one of their grievances against him.[4] As it was he was not free to make wholesale appointments, and in any case Maupeou and Isaac Arnauld – at first sight the best two examples for the *Banque* theory – were, like so many of their contemporaries, both converted to Catholicism long before Sully was dead.

Many of the letters quoted above will have made it clear how closely he personally supervised the financial work. A large number of the *arrêts du conseil* which survive have alterations and additions in his distinctive hand, and in the *conseil des finances*, at any rate by 1605, 'he was the sole director of affairs'.[5] In comparing his letters to the *trésoriers* with those of his predecessors – the sieurs d'O, de Sancy and d'Incarville – it seems that his concept of control was much more advanced than theirs. Where they were content to send occasional routine letters of receipt or encouragement, he writes frequent dispatches demanding statistics or giving clear details about the action to be taken.[6]

---

[1] See his *Relation of the state of France*, 487.
[2] Sully to the king, Paris, 9 September 1604; BN ms. fr. 23198, fo. 193.
[3] See for instance, E. G. Léonard, 'Le Protestantisme français au XVIIe siècle', *Revue Historique*, cc (1948), 153–79.
[4] Élie Benoist, *Histoire de l'édit de Nantes* (5 vols, Delft, 1693), iii, 139.
[5] A. Chéruel, *Histoire de l'administration monarchique en France* (2 vols, Paris, 1855), i, 357, quoting a contemporary.
[6] This statement is based on the records of the Bourges, Caen and Paris *généralités*, for which some registers of the early 1590s survive.

This increased activity was chiefly possible because at Paris he had built up a secretariat of his own, for which there had been no provision in the older organization. The existence of this special organ emerges best from the accounts of *deniers comptants*, where after 1599 there are often substantial payments to the 'clerks who have worked under M. de Rosny'.[1] There are also occasionally special settlements with individuals, like the 4,566 *livres* paid in 1608 to the sieur Du Maurier for analysing various papers.[2] The existence of this special branch has sometimes been mentioned by authors who relied on stray references in the *Économies Royales*;[3] it is interesting to be able to confirm it from the accounts. However, this structure was the result of Sully's private enterprise, and when he retired in 1611 it was dissolved, some of the secretaries accompanying him into 'exile', where they could work on the memoirs, and others finding jobs at Paris under the new men.[4] The death of the king in May 1610 was felt as sharply in the financial sphere as in the political and military ones. Some *bureaux* refused to send their monies to Paris, fearing the insecurity of the roads,[5] and although there was a certain recovery towards the end of the year, Sully's fall early in 1611 led to the destruction of his work.

We shall see in the next two chapters how the treasure which he had saved was squandered, and how his regulations came to be disregarded. As has often been pointed out, his work on the financial structure showed no very original ideas. In any case, having started with entrenched provincial hierarchies used to certain methods it was not possible for him to undertake sweeping reforms. Moreover, the existing system was much less chaotic than is often claimed, and was indeed both well understood and workable.[6] What he did was to breathe fresh life into the old

[1] For example, AN 120 AP 10, fo. 23v⁰.

[2] AN 120 AP 6, fo. 247–8.

[3] See King, *Science and rationalism in the government of Louis XIV*, 68–73 and 173, and John Koren, *The history of statistics* (New York, 1918), 244–7.

[4] Maupeou and Arnauld, for instance, stayed on as *intendants des finances*.

[5] Those of Bordeaux and Caen, for instance; see respectively AD Gironde, C 3875, and Romier, 'Lettres inédites de Sully', *Bulletin Historique et Philologique* (1909), 582–3.

[6] See the remarks on this point by Alphonse Callery, *Histoire des institutions financières de l'ancienne France* (Fontainebleau, 1878), 38–40.

regulations, and so to supervise the existing provincial officials that the worst abuses were made more difficult to carry off. But Sully was only given twelve years, too short a time for any lasting reform of the inveterate institutions of the *ancien régime*.

CHAPTER IV

Surintendant des finances
analysis of the budgets

Before the 'Papiers de Sully' became available there was no
reliable means of establishing the income and expenditure of the
trésorier de l'épargne; as the historian Jean-Henri Mariéjol put it,
'Sully's financial administration, which we think we know so
well, is in reality very obscure'.[1] Historians of the reign had only
fragmentary accounts at their disposal, and to supplement these
had to rely on the inaccurate estimates of foreign ambassadors
and other garrulous contemporaries.[2] Now, however, one
volume in the 'Papiers de Sully'[3] provides us with the *états-
généraux des recettes et dépenses de l'épargne* between 1605 and 1609.
These are the *états au vrai*, submitted during those years by
successive *trésoriers de l'épargne* to the council for approval at the
end of their terms of office, and therefore give a very accurate
account of all income and expenditure. We saw in chapter III
how income and expenditure were regulated by the *état du roi*
sent out to each generality in January, and how the *états au vrai*
sent in to Paris by the *trésoriers* of each *bureau* had to correspond
with this. Similarly the general *état au vrai* thereafter made up by
the *trésorier de l'épargne* had to correspond to the general *état du
roi*, of which he had received a copy when the extracts were sent
out to the provinces in January. The *trésorier de l'épargne* checked
that it did so, had it approved by the council, and then changed
the rather uninformative arrangement of entries of expenditure
by chronological 'rolls' into a more meaningful version recording

---

[1] *Henri IV et Louis XIII*, 52.
[2] See for instance, the figures quoted by Auguste Poirson, in his otherwise still valuable *Histoire du règne de Henri IV* (4 vols, Paris, 1865).
[3] AN 120 AP 2.

it by subjects; expenditure to the *trésoriers* of the navy, of the fortifications, of the artillery and so on. This fair copy was then sent in for checking to the *chambre des comptes*, whose *asséeurs* and *correcteurs* examined it carefully before approving it (or such was the theory).[1] The cycle ran thus:

January   *Surintendant* sends out appropriate extracts of the **état du roi** to each *bureau des finances* (and a copy to the *trésorier de l'épargne*).

The *trésoriers* collect taxes and make payments (**particular**) in accordance with this, and send in their **état au vrai** recording the work;

the *trésorier de l'épargne* receives all these provincial (**general**) *états au vrai* and establishes the **état au vrai** preserved in the 'Papiers de Sully' (120 AP 2);

he then reformulates the expenditure, leaving the income unchanged, and submits this **fair copy** to the *chambre des comptes*.

It was these fair copies which perished in the disastrous fire of 1737 at the Paris *chambre des comptes*, as a result of which it seemed impossible ever to re-establish the budget with certainty. Some time before 1737, however, a clerk of the financial administration called J. R. Mallet had abstracted from these fair copies a summarized version of the income and expenditure which he claimed to be accurate and which covered the years 1600-1700.[2] The interest of this version from our point of view is that in comparing its figures with those of the original *états au vrai* – no mean task in view of the reformulated expenditure – we find them to correspond (see appendix 1). We are therefore justified in using for the years 1600–4 a set of figures which have been proved accurate for the succeeding five years, and Mallet's version of the income and expenditure for the whole period 1600–10 is accordingly reproduced as tables 3 and 4, respectively. The first line in table 3 shows that income from the *recettes*

---

[1] See A. M. de Boislisle, *Chambre des comptes de Paris* (Nogent-le-Rotrou, 1873).

[2] The *Comptes rendus de l'administration des finances du royaume de France*, published at London in 1789. Mallet's figures are discussed by Poirson, *Histoire du règne de Henri IV*, iv, 609–13, and by A. M. de Boislisle in his edition of the *Correspondance des contrôleurs généraux des finances* (3 vols, Paris, 1874–97), i, xviii–xix.

générales in the *pays d'élections* fell between 1600 and 1610 from about ten million to about nine million *livres*. Although this reduction in *tailles* in the *pays d'élections* was somewhat offset by an increase in the contribution of the *pays d'états*, under Sully the total income from this levy, the chief form of direct taxation, was slightly reduced. The contributions of the *pays d'états* were not as small as appears from the table, for they were subject to numerous other charges, imposed in agreement with the estates. Thus although Languedoc directly contributed only about 200,000 *livres* yearly, in fact the king drew about 1,200,000 *livres* from that province, in the form not only of salt- and customs-duties payable by all *pays*, but also in that of payments for garrisons, of salaries for the governor and of similar expenses.[1] No doubt the other *pays d'états* made contributions to the *épargne* on a like scale.

Under *parties casuelles* came sums derived from sale of office and from the *droit annuel* or *Paulette*.[2] The *droit annuel* was a tax voluntarily paid by office-holders to ensure the transmission of their offices on their death to a person chosen by them; before the institution of this tax by Sully the forty-day rule had applied, by which offices could not be freely exchanged unless the former holder survived the exchange by forty days. The duty was hotly opposed by Bellièvre and by others who feared that it would set up an incompetent and uncontrollable hereditary caste; Sully himself in his later years perhaps regretted his part in proposing the measure, for he gives it only an inconsequential mention in the *Économies Royales*.[3] Its effect was to institutionalize that venality which custom had long permitted, and even though a small income was derived from it, the price was high; reform of venal practices was made even more difficult. After 1598 there were only a few creations of offices, and some were suppressed; the *parties casuelles* played a relatively minor part in the finances at this time.

Income from both salt- and customs-farms rose steadily

---

[1] BN ms. fr. 16658, fo. 523; the share of the *pays d'états* is discussed by Avenel, *Richelieu et la monarchie absolue*, ii, 213–17.

[2] See the work of Roland Mousnier, *La vénalité des offices sous Henri IV et Louis XIII* (Rouen, 1945), for much of what follows.

[3] *Économies Royales*, ii, 332b.

TABLE 3 INCOME OF THE *TRÉSORIER DE L'ÉPARGNE*, 1600-10

	1600	1601	1602	1603	1604	1605	1606	1607	1608	1609	1610
1 *Tailles* –											
(a) *pays d'élections*	9,949,999	10,191,031	9,394,647	9,666,235	9,665,645	9,863,995	9,650,692	9,626,083	9,274,105	9,004,643	9,169,759
(b) *pays d'états*	893,545	978,182	1,133,381	1,177,392	1,303,686	1,219,856	1,346,674	1,179,200	1,202,196	1,247,518	1,121,215
Total	10,843,544	11,169,213	10,528,028	10,843,627	10,969,331	11,083,851	10,997,366	10,805,283	10,475,301	10,292,161	10,290,974
2 *Parties Casuelles*	1,644,046	625,006	1,314,312	1,967,530	1,551,674	2,324,394	1,918,067	1,842,638	3,479,592	2,263,751	1,668,108
3 *Gabelles*	1,193,083	947,902	1,213,665	1,540,410	1,429,382	1,650,871	2,358,500	2,375,137	2,570,495	2,613,010	2,262,898
4 *Fermes*	1,904,261	1,606,466	2,283,991	2,399,969	2,017,534	3,167,194	3,747,178	3,214,574	3,517,607	3,525,381	3,261,300
Tota	4,741,390	3,179,374	4,811,968	5,907,909	4,998,592	7,142,459	8,023,745	7,432,349	9,567,694	8,402,142	7,192,306
5 *Bois*	33,651	166,880	241,730	123,285	108,550	160,115	162,600	447,957	278,636	282,271	267,533
6 *Deniers extraordinaires*	4,924,232	1,603,059	3,983,703	4,166,519	5,497,987	8,492,643	9,194,648	11,156,470	12,465,665	13,486,864	15,905,008
Grand total	20,542,817	16,118,526	19,565,429	21,041,340	21,574,460	26,879,068	28,378,359	29,842,059	32,787,296	32,463,438	33,655,821

during Sully's period as *surintendant des finances*. If, as we have
seen, his boast that he relieved the peasantry of the *taille* is true,
it is none the less clear that the country as a whole was more
heavily burdened with indirect taxes, whose weight roughly
doubled during these years.[1] The following graph, drawn up in
accordance with the figures set out in table 3, makes this development plain:

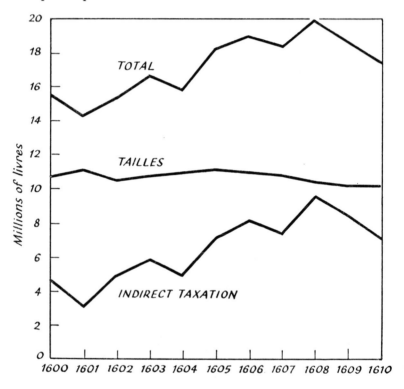

The income from *bois* was of little importance, and the in-
clusion of such small sums under a major heading was by now
only a relic from the days when such domain revenue formed a
major part of the royal income. The steady rise in the totals of
deniers extraordinaires is due to the practice of including on both

[1] Assuming of course that the increased revenue coming into the
treasury was not merely the result of more efficient methods of collection;
it is hard to know about this.

sides of the budget, in income as well as in expenditure, the sums in hand and paid over to the keeper of the treasure in the Bastille (see below). This method of accounting makes it necessary to be cautious when speaking of total income, for the annual true revenue rose only slightly to about eighteen million *livres*, in spite of an apparent increase to thirty-three million.

Table 4 sets out the expenditure. The household still took as much as one-tenth of the total, and the palace-guards almost as much as the navy. The figures for *guerres* reflect the wars and rumours of wars which troubled the reign; normal expenditure was almost doubled during the Savoy campaign of 1600 and more than doubled in 1610. The entries for the navy, the artillery, the fortifications, the buildings and the communications are analysed in the appropriate chapters. Most of the detailed accounts of the *trésoriers* in this section perished in the great fire at the *chambre des comptes*, but those of the *extraordinaire des guerres* for 1599–1610, of the *ponts et chaussées* for 1605–10, of the *ambassades* for 1606, of the *marine de Ponant* for 1610, and of various household funds,[1] can still be traced. From them we can often derive interesting information; the ambassadors' account for 1606, for instance, contains a full list of ambassadors' expenses in the various countries. Much the best-paid post was that of the sieur d'Alincourt, Villeroy's son, at Rome with 36,000 *livres*; after him came the baron de Salignac at the Turkish court with 25,000 *livres*, and then the ambassadors to England, Spain and Venice, each with 18,000 *livres*.

Under the heading *Ligues des Suisses* appear the payments nominally made to the Swiss soldiers who had served Henri IV in his early years. Chamberland has shown how this expenditure forms part of a 'comptabilité imaginaire';[2] although nearly twenty million *livres* are shown as paid between 1600 and 1610, in fact compositions for this amount were made with various Swiss colonels, who often accepted payment of as little as one-seventh

---

[1] See respectively BN ms. fr. 16697–16705, AN 120 AP 38–42, AD Calvados, acquisition Prévost 1905, fo. 90–2, BN nouv. acq. franç., 999 and AN KK 150–3 (*officiers de la maison du roi*, 1593–1601), KK 151 (*maison du roi*, 1608) and KK 154–6 (*écurie* 1599–1610).

[2] See his article on 'La comptabilité imaginaire . . .', *Revue Henri IV*, ii (1907–8), 50–60.

of their due.[1] This expedient is described in the *Économies Royales*, where Sully's 'secretaries' claim that he had paid off Swiss debts to the value of 17,350,000 *livres* 'from the time when you began to look into them until 1607';[2] table 4 shows this figure to be approximately correct. Apart from the sharp rise in 1610 when Marie de Medici was buying friends, there is little of significance in the lists of *états et pensions*, which, like the lists of *dons par acquits*, are useful chiefly in tracing the rise in favour of various individuals, such as the *intendant des finances* Isaac Arnauld, or the engineer Claude de Chastillon.[3] Nor are the expenses grouped under the heading 'miscellaneous' of great consequence.

The *deniers payés par ordonnance* record the progress of Sully's economies, for they comprise not only the yearly surplus, but also the sums paid over from one *trésorier de l'épargne* to another at the end of the year, as well as the treasure held in the Bastille. Sully saved consistently after 1602, and while some of the totals of treasure given in the *Économies Royales* are wildly exaggerated, others are near the mark.[4] At the beginning of 1610 there were about ten millions of *livres* on hand, and a further five million in the Bastille. The money in hand was soon dissipated, but the treasure of the Bastille was safeguarded by edicts forbidding the *surintendant des finances* and the *trésorier de l'épargne* who each, like the sovereign, held a different key to the final door, to open it without letters-patent verified by the *chambre des comptes*. Marie de Medici was unable to get such letters-patent authorized, and so on 15 July 1615 she bade the *surintendant* and the *trésorier* to come to the Bastille, where in the presence of the king, princes, dukes and great officers she made them hand over their keys.[5]

---

[1] The average was about one-fifth according to Chamberland, whose figures are confirmed by Bernard Barbiche, *Étude sur l'œuvre de restauration financière de Sully (1596–1610)*, summarized in *Positions des Thèses* . . . [of the École des Chartes], 1960.

[2] *Économies Royales*, i, 558a, and ii, 171.

[3] See for example, AN 120 AP 2, fo. 50v°, 95r°, 244r°, etc.

[4] Here the work of Barbiche, *Étude sur l'œuvre de restauration financière de Sully*, confirms that of Louis Batiffol, 'Le trésor de la Bastille de 1605 à 1611', *Revue Henri IV*, iii (1909–12), 200–9. See the *Économies Royales*, ii, 106, 305, 414 and 436 for conflicting estimates.

[5] For an account of this scene, see Louis Batiffol, *La vie intime d'une reine de France au XVIIᵉ Siècle: Marie de Médicis* (2 vols, Paris, 1931), ii, 206–10.

TABLE 4 EXPENDITURE OF THE *TRÉSORIER DE L'ÉPARGNE* 1600–10

	1600	1601	1602	1603	1604	1605	1606	1607	1608	1609	1610
Household[1]	2,074,559	1,998,722	1,950,241	1,942,879	1,934,058	1,857,750	2,445,892	1,867,813	2,303,203	2,262,272	3,514,348
Guards[2]	294,322	347,299	310,287	300,082	297,071	296,421	297,901	296,375	294,951	296,351	308,051
Guerres[3]	4,946,360	2,581,513	2,792,934	2,602,312	914,580	3,671,391	3,665,414	2,930,083	3,726,003	3,012,746	6,999,690
Marine de Levant	194,523	194,912	226,500	293,600	330,400	311,400	384,400	336,175	383,269	426,500	423,420
Marine de Ponant	21,000	21,600	28,600	35,300	78,500	24,300	24,000	18,000	37,875	38,675	39,675
Ligues des Suisses	1,038,000	2,737,892	2,434,446	1,841,225	1,971,299	1,352,741	1,281,600	3,123,777	1,361,573	1,243,648	1,209,400
Artillery	927,622	382,795	487,385	405,332	287,001	374,697	608,565	370,096	286,400	288,995	1,154,218
Fortifications	478,727	611,018	465,295	465,542	368,359	423,230	424,577	494,080	532,782	570,593	363,022
Buildings	558,352	649,943	796,487	876,926	770,311	598,473	573,511	688,166	536,223	633,298	476,653
Ponts et chaussées	6,000	5,765	15,570	4,000	40,600	595,469	749,800	842,227	1,224,153	1,149,150	991,563
États et pensions	1,812,787	1,767,820	1,794,195	2,009,068	1,768,869	1,941,570	2,010,685	2,024,536	2,117,553	2,184,760	3,130,898
Deniers payés par ordonnance	1,055,556	886,803	2,489,556	5,000,537	7,537,801	7,861,303	9,014,772	10,018,700	13,228,318	14,931,917	9,668,414
Miscellaneous[4] (end of rôles)	551,717	390,019	456,257	440,077	505,417	472,117	376,398	388,357	479,450	384,983	594,661
Dons par acquit	475,155	559,100	564,983	680,475	876,790	1,339,470	1,539,032	995,210	1,205,981	1,684,522	1,559,931
Deniers payés par acquit	3,865,988	1,405,231	3,063,812	2,134,579	1,282,906	2,685,216	1,600,930	2,191,231	2,203,715	963,057	2,060,269
Deniers payés comptants	2,146,141	1,648,901	2,135,058	2,009,413	2,510,500	3,067,827	3,446,079	3,345,192	2,251,175	2,501,982	1,685,853
Total	20,446,819	16,189,333	20,011,606	21,041,347	21,474,462	26,873,375	28,434,556	29,930,018	32,172,624	32,573,449	33,580,066

[1] Includes *offrandes et aumônes, chambre aux deniers, écurie du roi, maison du roi, argenterie du roi, menus plaisirs, venerie et fauconnerie* and *maison de la reine.*
[2] Includes *cent gentilhommes, gardes écossaises, gardes du corps du roi, prévôt de l'hôtel* and *cent suisses.*
[3] Both *ordinaire* and *extraordinaire.*
[4] Includes *voyages, menus dons* and *ambassades.*

F

2,500,000 *livres* had already been taken legally, to cope with the troubles of the previous year; soon nothing of Sully's treasure was left.

The *deniers payés par ordonnance*, the penultimate line in this first section, record payments for various presents and on old debts; like the expenses listed under 'miscellaneous', they contain little information of interest.

The *deniers payés comptants* cover secret payments by the king, summarily recorded in the general *état au vrai*, but amply described in three other registers,[1] which account for the years 1597–1610. These registers, which are the work of Sully's secretariat, can be combined with those of a manuscript in the Bibliothèque Nationale,[2] which contains the original *état de distribution de comptants par le roi (1599–1610)*, to provide an adequate description of secret expenditure. The largest single object of expenditure was the subsidy to the United Provinces, which between 1598 and 1610 reached the following totals:

1598	333,000	1605	1,950,000
1599	300,000	1606	1,950,000
1600	450,000	1607	1,950,000
1602	900,000	1608	600,000
1603	1,350,000	1609	300,000
1604	1,350,000	1610	900,000

(Total: 12,783,000 *livres*)

The French paid as much to the United Provinces as they could yearly afford – nearly two million *livres* being about one-tenth of the total income – until in 1608 the Dutch began to feel their way towards the truce with the Spaniards which was concluded in 1609. Hitherto the chief source of information about these payments, so significant for the diplomatic history of the period, has been fragmentary references in contemporary memoirs and letters.[3]

These figures from the *comptants* are confirmed by those of a

[1] AN 120 AP 9 (1593–7), 10 (1598–1608) and 11 (1594–1604).
[2] BN ms. fr. 4559; see plate 3.
[3] For example, the figures in Nouaillac (ed.), *Un envoyé hollandais*, 54, 59, 111 and 136; in the *Lettres Missives*, vii, 697; and in the *Économies Royales*, i, 378b.

document setting out the state of French debts to the English crown in 1612.[1] For in 1603 during his embassy Rosny had agreed that one-third of the subsidies for the United Provinces should count towards the reduction of the English debts.[2] In 1596 these debts, which were for the provision of English troops to help Henri IV against the League in Brittany, Normandy and Picardy, had amounted to about four million *livres*.[3] Between 1603 and 1607, when James I abrogated the agreement, the French had paid off nearly three million of them in supplying the Dutch with nearly nine million *livres*. English statesmen were unwilling to see the debts cancelled off in this way, calling it a 'Bravery of the Financer's [that is, Sully]', which the French king would never support.[4] Sully was particularly criticized by them as 'stretching the treaty [of 1603] beyond all reasonable construction, because he made it himself'.[5] All the same, these payments to the Dutch seem to have been counted against the debts to the English, which had thus been paid off by 1613.[6]

The other Protestant power subsidized by the Very Christian King was the city of Geneva, to whom payments began after the duke of Savoy's unsuccessful surprise attack in 1602,[7] and whose deputies were among the most clamant of Sully's suitors.[8] Within the realm too the Protestants of the Midi were paid large sums for the maintenance of the garrisons agreed in the edict of Nantes. No precise information has hitherto been available on either of these kinds of payment,[9] details of which follow:

[1] BN ms. fr. 4827, fo. 110–12.
[2] BN ms. fr. 17919, fo. 89r⁰.
[3] BN ms. fr. 4827, fo. 27–9.
[4] *Memorials of affairs of state*, ii, 403; letter of 19 May 1608 from Greenwich, earl of Salisbury to Sir Charles Cornwallis.
[5] Sir George Carew, *Relation of the state of France*, 487.
[6] Two further payments were made in 1612 and 1613; see Frederick C. Dietz, *English public finance, 1558–1641* (New York, 1932), 459.
[7] See de Crue, *Les derniers desseins de Henri IV*, 9–10.
[8] Arch. Aff. Étr., France 766, fo. 162–3, letter from Sillery to Villeroy, Paris, 30 June 1603. See also Francis de Crue, *Henri IV et les députés de Genève* (Geneva/Paris, 1901).
[9] The indications of de Crue, *Les derniers desseins de Henri IV*, 10, are inaccurate, and Benoist much underestimates this aid: *Histoire de l'édit de Nantes*, i, 421.

	French Protestants	*Geneva*
1598	171,930	
1599	379,350	
1600	353,040	
1601	346,896	
1602	346,896	
1603	350,062	101,000
1604	347,902	24,000
1605	350,903	72,000
1606	360,000	72,000
1607	374,000	82,000
1608	366,364	72,000
1609	371,545	72,000
1610	382,817	72,000

Some payments were also made to German princes who were creditors of Henri IV, like the marquis of Brandenburg and the duke of Würtemberg. But the sums involved were small and are found in the *deniers en acquit* and the *deniers par ordonnance par acquit*.[1]. Other money went on the embellishment of buildings, especially of the château at Montceaux-lès-Meaux. This expenditure escaped the cognizance of the *trésorier des bâtiments*, whose general accounts are discussed in chapter VII.

Throughout the reign the *comptants* record payments to a variety of mistresses; 'mademoiselle Des Fosses', the comtesse de Moret, the marquise de Verneuil and so on. In his latter years Henri IV lost very large sums at the gambling-table; in 1608 it was a mere 21,000 *livres*, but in 1609 he paid out at least 150,000 *livres* to the 's' Edouard, portugais'.[2] Sully can hardly have approved of this, and he took care to write 'pour jouer' on such entries. He inserted other autograph comments, some showing his humanity in providing money for a poor woman in the Bastille 'for her lying-in and food for herself and for her husband and children', and others revealing, perhaps, a grim sense of humour in recording that 'these items of furniture [bought for

---

[1] For instance, AN 120 AP 2, fo. 53v°, 97r°, 138r°, 185v°, etc.

[2] See AN 120 AP 10, fo. 106v°, for the 21,000 *livres*, and BN ms. fr. 4559, fo. 93v°, for the rest. The 150,000 *livres* checks well with the figure given in the *Lettres Missives*, vii, 707 and 754, and with the *Mémoires* of Bassompierre, i, 200–1.

the apartment of the doomed duc de Biron] must be kept for another time'.[1]

Technically the accounting system shows no advance under Sully, who sometimes used Arabic numerals himself but allowed his clerks to continue to use the clumsy and misleading Roman system. According to this 1,475, for instance, was written xiiii^{c}lxxv (see plate 3); mistakes in calculation were frequent. In the United Provinces at this time Simon Stevin, who worked as an engineer for Henri IV, was developing the application of double-entry book-keeping for the finances of Maurice of Nassau. Stevin is said to have offered the system to Sully, who allegedly refused to take it up;[2] it would not be applied to the French public finances before the early eighteenth century, though the Swedish state, for instance, had adopted it in 1623, under the direction of the Dutchman, Abraham Cabeljau.[3] It is inaccurate to claim that Sully prepared the first French budget (in the strict sense of the word as an annual estimate of income and expenditure), for, as we have seen, the establishment of an *état du roi* was standard procedure long before his time. However, the earliest *états du roi* omitted numerous important items especially among the *assignations*; Sully made his much more inclusive and so prepared the way for Colbert, in whose time the figures became fully comprehensive.

His financial achievement is best appreciated by comparing estimates of the early 1590s with those of the years of his administration. In 1594 expenditure was calculated to be more than twice as great as income,[4] and in 1596 a responsible estimate made it more than three times as much.[5] By 1600 Sully had brought the income and expenditure into equilibrium, preparatory to setting aside up to one-tenth of the revenue each

[1] For these entries, see BN ms. fr. 4559, fo. 15 and 17.
[2] See the article 'Sur l'administration et les réformes financières de Sully', *L'investigateur, journal de l'Institution Historique*, iv (1844), 220, note 1; also Steichen, *Mémoire sur la vie et les travaux de Simon Stevin* (Brussels, 1846), 96. I have not been able to find any more recent references to this part of Sully's work.
[3] See the work edited by A. C. Littleton and B. S. Yamey, *Studies in the history of accounting* (London, 1956), 236–46.
[4] BN ms. fr. 4680, fo. 15–19.
[5] Charlier-Meniolle, *L'assemblée des Notables*, 4–24.

year. Naturally he was helped in this by the establishment of peace and order, which made it easier to collect revenue. But his more equitable distribution of taxes counted for much, as did his relentless pruning of useless expenses. The list of contemporaries whom he offended by his parsimony is very long; to take the literary world alone, he had a testy brush with Malherbe, while the eminent scholar Casaubon called him an 'intolerable bumpkin' for failing to pay an allowance.[1] Tactful suppliants learned to approach him 'after dinner, when he is most amenable'; some deputies from Geneva, entering his room at this hour, were surprised to be greeted with: 'Well, how is the holy city of Jerusalem the Holy?'.[2] The importance of Sully's personal effort, backed by the king, is shown by the fact that three years after his dismissal Jeannin, his successor and an honest and competent man, disposing of two of the old *intendants des finances*, had to report to the States-General that the treasure in the Bastille was exhausted and the *épargne* running into debt once more.[3]

[1] See respectively, René Fromilhague, *La vie de Malherbe* (Paris, n.d.), 267–72 and O. Fox, 'Notice sur Isaac Casaubon', *Bulletin de la Société de l'histoire du Protestantisme français'*, xiv (1865), 267.

[2] De Crue, *Henri IV et les députés de Genève*, 400.

[3] See the 'Propos tenus par M. Jeannin' in the *Négotiations du président Jeannin*, ed. J. A. C. Buchon (Paris. 1838), 714–17.

CHAPTER V

Surintendant des finances

relations with the provincial authorities

As an energetic *surintendant des finances* Sully was bound to come into conflict with the provincial authorities: *parlements, chambres des comptes, cours des aides,* estates, municipalities and governors. A contemporary observed that he was 'much feared by all the courts, upon whose jurisdiction he was always trespassing',[1] and he himself wrote out a 'summary of the encroachments of the courts upon the financial structure, which must be set right'.[2] Much of his time was spent in controversies with these various 'courts'.

The greatest of the provincial authorities were the *parlements,* concerned as we have noticed earlier with judicial affairs and composed of lawyers who formed a compact group with common aspirations and privileges. Officers from one *parlement* would be sure of a welcome in another, and they consciously nourished their corporate spirit. Thus when Pierre Jeannin, first president of the Dijon *parlement,* took his leave in July 1598 of the Rennes *parlement,* the spokesman for the latter thanked him, 'offering him their continued co-operation in the unity and collaboration which exists between the *parlements* of the realm'.[3] Like the *trésoriers de France,* the members of the *parlements* resisted attempts by the central government to break up their unity; for example, when in June 1601 certain members of the Bordeaux *parlement* had personally accepted and carried out royal commissions they were reprimanded and 'it was decreed that no councillors of the court might undertake extraordinary

---

[1] *Sommaire mémorial de Jules Gassot,* ed. Pierre Champion (Paris, 1934), 244–5.
[2] AN 120 AP 37, fo. 120–1.
[3] BN nouv. acq. franç., 733, fo. 348r°.

commissions without the court's permission'.[1] In every province they meddled with the affairs of the *trésoriers de France*, disputing the latter's right to collect taxes, to award leases for farms and so on.[2] In Burgundy in 1608 the *trésoriers* replied in an unorthodox but effective way by threatening to cut the salaries of the members of the *parlement*,[3] but more often Sully tried to protect the *bureaux* by obtaining *arrêts* against the offending *parlement*.[4]

The occasions of conflict between the central authority and the *parlements* were many. The contracts for the farms were generally published at Paris. Often, however, the *parlements* contested the authority of the central power to provide for levies of this kind to be made within the provinces, and refused to register the contracts, encouraging the relevant *cour des aides* also to refuse. The result of such obstruction was usually that the local *trésoriers* were unable to find anyone to take the lease on at a reasonable price, for the eventual farmer would find it difficult to collect the duties if his warrant could be legally challenged. As the *trésoriers* at Caen wrote to Maupeou on 13 August 1601, the lease of the new taxes had been published, but

> we feel that we must warn you that in order to reassure possible bidders the verification must be passed in this province's *cour des aides* . . . for otherwise it will be hard to find any bidders.[5]

Sully's next step would be to obtain from the king *lettres de jussion*, by which the resistance of the *parlement* or other court would be overridden – in legal theory. In practice the lease would still be hard to let, and this local resistance was one of the reasons why attempts to centralize the gathering of customs and other taxes, in the manner of Colbert's great reform of 1664, were bound to fail. When, for instance, in May 1604 Sully consolidated the *aides* into a *bail général* and leased it to Jean de

[1] Bib. Bordeaux, ms. 371, fo. 58v⁰.
[2] See for example, a letter from the *procureur général* of the Rouen *parlement* to Bellièvre (BN ms. fr. 15898, fo. 604), asking him to support the *parlement* against the *trésoriers* – and against Sully.
[3] Bib. Dijon, fonds Saverot 1499, 200.
[4] See for example, Valois, n⁰ 3568 (Bordeaux), and n⁰ 12062 (Dijon).
[5] Romier (ed.), *Lettres et Chevauchées*, 130.

Moisset, the latter soon had to give it up, largely because of these complications.[1] Although the tax-farmers at this period could provide large sums of ready money for the crown, they had little hold over government, and if at a certain stage 'revenue farming is scarcely to be distinguished from farming the actual administration of a district to the person responsible for collecting the royal revenues in it',[2] this stage was by no means reached in the France of Henri IV.

Another subject of controversy was the payment of the *rentes*. These were annual payments made to individuals who had in the past paid sums of money to the kings. Such interest-bearing loans to the Crown dated back to the fourteenth century, but after 1522 there also existed in France the *rentes de l'hôtel de ville* [of Paris. Some other large towns had a similar arrangement], investments guaranteed by the Parisian municipality, to whom the king alienated certain customs-farms. Payments on both these categories of *rentes* became increasingly sparse after about 1580, as a result of the dislocations of war, so that by 1600 some *rentiers* had had no interest for fifteen years.[3] To tackle this situation, in November 1603 the king and Sully appointed Jean de Moisset to replace the six former *receveurs des rentes*. This was a step which aroused great opposition in Paris, where the municipality did not wish to see a royal nominee in control of their revenues. Moisset was eventually admitted to his office in March 1604, but his attempt to carry out an *arrêt* the following August, which provided for the payment only of current *rentes* from current income, had to be abandoned. On 9 September there was a general remonstrance, led by *prévôt des marchands* François Miron, against this 'retranchement des rentes'; Sully was also thinking of disavowing some titles altogether, but the following April was forced after another rousing speech by Miron to abandon his scheme.[4]

[1] Permezel, *La politique financière de Sully*, 70.

[2] Quoted from G. E. Aylmer, *The King's Servants: the civil service of Charles I, 1625–1642* (London, 1961), 450.

[3] This passage is based on Bernard Schnapper, *Les rentes au XVIe siècle; histoire d'un instrument de crédit* (Paris, 1957).

[4] On this opposition, see Miron de l'Espinay, *François Miron et l'administration municipale de Paris sous Henri IV de 1604 à 1606* (Paris, 1885), and also, Paul Robiquet, *Histoire municipale de Paris* (3 vols, Paris, 1880–1904).

In the provinces on the other hand Sully seems often to have prevailed. The municipal officers of Toulouse were complaining as early as July 1601 that their interest had been cut, and in November 1604, during his visit to court, the bishop of Carcassonne, representing the estates of Languedoc, was able to obtain only one year's grace for the province from the general 'retranchement'.[1] As well as examining and disavowing some *rentes*, and cutting the interest on others, Sully was considering a general buying-up of titles.[2] This is inseparable from his other project, of *rachat du domaine*, for which he studied and annotated with his usual thoroughness much previous legislation concerning the royal *domaine*, royal estates forming part of the crown patrimony (see plate 4). In the case both of *rentes* and of *domaine* certain individuals had claims on the royal revenues as a result of past payments to the crown, whether they received in return annuities from customs-farms or land producing a certain income. After 1607 Sully passed many contracts with *partisans* (persons undertaking such *partis*), who engaged to make the payments either on *rentes* or *domaine* (or both) for a limited period, often sixteen years. During that time they enjoyed any surplus income and at the end of it the *domaine* reverted to the crown or the *rentes* were annulled. Many of the contracts agreed in this way did not mature, because they were cancelled after 1610. But in pressing through *arrêts* for such *rachats* Sully often seems to have overcome the resistance of the *parlements*, whose members frequently had an interest in the continuation of the existing system of *rentes* and *domaine*. He encountered great difficulties in attempting to enlist the support of members of the *parlements* for financial reform of any kind. In November 1604, for instance, an *arrêt* was sent to the *parlement* at Dijon authorizing some of its members to investigate the abuses of the 'officiers comptables'.[3] We read in the account of the proceedings of the *parlement* for December 1604 that the

sʳ de La Berchère got up and said that he had not asked to be

---

[1] AN H 748/20, fo. 12vᵒ.
[2] For what follows, see Barbiche, *Étude sur l'œuvre de restauration financière de Sully*.
[3] AD Côte d'Or, C 3419 (under this date).

selected for the commission in question, and that he neither intended nor wished to go forward with it unless so requested by the court.[1]

In this case as in many others, provincial and corporate solidarity came before other considerations; eventually no investigations were in fact carried out at Dijon, because the *parlement* refused to register letters-patent providing for the examination of the accounts of the *chambre des comptes*.

It was in theory possible to organize investigations of this kind through a *chambre de justice*, and four of these specially-convened judicial bodies met during Henri IV's reign, in 1597, 1601, 1604 and 1607. The account of their proceedings is not very creditable either to the king or to Sully.[2] The normal procedure was for one or more persons to be authorized to investigate the books of all *comptables* handling royal money, with power to fine them when irregularities were discovered. The king of course received a considerable payment for the granting of this authority; in 1607 for instance the English ambassador Carew wrote that 'it is thought the king will draw an exceeding great profit'. He went on, however, to add that 'some think the matter is likely to be compounded . . . they [the financiers] have already offered 300,000 crowns'.[3] In fact before the inquiry had gone very far such a *composition* was generally agreed upon; the financiers paid over a certain sum in return for the abandonment of the investigation. The British Museum preserves an interesting copy of one of these offers of a *composition*, annotated by Sully.[4] It concerns the *chambre de justice* of 1601, for the revocation of which the financial officers make an offer of 600,000 *livres*. Sully has made a good many erasures and simplifications in the elaborate method proposed for payment, all summed up in his phrase: 'sans diminution des deux cens mil escus promis au roy' (without any reduction in the 200,000 *écus* promised to the king).

[1] Bib. Dijon, fonds Saverot 1499, 118.
[2] The work of the 1607 *chambre* is well summarized by Alfred Des Cilleuls, *Henri IV et la chambre de justice de 1607* (Paris, n.d.).
[3] Carew to Sir Thomas Edmondes, [Paris?] 7 April 1607: BM Stowe 169, fo. 9.
[4] BM add. mss. 21512, fo. 25–6.

The terms of the *arrêt* establishing these *chambres* generally provided for simultaneous investigations in the provinces, which ended with the same kind of blackmail disguised as a *composition*.[1] A letter to the king from a certain 'de Vuyon', written from Toulouse in April 1604, makes it clear how this arrangement worked.[2] The municipal authorities of the region, says Vuyon, offer the king 90,000 *livres* if he will exempt them from investigation; he adds that

> like this Your Majesty will be much better served than by an investigation which will demand a great deal of time, trouble and expense, whereas [through the suggested arrangement] the financiers will pay over this sum freely and without constraint.

Generally the inquiry was diverted in this way, but even when there was no *composition* it was not the dishonest high officials who suffered, so much as the small men who could not so well protect themselves. As the Brittany estates complained of a certain *commissaire* in 1603,

> the s[r] de Trelon, instead of investigating the high financial officers, has turned on poor clerks and the officers of the small towns.[3]

In short, both at Paris and in the provinces the *chambres de justice* represented a thoroughly disreputable fiscal expedient.

The 'juge naturelle de telles recherches'[4] should have been the *chambre des comptes* at Paris, working with its adjuncts in the provinces. Sully, however, does not seem to have trusted the *chambre*, which he described as being hand in glove with the *trésoriers de France*.[5] In September 1598 he was working on the accounts of the *chambre* with two of its officials; to a suggestion that members of the staff of the *chambre* might make the extracts (of *dons* or gifts) just as well as Rosny, the king replied that 'the

---

[1] The procedure is well described by Permezel, *La politique financière de Sully*, 30, et seq.

[2] BN ms. fr. 23198, fo. 7.

[3] BN ms. fr. 22315, fo. 24v⁰.

[4] In the words of a complaint by the *chambre des comptes* in 1607: AN P 2669, fo. 123–4.

[5] *Économies Royales*, ii, 192–3.

sieur de Rosny was always at his side and could better answer for it'.[1] This work survives as the volume entitled 'Dons du Roi, 1589–1596', among the 'Papiers de Sully'.[2] Throughout the reign he continued to check over the registers of the *chambre*. Its delegates remonstrated with him in October 1604 that the *correcteurs* could easily reckon up the illegal expenses claimed by the *élus* since 1599 – the subject on which he was working – but he replied that 'the correctors did nothing and that it was the king's wish that the *commissaires* whom he had named should work at it'.[3] Often too he would borrow registers. In March 1606 he obtained letters-patent for such accounts as he needed to be brought to him at the Arsenal;[4] this authority was limited to accounts dealing with the years after 1598, but in June 1608 he wrote to the king asking it to be extended to 'all those I may need'.[5] To this letter the king replied at once that he had ordered this to be done.[6] The *chambre* accepted this borrowing with surprising docility, taking great trouble in 1608 to obtain as quickly as possible a document which Sully particularly needed.[7]

Their helpful attitude contrasted sharply with that of the *chambre des comptes* at Rouen. In August 1604 the king drew up a commission for two investigators to visit that court, whose co-operation in handing over documents Sully was to ensure.[8] On 11 September 1604 the *gens des comptes de Normandie* wrote to chancellor Bellièvre complaining that the 'communication of the accounts and receipts requested by the commissaires [was] against the regulations for the *chambres des comptes*', and adding that they had nevertheless decided to allow the *commissaires* to see some of the relevant documents.[9] The next day the *commissaires* themselves wrote to Bellièvre describing the obstructive attitude of the 'gens des comptes', and adding that the first

[1] AN P 2666, fo. 150v°.
[2] AN 120 AP 12.
[3] AN P 2668, fo. 103.
[4] AN P 2669, fo. 45r°; for the letters-patent, BN Dupuy 854, fo. 149.
[5] BN Dupuy 194, fo. 156.
[6] *Économies Royales*, ii, 243a, a transcript of the royal letter.
[7] AN P 2669, fo. 153–4.
[8] *Économies Royales*, i, 593–4.
[9] BN ms. fr. 15899, fo. 35r°.

president 'wants so to reduce the number of documents shown to us that he may discover the object of our investigation'.[1] It is not easy to say how this investigation ended; perhaps in some form of *composition*. Although in his early years Sully had often to rebuke the *chambre* at Paris, his relations with it were greatly improved after about 1605.[2] In January 1610, for example, he came to an agreement with first president Nicolay over the 'expenses and perquisites' ('épices et menuz necessitez') of its members;[3] this was a subject for much acrimonious dispute with other courts. This relative harmony may have been the result of Sully's attempt to subordinate all the provincial *chambres des comptes* to the one at Paris. In February 1602 an *arrêt* was promulgated in order, as Sully himself wrote, to 'oblige the *chambres* at Dijon, Grenoble, Aix, Montpellier, Nantes and Rouen to send copies of their accounts for 1595–1600' to Paris, for 1602 to the council and thereafter to the *chambre des comptes*.[4] In August 1602 a further *arrêt* transferred jurisdiction over certain financial areas in the south from the Montpellier *chambre* to that at Paris,[5] and in January 1603, during an audience with the king, the first president of the Paris *chambre* complained of the encroachments by the men of Montpellier, who had taken advantage of the confusion of the war period –

> To which His Majesty replied that he believed it to be so . . .
> that his intention was eventually so to arrange things that he
> could have not only all the generalities, but also all the
> *chambres*, depending on the one at Paris.[6]

Such an aim was bound to meet with much opposition. In January 1603 the *arrêt* of August 1602 mentioned above was cancelled in favour of Montpellier,[7] whose 'gens des comptes' wrote an interesting letter to the king the following April. They thanked him for favouring their case in spite of the representa-

---

[1] Loc. cit., fo. 325r⁰.
[2] See for example, AN P 2667, fo. 112r⁰.
[3] AN P 2670, fo. 3–7.
[4] AN 120 AP 1, fo. 1, for the *arrêt* and Sully's comments.
[5] Valois, n⁰ 7438, mentions this *arrêt*.
[6] AN P 2667, fo. 6–13.
[7] Valois, n⁰ 7438; see also the further *arrêt* of October 1603, Valois, n⁰ 7868.

tions of 'messieurs les comptes de Paris', but complained that the documents needed to establish their authority in the disputed case had not reached them, as 'monsieur de Rosny . . . has withdrawn them and now holds on to them without explaining why'.[1] It is possible that the king was bluffing, and that he and Rosny had agreed not to let the Montpellier *chambre* have the *arrêt* passed in its favour; unfortunately we can follow the incident no further.

In a letter of uncertain date to the king Sully once boasted that he had

> so hustled on [a certain declaration] that in the same morning it had been verified both at the *chambre des comptes* and in the *cour des aides*, so that it only remained to name the *commissaires*.[2]

The *cour des aides* had been notably obstructive over fiscal legislation in 1597, just when the king needed all his resources for the siege of Amiens.[3] But after that there are few traces of resistance, except for the incident in 1605 when it opposed the attempt of some 'gens du roy' to borrow some of its registers.[4] Sully's dealings with the *cour des monnaies* at Paris were more eventful. In 1602 its officials opposed him when he enacted legislation recognizing *monnaie de compte*; this was the *livre* which, valued at three to the *écu*, now replaced it. In 1609 he had been the moving spirit behind the drawing-up of a new edict, designed again to counter the rising prices, to prevent the debasement ('empirance') of the French coinage. The *cour des monnaies* again opposed him and this time it was successful; although the edict was published by the crown in 1609 it was never verified by the *parlement* and remained a dead letter.[5]

These lesser courts, like the *parlements* from which they derived, were bodies permanently in session. This was not the case with the provincial estates which met for only about a fortnight

[1] BN Dupuy 562, fo. 158.
[2] Bib. Institut, fonds Godefroy 265, fo. 206–7.
[3] See Chamberland, 'Jean Chandon et le conflit entre la cour des aides et le conseil du roi', *Revue Henri IV*, ii (1907–8), 113–25.
[4] AN Z 1A 159, fo. 2r°.
[5] See Bernard Barbiche, 'Une tentative de réforme monétaire à la fin du règne d'Henri IV', *XVIIᵉ siècle*, lxi (1963), 3–17.

once a year. At their assemblies the delegates of the three orders discussed matters concerning the province and drew up a *cahier* of grievances, which was sent to Paris with a representative to press home its points. The king and council would then reply to these points one by one and return the *cahier* for the consideration of the next session of the estates. Often the replies did not give satisfaction, particularly on questions for which Sully was responsible. Thus in November 1604 the Languedoc estates, meeting at Albi, declared that

> the replies which monsieur de Rosny and other lords of the council had put forward on the *cahier* sent to them . . . did not in any way meet the wishes of the province.[1]

Likewise in December 1609 the Normandy estates pointed out that

> the routine of making requests has led to a habit of refusing them . . . for it looks as though the replies on the past year's *cahier* are a straightforward copy of those for the previous year.[2]

Although the Normandy estates, in Sully's words, were but 'une ombre au prix des six austres',[3] it is the series of their *cahiers* which is the most readily available and so the most often quoted. There are many complaints that the *rentiers* of Rouen are not being paid, complaints which find their counterpart in the proceedings of other estates; there are also laments of a medieval eloquence about heavy taxation. In theory the estates alone could approve financial levies on their provinces; as the Languedoc estates pointed out at Pézenas in April 1599,

> By the ancient privileges and freedoms of this region no sums may be imposed or levied on it without the consent of the estates.[4]

This was a claim repeated many times, but Sully, as we have noted, was slowly forcing up the *taille* contribution of the *pays*

[1] AN H 748/20, fo. 7-8.
[2] Beaurepaire (ed.), *Cahiers des états de Normandie*, ii, 160.
[3] See his 'Relation', BN ms. fr. 23042, fo. 135r°.
[4] AD Lozère, C 536, fo. 562r°.

1. Anne de Courtenay, first wife of Sully, engraved by Pieter Louis van Schuppen (*BN Estampes*).

ANNE DE COVRTENAY DAME
DE ROSNY ET DE BONTIN

2. The locks of the *canal de Briare* at Rogny (Yonne) (*Author's photograph*).

3. A marginal comment in Sully's hand; '*je ne say que c'est de cest article*'. This refers to the entry for 400,000 *livres*; the preceding entry amounts to 1,477 *livres*, 14 *sols* (*B.N ms. fr. 4559, fo. 103*).

d'états, and had obtained control over the *trésoriers* of some estates. Thus in 1602 the estates of Brittany wrote to him from Saint-Brieuc that he should send authority for a certain payment, as the treasurer

> has told us that without your express consent he cannot pay [it].[1]

Sully's methods for establishing his administration in a province which was hitherto *pays d'états* emerge well from a study of his struggle to set up a system of *élus* in Guyenne; we can follow the contest in detail through the letters sent back home by a certain M. de Selves, deputed by the province to oppose the innovation.[2]

In his 'summary of the encroachments of the courts . . .', mentioned at the beginning of this chapter, Sully had written that 'in Guyenne there are six financial sub-divisions which claim to be *pays d'états* and only impose as much in taxes as they care to';[3] he seems to have begun his attempts to set up *élus* in 1604. That December Selves arrived in Paris, and during the following January and February usually had two meetings a week with Sully. In the course of one 'furieuse contestation' the latter assured him that it would not only be Guyenne which would have *élus*, 'but that it was the king's wish that all over France the *taille* should be levied in a uniform fashion'. Selves adds that as for Languedoc, Provence and Dauphiné, 'those fellows will know better than us how to stand up for themselves', and goes on to remark that he has been threatened by Sully with the Bastille for his pertinacity.

Early in March he had his case brought before council, but

> when our business came up the sieur de Rosny got up and left in a rage.

Two days later the case was again brought before council, where it even found a sympathetic majority, but 'the sieur de Rosny is so absolute that none dares resist him'. Selves had obtained letters supporting his case from the maréchal d'Ornano,

[1] BN ms. fr. 22315, fo. 8r°.
[2] AC Agen, CC 123.
[3] AN 120 AP 37, fo. 120.

G

governor of Guyenne, and he hoped to use them to good effect. For with the aid of similar letters from their governor, the maréchal de Brissac, the deputies of Brittany had obtained a respite. But Rosny's rage was such that late in March Selves still dared not submit his *cahier*; early in April he wrote

> that it has never before been so bad for the provincial com- munities at Court as it is now . . . you may be sure that they are resolved to deprive you of all your privileges.

All the same, he maintained his pressure on Rosny and by 22 April was able to write that 'if we can hold on we may yet escape the establishment of *élus*'; it seems that Rosny was beginning to fear that general disaffection in Guyenne might lead to rioting.

In May the *surintendant* went to inspect the Briare canal, and in June Selves wrote that he had 'openly offered the king com- pensation, through madame de Moret; we must give her a lavish present'. Rosny returned to the court in August, having attended the Châtellerault assembly, and the following October, in one of his last letters, Selves wrote that although he was still eager to establish the *élus*, 'if he cannot manage this he will accept the compensation offered. So it is up to you and the other provinces to see to it.' No doubt some collusive compromise was reached that year, for the *élus* were not in fact established in 1606. How- ever, Sully was not easily deterred, and by 1609 he had had his way.[1] The Guyenne deputies protested then that it was 'no- torious that all novelties are and must be prejudicial',[2] but their objection was overruled. Slowly a uniform financial structure was being built up all over France, though there was much opposition yet to be overcome; Richelieu himself, for instance, failed to establish *élus* in Brittany, Burgundy or Provence.[3]

When Sully or the king wished to enforce a particular point of legislation, they would often send special representatives into the provinces. The activities of these *commissaires départis* have sometimes been described as making Sully the founder of the

[1] AD Gironde C 3875, fo. 11v°.
[2] Valois, n° 14688.
[3] Avenel, *Richelieu et la monarchie absolue*, i, 209–12.

intendants, and in view of the later importance of these officials it is worth looking closely at the history of their predecessors. About the middle of the sixteenth century there began to appear commissions for *intendants*, – *de l'armée, de la justice* and so on.[1] These commissions were granted for a specific purpose and for a limited period, and continued to be used under Henri IV. Many provinces had their temporary *intendants des finances*, often sent to re-establish normal procedures after the wars, and *commissaires* were also sent to towns to check their debts.[2] Others were appointed for even more limited purposes; in 1604, for example, Sully was ordered by the king to send 'someone of whose standing, intelligence and industry you can be certain enough to answer to me'[3] to check on the violations of the Spanish trade embargo. Sully chose one of his secretaries, the s[r] de La Fond, who reported back to him a month later with details of the situation.[4]

Commissions of these kinds were useful and even popular; the Rouen Assembly of Notables recommended their use,[5] and in March 1608, for example, the first president of the Toulouse *parlement* thanked Sully for sending him the sieur de Colange, 'as worthy to handle great and important affairs as any person of my acquaintance'.[6] They are to be distinguished from those *commissions extraordinaires* which, as the equivalent of the contemporary English monopoly-grants, imposed a heavy burden on the people to little effect. Sometimes the alleged aims of the *commissaires* would be laudable; as the *procureur syndic* of the Normandy estates put it, they would bear 'apparently all the indications of being most useful', when in fact they were 'infinitely pernicious'.[7] Thus *commissaires* were appointed to check the weights and measures, for instance, or to recover

---

[1] For the chronology, see Gabriel Hanotaux, *Sur les chemins de l'histoire* (2 vols, Paris, 1924), ii, 1–112 [chapter on the 'Origines de l'institution des intendants des provinces'].

[2] Valois, n⁰ 4614, 5099, 6572, and so on.

[3] *Économies Royales*, i, 555a and 583b.

[4] See Rosny's letter to the king, Poitiers, 25 June 1604; BN ms. fr. 23198, fo. 189.

[5] Poirson (ed.), *Mémoires de Villeroy et de Sancy*, 57 and 66.

[6] *Économies Royales*, ii, 231b.

[7] In a memorandum to Sully, BN Dupuy 240, fo. 160.

domain. But they generally ended by levying fines on such people as they were able to threaten with impunity, fathering the proverb: 'ce n'est pas par justice, c'est par commissaires'.[1] It seems to have been the weakness of the king which allowed these *commissaires* to flourish. Members of his council several times requested their abolition,[2] and Sully himself wrote to the king for this purpose.[3] Unusually for him, Sully tried to dissociate himself from this aspect of royal activity, writing for example to the municipality of Rouen in January 1603 that he tried to annul *commissions*, but that they continued to be imposed 'sometimes through an authority greater than mine, and sometimes by a majority in council'.[4] In a curious letter of October 1607 to the *trésoriers de France* in Burgundy he even encouraged them to oppose the abusive commissions, following this up in May 1609 with a request to the same *trésoriers* to send a list of all *commissaires* in their generality.[5] These efforts do not seem to have had any success, to judge by the frequency with which legislation on the subject had to be repeated.[6]

So much for the abusive *commissaires*; it is time to return to their more constructive colleagues. Permezel, arguing from his knowledge of the generality of Lyons, claimed that 'Sully methodically allocated to the *intendant* functions which became more and more numerous and varied'.[7] It would be mistaken to extend this judgement to France as a whole. Lyons was a special case, as a great industrial and commercial centre which yet lacked *parlement*, estates or other sovereign courts; its governor thus held an exceptionally responsible position, and it

[1] Quoted by Zeller, *Les institutions de la France au XVI⁰ siècle*, 188.

[2] For instance, in March 1596, in the letter quoted by Chamberland, 'Le conseil des finances', *Revue Henri IV*, i (1905–6), 28–32, and in 1602, in a letter signed by six council-members; Bib. Institut, fonds Godefroy, 263, fo. 89.

[3] On 2 May [probably] 1604; Bib. Institut, fonds Godefroy, 284, fo. 206–7.

[4] *Inventaire sommaire des Archives Communales de la ville de Rouen* (i, Rouen, 1887), reference A 22. See also *Économies Royales*, ii, 260b.

[5] AD Côte d'Or, C 2082 bis, fo. 26r⁰; see also Permezel, *La politique financière de Sully*, 23.

[6] See for example, AD Marne C 2491; fo. 1 contains an *arrêt* for the suspension of a long list of *commissions* (Valois, n⁰ 11199), most of which are again revoked by a *déclaration* of September 1610 (fo. 246, et seq).

[7] *La politique financière de Sully*, 18.

is the only centre in which throughout the reign we find an *intendant* at the governor's side.

Elsewhere the *intendants'* commissions were given for specific tasks and limited periods. Roger Doucet has criticized the argument of Hanotaux that *intendants* first appeared with the first use of that term,[1] and it should be emphasized that the early *intendants'* powers do not compare with those of their successors. It was only towards the middle of Louis XIV's reign that the *intendance* was fully established all over France. The latter years of Richelieu's administration saw the *intendants des armées* becoming increasingly important,[2] but in the time of Henri IV the most numerous and effective local agents of the central power were probably not those who were called *intendants*, but rather the *lieutenants* of Sully in his capacity as *grand voyer* and *grand maître de l'artillerie*.[3]

Sometimes the towns welcomed the *commissaires* whom Sully sent to check their debts, for these officials might well judge against the municipality's creditors. But they nearly always resisted his attempts to check on their income (from various duties) and expenditure. It was only after a long struggle that the *bureau de la ville* at Paris would give up accounts of *dons et octrois*,[4] and the municipality of Bordeaux, like many others, protested strongly at Sully's commission for the *trésoriers de France* there to lease a new customs-farm.[5] All the same, Sully steadily tightened his grip on municipal finances. For as he once remarked to a representative from the *chambre des comptes*, he knew that these often concealed 'beaucoup de malversations'.[6] He checked with great care the accounts which were sent to him, reducing the expenditure of Mâcon, for example, from 2,404 to 1,870 *livres* in 1607.[7] He was also inflexible in refusing

[1] *Les institutions de la France au XVIᵉ siècle*, i, 422, note 1.
[2] See Roland Mousnier's chapter, 'État et commissaire . . .', in *Forschungen zu Staat und Verfassung : Festgabe für Fritz Hartung* (Berlin 1958) 325–44.
[3] I have argued this in an article on 'A phase in the development of the intendants; the reign of Henri IV', *The Historical Journal*, ix (1966), 27–38.
[4] *Registres des délibérations du bureau de la ville de Paris* (part of the *Histoire Générale de Paris*), xii, 238–9, and xiii, 26–7.
[5] See their letter to Bellièvre, August 1602; BN ms. fr. 15899, fo. 577.
[6] AN P 2668, fo. 266–7.
[7] AC Mâcon, CC 103, n⁰ 31.

concessions, as the representative of Avignon learned in 1604, when his representations at court were frustrated 'par la seule opinion et cruauté de monsieur de Rosni'.[1] The *députés en cour* of other towns came up against his rigorous investigations; in 1601 the mayor of Lyons had a very hostile reception from him, in spite of enjoying the support of Bellièvre, 'who is our friend, but who dares not open his mouth in council',[2] and in 1604 a councillor of Dijon, after observing that 'no business can be done here without monsieur de Rosny', had to send back to Burgundy for a copy of his town's accounts.[3] By the end of the reign many of the towns of France were in his grip, even a provincial capital like Rouen receiving him with great honour because 'through his favour he could greatly forward the interests of the town'.[4]

It may seem strange that, in a summary of the effect of Sully's financial activity on the provincial authorities, no mention should have been made of the governors, who were nominally in charge of each province. Their authority, however, seems at this time to have been overshadowed by that of the *parlements*;[5] sometimes they would write directly to the king to complain of the rigours of Sully's methods, as for instance the maréchal d'Ornano, governor of Guyenne, did in 1603,[6] but they remain for the most part in the background. We hear of them only at the annual meeting of the estates, when they put the king's case, or in emergencies, when they mobilize the military forces of the province.

We have noticed that Sully did not alter the basic financial structure and that he made no technical innovations in the finances. This chapter has shown that, although he gained a firm hold over the finances of some municipalities, and here and

---

[1] AC Avignon, AA 46.

[2] Antoine Péricaud, *Notes et documents pour servir à l'histoire de Lyon . . . (1594–1610)* (Lyon, 1845), 174.

[3] Joseph Garnier (ed.), *Correspondance de la mairie de Dijon* (3 vols, Dijon, 1870), iii, 84.

[4] *Inventaire sommaire des Archives Communales de la ville de Rouen* (i, Rouen, 1887), reference A 22.

[5] See Gaston Zeller, 'L'administration monarchique avant les intendants', *Revue Historique*, cxcvii (1947), 180–215.

[6] BN ms. fr. 23197, fo. 274 and 276.

there was encroaching on the privileges of the estates, he had scarcely begun to challenge the authority of the *parlements*. If he had been able to maintain his pressure for twenty years instead of ten, he might have appreciably reduced the deadening authority of the sovereign bodies. As it was, the effect of his work was short-lived; with his fall corrupt provincial officials went free again, just as the secretariat built up by him broke down and the budgetary equilibrium which he had so painfully established was shattered.

To such general questions as the extent to which the French crown was obliged to rely during his administration on loans and anticipations it is difficult to give an answer. The figures quoted in chapter IV do not fully account for all the state's financial operations, because some payments are not included. Apart from the collection-expenses for various taxes there were allowances for the holders of *rentes*, usually assigned to *fermes*. We can never know how much of the income from *fermes* was thus paid over by the farmers directly to the creditors of the monarchy, although of course the weight of this obligation was reflected in the price the Crown received – or failed to receive – for the contract. Similarly there is no means of accurately calculating the proportion of income devoted to the payment of holders of various offices, although these had to some extent taken the place of *rentes* as a safer investment for individuals and as an equally sure source of income for the crown.[1] It is not necessary to emphasize the social and economic importance of this development, seemingly natural to an absolute monarchy in which, as Mousnier has said for a later period, 'there seems to be a necessary connection between instruments of finance and the form of government'.[2] What would later be known as 'Dutch finance' could not take root alongside a rapacious crown, whose abuse of the 'grand parti de Lyon' of the fifteen-forties[3] was a

---

[1] On the wider implications of the spread of venality, see K. W. Swart, *Sale of offices in the 17th century* (The Hague, 1949).
[2] See his article, 'L'évolution des finances publiques en France et en Angleterre . . .', *Revue Historique*, ccv (1951), 1–23. See also Robert Ashton, *The Crown and the money-market, 1603–1640* (Oxford, 1960), 190.
[3] On this, see Doucet, 'Le grand parti de Lyon', *Revue Historique*, clxxi (1933), 473–513, and clxxii (1933), 1–41.

standing warning against loans to the monarchy by private
individuals lacking the means to enforce their claims for repay-
ment. Hence the French crown's reliance on sale of office and
other ultimately ruinous financial expedients during the long
wars of the seventeenth century.

Sully's influence on these general developments was not great;
he cut back the *rentes* payments and institutionalized office-
transmission by the *Paulette*, as we have seen, but these were
superficial measures. The first has been well described as
forming part of a 'banqueroute partielle', and the second merely
acknowledged that an inveterate ill had come to stay. If Sully
lightened the crippling load of interest with which the royal
finances were charged, and made some progress towards re-
deeming the principal by his plans for *rachat du domaine*, he was
all the same obliged, as we have seen, to jeopardize his work by
himself selling offices when he needed ready money. No one
reformer could make headway against the great currents of
financial abuse within the French monarchy, as Colbert and
Turgot were to discover after Sully.

CHAPTER VI

Grand voyer

By 1500 Paris was already the centre of the system of roads in France. In Roman days the hub of the roads in Gaul had been Lyons, but in the centuries following the decline of the empire the influence of this Italian outpost had much diminished. In medieval times the Roman pattern became obscured by an erratic network of routes serving various purposes; ways for pilgrims, walks for sheep, tracks for merchants, and so on. Then, when the kings of the Ile-de-France slowly became rulers of France, it was from their chief town at Paris that messengers fanned out, devising new routes and slowly establishing Paris as the road-centre.[1]

To talk of 'road-centres' is, however, rather anachronistic, given the circumstances of the sixteenth century. The first map showing the network of French roads dates only from the 1630s, and men of the sixteenth century thought rather in terms of safe bridges over rivers and climbable passes over hills, than in terms of actual roads. The boggiest stretches of route sometimes had stone paving, as we shall see, but for the most part 'roads' were mere tracks, thick in mud after rain and deeply pitted during the dry seasons. Bridges were constructed only where traffic was likely to be very heavy – elsewhere fords and ferries were used whenever possible – and during the civil wars many had been ruined. Some were deliberately destroyed for tactical reasons, 'to prevent the passage of canon', for instance; others had given way under the great weight of the guns which

[1] See *Les routes de France*, published by the *Association pour la diffusion de la pensée française* (Paris, 1959). This chapter is based on my article, 'The communications of France during the Reconstruction of Henri IV', in *The Economic History Review*, second series, xviii (1965), 43-53.

repeatedly passed over them.[1] Conditions in general were such that in the late autumn of 1599 a messenger from the king at Dieppe, wishing to reach Saumur on the Loire, thought it best to take ship to Saint-Malo and thence to strike southward. When we read that it took him fifteen days to reach Saint-Malo, having first been blown to Portsmouth, it is astonishing to contemplate the rigours of a route thought to be even less practicable than this.[2]

It was to tackle the problem that the office of *grand voyer* (director of communications) was created for Sully in 1599. During the years which followed, his jurisdiction was systematically extended; in June 1603 a declaration united the offices of *voyer de Paris* – a post which Sully had purchased the previous March – and *grand voyer* – authorizing the latter to

> establish in each generality of the kingdom a person, chosen from among our local officers, to be his *lieutenant*;

under this declaration a network of subordinate officials would be established. In June 1604 a further declaration clarified these orders, in January 1605 Sully himself drew up an edict concerning administration which we shall analyse shortly, and in December 1607 a final edict added certain perquisites to the exercise of the *grand voyer's* office.[3] The title itself reflected the developing need for a unified supervision of all the communications in France. For although in the declaration of 1604 the king spoke of his desire to 're-establish . . . the office of *grand voyer*, which has been long in abeyance and seemed abolished', in fact this was a new creation responding to new political needs and fresh economic possibilities; never before had there been a single officer having the 'power to superintend all the local *voyers* in all the towns of the realm'.[4] The novelty of the creation was clear in the terms of the 1599 edict, which spoke of wishing to

---

[1] AN 120 AP 46, fo. 38v⁰ and AD Cher C 973, fo. 45v⁰.

[2] Journey described in the memoirs of Aubery Du Maurier, Bib. Poitiers, Ms. 298.

[3] For these enactments, see E. J. M. Vignon, *Études historiques sur l'administration des voies publiques de France* (3 vols, Paris, 1862), i, 89, and F. A. Isambert, *Recueil général des anciennes lois françaises* (29 vols, Paris, 1821–33), xv, 335–41.

[4] In the words of the 1599 edict.

'establir un grand voyer'; the later fiction of revival no doubt
crept in either to offset the claims of the *trésoriers de France*,
traditionally responsible for *voirie*, or to exempt Sully from the
tax on newly-created offices.[1]

He remained *grand voyer* until August 1616, when he resigned
in favour of the comte d'Orval. For the years 1605 to 1610 we
now have accounts giving the income and expenditure of the
trésorier des ponts et chaussées, who was directly responsible for the
pays d'élections.[2] These accounts are not as useful as would have
been the list, mentioned in the *Économies Royales*,[3] of all expenditure on the communications, for they do not account either for
the great towns or for the *pays d'états*, but they do enable past
estimates of direct royal spending to be corrected. These
estimates were generally based on a passage from the *Économies
Royales* in which are given the purposes for which the *tailles
extraordinaires* were levied between 1599 and 1609.[4] The fuller
accounts naturally show the total expenditure to have been
much greater, but it is possible to show from the other figures,
analysed in chapter IV, that the old tables were at least correct
in showing little expenditure before 1605; as Sully himself
pointed out in a letter of January 1605 to the *trésoriers de France*
at Caen, he had put off the drawing-up of the enclosed *voirie*
regulations until he had had time to work on the general
financial structure.[5]

Table 4 brings out the pattern of expenditure; a steady rise
after 1605 until 1609 and then a faltering in 1610, when preparations for war caused the diversion of funds. After that there
was a tailing-off in 1612 before the sudden drop of 1616, the
year of Sully's resignation. There was very heavy expenditure
in the generality of Paris on the bridges at Mantes and Saint-
Cloud; in the generalities of Bourges and Poitiers, as we shall see,
there were considerable canal-works, and in that of Orleans the
heavy expenditure of 1609 went to repair the great damage
caused by that year's floods. Bridges and canals accounted for a

---

[1] The theory of Paul Viollet, *Le roi et ses ministres* (Paris, 1912), 479.
[2] AN 120 AP 38–42.
[3] *Économies Royales*, ii, 290b.
[4] Ibid., ii, 271–3.
[5] Romier (ed.), 'Lettres de Sully', 553–4.

very high proportion of the money compared with the roads; the reason for this will become clear when the nature of the work on the roads is considered. The detailed accounts show how money was being levied in the various generalities and then spent in accordance with the orders of the central directorate, and not necessarily on works of primary importance to the region concerned. Thus all the generalities contributed to the building of the Briare canal except those of Bordeaux, Limoges and Poitiers.[1] These three were, however, responsible for the completion of the Tour de Cordouan, a lighthouse at the mouth of the Gironde, begun by Louis de Foix and completed by Claude de Chastillon;[2] some of the *pays d'élections* also contributed to this, and in the debates of the estates of Languedoc we hear a strong provincialist response from some *diocèses*,[3] who are unwilling to pay, as they say, because 'ilz ne font aucun pastel'[4] (and consequently do not need the Tour de Courdouan to guide the vessels exporting this dye for them). Sometimes indeed *voirie* money was entirely diverted from the purpose for which it was ostensibly levied. Thus an account in Sully's own hand concerning the generalities of Bordeaux, Limoges and Poitiers estimates income at 140,090 *livres*; 45,000 of these went on *voirie* work within the provinces, 6,000 on the Tour de Cordouan, 51,090 on the communications of other regions – the 'canal de Vesle' near Rheims, for instance, and the 'pont d'Avignon' – and 38,000 'straight to the Treasury'.[5] There were constant complaints about this kind of diversion, like those of the estates of Normandy in their *cahiers* between 1605 and 1608, that heavy taxes were being levied 'under the pretence of completing Rouen bridge' – on which in fact no work was being done.[6]

But if some of the monies escaped into the central treasury, to be used for cannon, fortifications or mistresses, at any rate funds which reached the *trésorier des ponts et chaussées* were spent in a systematic way. The ruling of 1605 set out a detailed procedure

---

[1] See the 'état des recouvrements', AN 120 AP 48, fo. 9–10.
[2] See chapter VII, and plate 9.
[3] term surviving to mean (civil) administrative sub-division.
[4] AD Tarn, C 55, fo. 171v⁰.
[5] AN 120 AP 48, fo. 9.
[6] Beaurepaire (ed.), *Cahiers des états de Normandie*, ii, 57, 109, 121, 145, etc.

which seems to have been scrupulously followed; the *lieutenants* of the *grand voyer* were to tour their districts in February, 'when the floods are normally at their height and the roads at their worst', in order to see what needed to be done. Having submitted a general state of priorities to the *grand voyer* the previous November, and received his authorization for certain projects, the following September or October they were to make another tour to estimate the value of the work carried out during the summer. With their *réceptions d'ouvrages* completed, they were then to verify the receipts and payments of the local *trésoriers*, making sure that the accounts went to the *grand voyer* before being checked by the *chambre des comptes*.

This edict, which regulated *voirie* work throughout the rest of the reign, spoke of the '*grand voyer* or his *lieutenants, trésoriers de France, intendants* or other officers'.[1] In fact most of the *lieutenants* were *trésoriers de France*, often indeed the senior members of each *bureau des finances*, though some too were *lieutenants* of Sully as *grand maître de l'artillerie*, or else *intendants des turcies et levées* (see appendix 2). It has often been remarked, with an eye to the *corps d'ingénieurs* set up in 1747 for the *ponts et chaussées*, that the great weakness of this branch of the administration had been the absence of a trained body of engineers. However, the *trésoriers* were specialists of a kind, and the accounts of *voyages et taxations* make it clear that for technical tasks such as the *réception d'ouvrages* they were often helped by 'expertz', usually mastermasons. Moreover, for difficult projects like major bridges Sully could call on his *ingénieurs du roi* from the artillery; men like Claude de Chastillon and Humphrey Bradley, who were among the foremost experts of the age.

It was not so much technical or administrative deficiencies as the resistance of the provincial authorities which hampered the fuller development of communications at this period. The traditional guardian of the rights of the sovereign courts was the chancellor, and chancellor Bellièvre put up a stiff fight before consenting to the declaration of June 1603.[2] The *parlements* were

[1] Mallevoüe (ed.), *Actes de Sully*, xxxii.
[2] BN ms. fr. 15897, fo. 522, and ms. fr. 15894, fo. 573; letter from Sully to Bellièvre and the latter's reply.

equally obstructive; at Paris, for instance, the edict of May 1599 was not registered until the following September,[1] and at Bordeaux the *parlement* ratified the edict of June 1604 the following August, but only 'provided that those who are appointed do not trespass upon the jurisdiction of *voyers particuliers* and other officers'. Sully was not slow in obtaining *lettres de jussion* to override this nugatory clause, but even then the opposition remained stubborn.[2] In the Bordeaux generality the upshot was similar to that in most of the other *pays d'élections*; Sully and the king behaved as though their edicts had in fact been registered without opposition or comment.[3]

In the *pays d'élections* the most effective opposition came, paradoxically enough, from the *trésoriers de France*. For they claimed by immemorial right – which in fact dated from 1508 – to control all affairs of *voirie*. Sully may to some extent have disarmed them by choosing his *lieutenants* from among their number; certainly this was to be the way in which after 1669 their *voirie* jurisdiction was gradually taken over by *intendants*, who each selected a *trésorier* as his adviser on questions relating to *ponts et chaussées*. However, in most generalities Sully had to exert constant pressure to get his orders obeyed, and there are at least two instances of the *trésoriers'* overt resistance to his encroachments. Thus in May 1608 he had to write a very strong letter to the Caen *trésoriers* about their attack on the powers of his *lieutenant* 'd'Obigny',[4] who had been a member of the bureau but seems to have turned against his colleagues, and a little earlier he had had to support the sieur d'Escures, *lieutenant* for Moulins and Orleans, against the *trésoriers* of the latter city.[5] If, with the support of the king, Sully was able until 1610 to override this opposition, after that year he no longer made any headway against the *trésoriers'* pretentions, and they obtained first the restriction (1618) and eventually the abolition (1625) of the charge of *grand voyer*.[6]

[1] Mallevouë (ed.), *Actes de Sully*, xxx.
[2] See for instance, AD Gironde 1B 18, fo. 56–7, 61–2 and 124.
[3] *Économies Royales*, i, 593a: letter from the king to Sully, 19 August 1604.
[4] Guillaume Novynce, sieur d'Aubigny: see Romier (ed.), 'Lettres de Sully', 574–5.
[5] Valois, n° 12068, and Romier (ed.), 'Lettres de Sully', 575.
[6] BN Cinq Cents de Colbert, 225, fo. 74.

The greater towns had often received royal permission to levy various duties at their gates in order to undertake public works or to maintain public roads and buildings. Sully made a determined effort to check and control all these levies; as a note in his hand on a copy of a royal declaration of April 1605 puts it, the aim was:

> to oblige the towns imposing dues to present their accounts to the *trésoriers de France*, or if necessary to M. de Sully, every three years, and to submit to a check by the *chambre des comptes* every six years.[1]

In his *Histoire de la ville de Troyes*[2] Boutiot described how the *grand voyer* could encroach on the *voirie* responsibilities of a small town like that, and for Bayonne there survives an account of income and expenditure on the bridges and other installations which, annotated by Sully, shows how he was tracking down diversions of funds.[3] Even a great centre like Lyons was obliged to submit in the end; in March 1603 Sully failed in an attempt to reform the administration of the taxes, which he said had been 'appropriée à ceulx qui ont esté en charge',[4] but five years later we find him supplying the town with 5,000 *livres* to repair a bridge, in return for which they must provide a further 5,000 and also submit copies of their accounts.[5] In each provincial centre the *lieutenant* did his best to control the allocation of funds in this way, with considerable success. Sometimes the municipality would interfere directly with the work of *voirie*, as in 1602 when the *prévôt des marchands* at Paris tried to forbid a contractor working under the Châlons *lieutenant* from repairing the bridge at Frignicourt (Marne). Then Sully merely told the contractor to get on with the work and discharged him from all 'hindrances, condemnations and injunctions' on the part of the *prévôt*.[6] This was easy in the area under the close control of the administration

---

[1] AN 120 AP 1, fo. 210v⁰.
[2] T. Boutiot (4 vols, Troyes/Paris, 1870–4), iv, 297.
[3] BN nouv. acq. franç., 23798, fo. 2.
[4] Péricaud (ed.), *Notes et documents*, 174.
[5] Bib. Lyon AA 54, letter of May 1606 from Sully to the municipality.
[6] AD Marne C 2490, fo. 161–4. For the *prévôt*'s viewpoint, see also *Registres du bureau de la ville de Paris*, xii, 592–3.

in Paris, but not so easy, as we shall see, in the outlying provinces.

Sully was also largely successful in regulating the rights and duties of *péagers*, private individuals who levied duties – theoretically under royal warrant – on certain routes, and were supposed to use the product for repairs. By the order of January 1605 the *lieutenants* had been ordered to check all *péagers*, and in April that year a further *arrêt* ordered them to draw up a list of *péagers* during their autumn *chevauchée*. One of these lists survives at the Archives Nationales;[1] nobody was spared, and even the prince of Orange, for example, was required in June 1607 to prove the right by which he levied a tax on 'all kinds of goods going up and down the Rhône'.[2] In his case letters-patent validating the levy were not granted until 1610.

In short, within the *pays d'élections* the centralized administration of the communications was making good progress. It was different in the five great peripheral provinces: Brittany, Burgundy, Dauphiné, Provence and Languedoc. In Brittany, for instance, the estates refused in 1607 and 1608 to consider an offer by Sully to double from the treasury any sum which they might set aside for *voirie*. In 1609 they did set aside 6,000 *livres*, provided that Sully kept his side of the bargain; unfortunately we cannot tell how this arrangement prospered.[3] In Burgundy the estates in 1608 prayed His Majesty

> not to make any innovation in the old and customary procedure for repairing bridges and roads, which is carried out by local officials at the expense both of those who use the bridges and of the neighbouring landowners.

However, in 1610 they did consent to the levy of 20,000 *livres*, to be distributed by the local officers and the *lieutenant*; as in Brittany, some progress had been made.[4]

In the remaining provinces resistance was more successful. In Dauphiné the duc de Lesdiguières ruled the province almost

[1] AN 120 AP 48, fo. 59–60.
[2] BN ms. fr. 16910, fo. 172–92.
[3] BN ms. fr. 22315, fo. 91–2 and 109–10, and also a letter from Sully to the estates' treasurer, AN 120 AP 36, fo. 3.
[4] AD Côte d'Or C 3076, respectively, fo. 82–3 and fo. 206v°.

Domain investigation in Sully's hand; an analysis of some of the regulations of Charles IX (*AN 120 AP 30, fo. 13*).

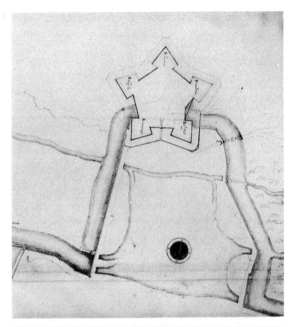

5. Plan by Jean Errard for the citadel at Amiens (*BM add. mss 21,117, fo. 25–6*).

6. Aerial photograph of the citadel at Amiens orientated in the same way as plate 5 (*Ministère de la Construction*).

as though it were a sovereign state, and Claude Expilly
explains in his *Plaidoyez* that the charge of *grand voyer*
has never been received in Dauphiné, for the governor and
his lieutenant have retained this authority.[1]
Lesdiguières in fact did a great deal for the public works of the
region.[2] In Provence the estates of 1605 and of 1609 both con-
demned the encroachments of the sieur de Châteauvieux,
Sully's *lieutenant*,[3] and by May 1615 they had successfully
reaffirmed the ancient traditions of the province.[4] The same
pattern is repeated in Languedoc; having decided at their
Pézenas assembly of 1602 that there was no money for bridges,
the estates so far relented the following year at Carcassonne as to
allocate 1,200 *livres* for their repair. In 1605 at Narbonne they
loaned the *recteur* of the bridge at Pont-Saint-Esprit 3,000
livres for its repair, but were careful not to make a straightfor-
ward grant 'a cause de la consequance'.[5] It was the conscious
policy of these estates so to localize levies as to avoid the danger
of a system which could 'commit the province to a general
contribution'.[6] They were even unwilling to support the work
which was set under way to establish a safe harbour at Sète, and
this project had to be abandoned in 1605.[7] In 1608 Sully
appointed as *lieutenant* a particularly enterprising official called
Miles Marion;[8] complaints of his encroachments began at once,
so that early in 1609 Marion was forced to declare that he
would be 'very unwilling to do anything against the rights and
privileges of the region as he will always make evident'.[9] Of

[1] *Plaidoyez de M. Claude Expilly* (Paris, 1612), 650–7.
[2] See Ch. Dufayard, *Le connétable de Lesdiguières* (Paris, 1892).
[3] AD Bouches-du-Rhône, C 11, *liasses* for 1605 and 1611.
[4] AD Bouches-du-Rhône, C 468.
[5] AD Tarn C 55, fo. 263r°; the *recteur* was the director of the bridge and hospice there.
[6] *Lois municipales et économiques du Languedoc* (2 vols, Montpellier, 1780–7), ii, 294–5.
[7] P. Boissonade, 'L'essai de restauration des ports et de la vie maritime en Languedoc de 1593 à 1661 et son échec', *Annales du Midi*, xlvi (1934), 98–121.
[8] I have investigated his career in 'A phase in the development of the *intendants*', 34–5.
[9] AD Lozère, C 538, fo. 142.

H

course to carry out his task he needed to erode precisely those
rights and privileges exploited by corrupt municipalities and
péagers, but there was little chance of his being able to do so at
this time in a province with estates as powerful as those of
Languedoc. It seems to have been only in the second half of the
eighteenth century that they realized the need for adequate
roads.[1]

In three of the five great *pays d'états*, then, Sully's work had
made virtually no headway, and this must be borne in mind
when we consider the results achieved in the country as a whole.
Traffic of course consisted of horsemen and of relatively light
passenger coaches, since heavy goods went by water whenever
possible, whether by sea, river or canal. For these categories of
traffic there was no question of straightening the roads, and if
they were widened it was not so much to allow an increased
volume of traffic as to offer a greater choice of terrain on which
to manœuvre, both to avoid potholes and to 'prevent the thefts
and murders'[2] which easily took place in close country, where
robbers could hide near the road. All the same, Gaxotte's ironic
description of seventeenth-century road-builders as seeing their
task being to 'fill the ruts with fagots and gravel'[3] was probably
too severe. Some width of paving often existed near the middle
of the route, especially in the more difficult boggy stretches.[4]

The crucial points of land-communications were the bridges,
and map 2 shows that royal bridge-work was extensive in the
pays d'élections. As we shall see, a good deal more was done by
private enterprise under licence from the *grand voyer*. Where
stone bridges could not at once be constructed wooden ones
were often provided as a temporary measure;[5] they lasted only

---

[1] See Robert Forster, *The nobility of Toulouse in the 18th century; a social
and economic study* (Baltimore, 1960), 66–8.
[2] Valois, nº 10053; quoted as the reason for widening a road.
[3] *Le siècle de Louis XV* (2 vols, Paris, 1935), ii, 162.
[4] See for instance, Vignon, *Études historiques*, i, 18–20, who quotes a
document as requiring a certain road to be 'eight and a half *toises* wide,
with in the middle a strip two and a half *toises* wide which shall be paved',
and also AD Gironde 4249, in which the contractor is to pave the road 'in
the more difficult places'.
[5] *Économies Royales*, ii, 259a, letter of 1608 from Sully to the king, and
Valois, nº 11169 and 12096.

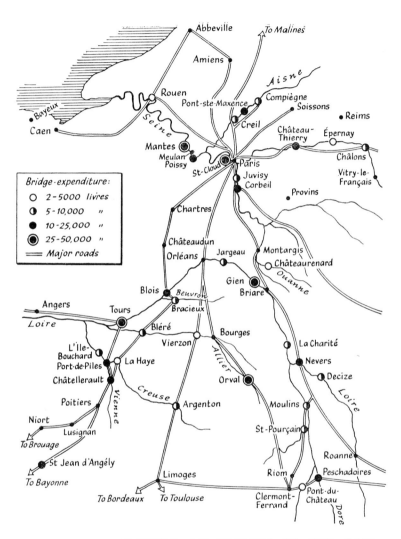

MAP 2 EXPENDITURE ON BRIDGES IN THE *PAYS D'ÉLECTIONS*, 1605–10, by the *trésorier des ponts et chaussées*. Roads from M. Tavernier, *Carte Géographique des postes* (Paris, 1632).

fifty or sixty years but they cost only one-fifth as much as stone ones.[1] Sometimes the work was undertaken for specifically economic reasons. Thus in September 1598 the *trésoriers de France* at Bourges wanted the bridge at Argent-sur-Sauldre (Cher) to be rebuilt so that cattle from the Limousin could pass conveniently from that region to the north, and so that cloth could enter Champagne and Lorraine.[2] But texts setting out such specific motives are rare, and the usual reasons stated for bridge-building or repairing are to keep the *grands chemins* open to couriers,[3] or merely because, as in the case of the bridge at Vierzon, it was the 'finest, shortest and safest road from all the towns of Guyenne to Paris, Orleans and Rouen'.[4]

Apart from the work summarized on the map, there were the efforts of the great towns; to consider only the main river-crossings, work was set under way for bridges at Avignon, Bayonne, Bordeaux, Nantes, Orleans, Rouen and Saumur.[5] Often the advice of the artillery engineers was sought, and sometimes the *grand voyer* was able to use his general powers to reconcile differing parties; we read for instance that at Avignon it was the 'duca di Suilli' who in 1607 helped arrange the sharing of expenditure on the new bridge between the principality of Orange and the neighbouring French provinces.[6] Sometimes too Sully took a hand in the actual construction; in 1608 he travelled to Rouen at the king's request to supervise the preparation of plans for a new bridge there.[7] The plans were drawn up by the artillery engineer Claude de Chastillon, but have been lost.[8] Two reports of 1605 and 1607 by *lieutenants* of the artillery

---

[1] AD Cher C 973, fo. 45r°.

[2] AD Cher C 973, fo. 45v°.

[3] See for instance, AD Gironde C 4239. 'Grands chemins' were those along which there was a regular service of messengers and for whose upkeep the king was responsible; they might also be called 'chemins royaux'. See AD Côte d'Or C 2082 bis, fo. 108v°, 'grands chemins, vulgairement appellez chemins royaux'.

[4] AD Cher C 978, fo. 28–9.

[5] Valois, n° 707, 5294, 5589, 6379, 7679, 9567, 11169, etc.

[6] Bib. Institut, fonds Godefroy, 375, fo. 173–85.

[7] This journey is well documented; see L. Lalanne (ed.), *Oeuvres de Malherbe* (4 vols, Paris, 1862), iii, 78–9; *Économies Royales*, ii, 246–7; and AN 120 AP 6, fo. 184r°.

[8] The last mention of them is found in Ch. Loriquet, *Catalogue historique et descriptive du musée de Reims* (Reims, 1881), 267–8.

are interesting for the light they throw on this work; in the first the Somme, whose bridges had suffered greatly during the wars, is reported to be bridged at Ham, Péronne, Corbie, Amiens and Abbeville, and in the second the bridges of Guyenne are described as being in 'very good shape except for the bridges at Grenade near Toulouse and l'Isle-Jourdan'.[1]

In the most thorough regional study of land-communications at this time, Boissonade concluded that in Poitou the work on roads and bridges was extensive and had a very stimulating effect on trade and traffic.[2] In the absence of similar regional studies it is perhaps dangerous to generalize, but expenditure in the generalities of Bourges and Orleans, as well as in that of Paris, ran at a similar figure, and one may assume that good progress was also made in them. Here and there, indeed, there is direct evidence of growth as a result of improved roads and bridges; thus the *Chronique bordelaise* speaks of a new road and bridge made in 1608 as having opened up a hitherto unfrequented area.[3] Such evidence is, however, rare.

We have already noticed the prominent part which the construction of canals took in the general expenditure. In France about 1600, statesmen were much attracted by canals from the strategic as well as from the purely economic point of view. Thus Sully pressed for the 'joining of the Seine to the Loire, of the Loire to the Saône, and of the Saône to the Meuse', because this would 'lose two millions of income to Spain and gain them for France';[4] he also talked of 'joining Maine and the Mose [Meuse], and so to convey merchandise from Holland to Marseilles by fresh water'.[5] When Humphrey Bradley, *ingénieur ud roi*, wanted to emphasize to Sully the attractions of the same project, he pointed out not only the advantage of drawing goods through 'eau calme' instead of over rough terrain, and of being

[1] AN 120 AP 45, and 120 AP 46.
[2] P. Boissonade, 'Les voies de communications terrestres et fluviales en Poitou sous le règne de Henri IV', *Revue Henri IV*, ii (1907–8), 193–228 and 295–311, and iii (1909), 65–102.
[3] *Chronique bordelaise* (Bordeaux, 1703), 129; for some other references, see Gustave Fagniez, *Économie sociale de la France au temps de Henri IV* (Paris, 1897), 188.
[4] *Économies Royales*, i, 558.
[5] Carew, *Relation of the state of France*, 432.

able to control a considerable source of revenue, but also the way in which troops could thus arrive wherever they were needed, without tiring themselves or harassing the peasants.[1] Hugues Cosnier, the contractor for the Briare canal, added to reasons like these the consideration that an Aisne-Meuse canal, for example, would enable the coal of the Liège district to be sold at Paris much more cheaply than English coal.[2] Sully took a keen interest in the Briare (Loire-Seine) canal, on which nearly 1,000,000 *livres* were spent up to 1610.[3] He not only provided the driving force in Paris for keeping the project going, but also paid at least one visit to the site. He seems to have behaved with typical high-handed enthusiasm on this occasion, carrying out a personal topographical survey[4] and disorganizing the contractor's estimates by ordering the locks to be made larger and of stone instead of wood. The set of locks at Rogny survives, telling evidence of the magnitude of the scheme (plate 2).

In the end the Briare canal was not quite finished and did not come into operation until 1642. But smaller canals were completed, often using the services of *ingénieurs du roi* like Humphrey Bradley and Claude de Chastillon. Among these smaller canals were the 'Clain et Vienne' (about 150,000 *livres* in all), the 'Vesle et Aisne' (about 60,000) and the Cher at Saint-Amand (about 60,000). Boissonade, in the article already quoted,[5] analysed the effects of the completion of the first of these and found that trade in agricultural produce was particularly stimulated. It is easy to visualize the great effect the opening-up of even a short length of well-sited waterway could have, for land-transport costs were between three and five times as great as those by water,[6] and many of the navigable rivers were blocked by mills.[7] The siting of the Paris arsenal, on the Seine near the Bastille, is interesting in this respect, since from it

---

[1] AN 120 AP 48, fo. 19-24.

[2] Quoted by Henri Pinsseau, *Le canal Henri IV ou canal de Briare* (Paris/Orléans, 1943), 40.

[3] See Pinsseau, *Le canal Henri IV*; his accounts are confirmed by those of the 'Papiers de Sully'.

[4] BN ms. fr. 16740, fo. 121.

[5] 'Les voies de communications', 65-73.

[6] To judge by the contracts printed by Mallevouë (ed.), *Actes de Sully*.

[7] See for instance, Valois n° 10733 and 11846.

supplies could be floated up the Marne to Châlons and thence distributed to the eastern frontier towns; an order from Sully to one of his artillery *lieutenants* survives in which he orders him to move his cannon 'by water if possible'.[1]

In the *pays d'élections*, then, in the heart of France, for the first time there was a unified network of officials directed from Paris according to standard procedures. Even if technical innovations were few, and even if the whole structure gradually disintegrated after Sully's disgrace in 1611, this was an administrative innovation of the greatest importance for the future. The staff of the *ponts et chaussées* at this time were more competent technically than has often been realized but it is very hard to assess the results achieved by them, especially when we consider that France was at that time enjoying a 'natural' recovery after forty years of war. Perhaps the best gauge may be found in the comparative figures for *voirie* expenditure under Richelieu, Colbert and Louis XIV. The 1,000,000 *livres* annually paid to the *trésorier des ponts et chaussées* during the last three years of Henri IV's reign was certainly not equalled before 1680,[2] and bearing in mind both the inflation and the disastrous years of war at the end of the century, it seems unlikely that the effort directed by Sully was surpassed before the days of Louis XV, with his *école des ponts et chaussées*.

[1] BN ms. fr. 16694, fo. 16–17.
[2] According to Mallet, *Comptes rendus de l'administration des finances.*

CHAPTER VII

Surintendant des fortifications *and* des bâtiments

It may seem strange that the royal buildings should be grouped with the fortifications rather than with the other civil public works described in chapter VI. However, to Sully's contemporaries this arrangement would have seemed natural; many of the civil architects were also military engineers – which has been held to account for the severe 'military' style of their buildings[1] – and when they wrote manuals they found it appropriate to deal in successive chapters with arithmetic, fortification, royal palaces and private houses.[2] Moreover, Sully was in charge of both fortifications and buildings; he became *surintendant des bâtiments* in 1600 on the resignation of Nicolas de Harlay, sieur de Sancy,[3] and the same year became *surintendant des fortifications*, a post which he resigned in 1605 in favour of his son, Maximilien II de Béthune.[4] However, Maximilien II worked under his guidance with the officers appointed by Sully, who may thus be considered as responsible for buildings and fortifications between 1600 and 1610.

The 'Papiers de Sully' are particularly useful for their details of work on the fortifications, especially when their information is related to a great series of maps and plans, drawn up by the engineers under Sully's guidance and now preserved in the

---

[1] For instance, by P. Du Colombier, *Le style Henri IV – Louis XIII* (Paris, 1941), 29.

[2] See for instance, Jacques Perret's 'Manuel d'un ingénieur-architecte', BN ms. fr. 14727.

[3] Mallevoüe (ed.), *Actes de Sully*, xxxvi. Sancy was compensated by a grant from the king; see BN ms. fr. 4559, fo. 18–19.

[4] Mallevoüe (ed.), *Actes de Sully*, xxxix–xl.

British Museum.[1] Sometimes too, in the regions like Picardy where the frontier of France later expanded, it is possible to study the surviving buildings; in other regions, like Provence, where the works of Henri IV remained in constant use and were much transformed, we may often obtain some notion of their original form from the models preserved in the Musée des Plans-Reliefs housed at the Invalides.[2]

Plate 11, showing the siege of Montmélian in 1600, gives us a good idea both of typical medieval fortifications and of the kind of work which began to replace them during the sixteenth century. The old town at the foot of the hill is surrounded by a high curtain wall, broken here and there by round towers; this is the traditional type of town-wall of which a magnificent if much-restored example survives at Carcassonne. This kind of defence was useful against thieves or lightly-armed robber bands. But the steady progress of artillery began to demand a different kind of structure to resist bombardment, which pierced the high walls and brought them crashing down on the heads of the defenders, who were without means of retaliation. It was the Italians who seem first to have developed a new form of fortification, in response to the need to protect their towns during the wars of the late fifteenth and early sixteenth centuries, when the artillery of the kings of France enjoyed such success in Italy. One of the earliest of the new systems to be constructed still survives, at Verona; the citadel which we see above the town at Montmélian has been laid out in accordance with the same general principles.

The great aim was so to dispose the defending guns as to catch the attacker with cross-fire from whatever direction he might come. This could best be done by constructing a series of 'bastions' projecting from the line of defence, designed so as to cover not only each other but also the adjacent wall. At first the bastions were flat, or nearly so:

[1] BM add. mss. 21,117; I have used this volume extensively in an article on 'Les *ingénieurs du roi* au temps de Henri IV', *Bulletin de Géographie*, lxxvii (1964), 13–84.
[2] The history of these *maquettes* is set out in the *Catalogue-Guide du musée des Plans-Reliefs* (Paris, 1928).

FIGURE 1   FIGURE 2

later it became clear that they were more efficient if they had
two faces:

FIGURE 3   FIGURE 4

Figure 3 shows a bastion with 'oreillons', or small ears to protect
the gunners on the flanks. This form, which was still in use in
France about 1600, became less common during the seventeenth
century, when the type of bastion shown in figure 4 became
general. Figure 5 gives a cross-section of the line of defence;
the attacking force had first to cross the glacis, swept by
the fire of the defending guns, and then gain possession of the
covered way, held by the defending infantry. Then it had to
cross the ditch before finally assaulting the rampart, whose
scarp would normally have been breached by the attacking
artillery before the foot-soldiers could go in. Behind the rampart
the town was laid out so that guns could be quickly moved to a
menaced sector; often supplies were held in reserve so that fresh
earthworks could be undertaken behind a breached section of
rampart. It goes without saying that the walls were all constructed as strongly as possible to withstand the guns, and that
fields of fire were cleared beyond the glacis, so that attackers
could be early engaged.

Such defences were scarcely within the reach even of the greatest
French towns; they were not only very expensive but they also
required the employment of skilled engineers for their construction, as each section formed an indispensable part of the general
defensive scheme. By the third quarter of the sixteenth century
many Italian towns had fine bastioned traces, and in northern

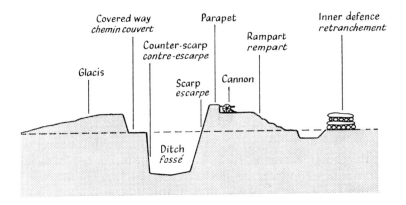

FIGURE 5   CROSS-SECTION OF A DEFENSIVE TRACE

Europe the Spaniards had completed several fortresses in the Low Countries. In France the north-eastern frontier had been extensively fortified during the 1540s, and there were strong modern works at Doullens, Guise, La Cappelle, Le Catelet, Sainte-Ménehould and Vitry-le-François.[1] But the other frontiers could offer little resistance to attack with modern weapons, if we except the strong-points of Brouage, Grenoble and La Rochelle. As Robert Dallington wrote in his *View of Fraunce* (London, 1604), '[apart from La Rochelle and Amiens] if a man will looke through all France, I thinke that hee shall not finde any Towne halfe perfectly fortifyed, according to the rules of Ingeners'.[2]

There was then much to be done when Henri IV was eventually free to attend to his realm's fortifications. The administrative structure which he inherited from the Valois was not very effective. Until the reign of François I the towns had themselves undertaken the construction and upkeep of their walls. Then during the wars with the emperor Charles V the royal treasury began to make contributions, but the king's treasurers shared the task – and the allocation of funds – with the captain of each town and with its mayor. Each of these three had one of

[1] Gaston Zeller, *L'organisation défensive des frontières du nord et de l'est au XVIIe siècle* (Paris, 1928).
[2] Op. cit., C2.

the three keys without which the chest containing the fortifica-
tion-money could not be opened. This was not a system making
for great efficiency, and it was in any case rarely put to the test
after 1560, with the onset of the civil wars. In 1598 the whole
system needed to be reorganized.

Sully, as we have noted, became *surintendant des fortifications* in
1600, but although he set to work at once, the first of his administrative regulations which survives dates from 1604.[1] In it he
shows the same spirit of method as in his work on the finances or
on the communications. His great principle is that the financial
allocations set down in the *états des fortifications*[2] shall be followed;
there is nothing very original in this, but what makes the system
work is his establishment of a network of local officers, whom he
supervises closely. In each of the great frontier provinces of the
east – Picardy, Champagne, Dauphiné and Provence – he
appoints an *ingénieur du roi*, who has as his deputy a *conducteur des
desseins*.

The *ingénieur* had to note down as he travelled round the
province the work which had to be undertaken the following
year, according to the general directions of the *états des fortifications*. Once this work had been approved by the governor of the
province – who often came with the *ingénieur* on these trips
– the contracts, following the plans drawn up by the *ingénieur* and
conducteur, were put out to tender by the *contrôleur-général*, of whom
there was one in each province. The *ingénieur* could check on the
progress of work during his tours of inspection, and there was a
clause in the regulation allowing him to refer unco-operative
captains of towns or fortresses to the royal council. Then once
the project was completed, or when the winter set in, the work
was measured up and the account settled by the *ingénieur* in the
presence of the *contrôleur-général*. This system seems to have been
followed pretty faithfully, to judge by odd references; it was
completed by an *arrêt* of 7 February 1608 which set out more
minutely the way of adjudging bids for contracts.[3]

[1] Copies are BN Cangé 20, fo. 114, and Arch. Aff. Étr., France, 766, fo.
10.
[2] Those for 1609 survive; see AN 120 AP 27, fo. 1–34.
[3] Valois, n° 11916.

The *ingénieurs du roi* did not receive any formal technical education, but were apprenticed like other artisans; Jean Errard perhaps with an Italian master, Jean de Beins with Raymond de Bonnefons and Louis de Foix with Spanish masters. In the course of their construction-work they drew up maps, and so made a considerable contribution to French provincial cartography. No doubt they used the so-called *cercle hollandais*, developed in the mid-sixteenth century to combine the functions of the earlier compass and astrolabe. Perhaps too they knew of the theodolite and plain-table, increasingly used in England after about 1570. Unfortunately their maps are all fair copies, lacking any indications of how they were drawn up.

The endpapers reproduce the magnificent map of Picardy and Artois drawn up by Jean Martellier, *conducteur des desseins* for the *ingénieur*, Jean Errard. Work in that province, which yearly consumed about 250,000 *livres*, was concentrated on the sites marked on map 3. The line of the fortifications passes well to the west of that later established by Louis XIV, and many of the works have consequently survived. We may take as a fine example of Errard's style the citadel of Amiens. The town had been captured by the Spaniards in March 1597, and after its recapture the following September he was commissioned to construct a great citadel there. Plate 5 shows his plan for it; a handsome pentagon with his distinctive feature, an acute angle between the wall and the bastion's flank:

FIGURE 6

Figure 4 (page 122) shows the more normal form of bastion, with a right-angle between the wall and the bastion's flank. Errard maintained on the contrary that there should be a right-angle between the face and the flank, and it was this which obliged him to have this acute angle. It was tactically mistaken, as the fire of some of the defenders on the flank was partially

MAP 3 SITES FORTIFIED UNDER HENRI IV

masked by the adjacent wall, but as a distinctive element in his style it is useful in attributing fortifications to him. The work at Amiens went forward throughout the reign of Henri IV, and yearly cost considerable sums. The citadel survives intact, and plate 6 allows us to see how closely its final form followed the plan of Errard, particularly in the acute angles between the wall and the flank of the bastions.

The other sites in Picardy which took most money were Calais and Doullens. At Calais considerable additions were made to the water-defences of the town and of the citadel, which dates from the mid-sixteenth century and still survives. At Doullens too extensive works were undertaken, involving the grafting of three great new bastions on to the small and rather irregular citadel set up by Henri II; here again the work of Errard survives intact, though it is being badly damaged by the trees and shrubs which now cover it. Errard was ennobled in 1599, and was active the following year in the campaign against the duke of Savoy. Sometimes he worked outside Picardy; he was certainly employed on the fortifications of Burgundy, notably at Langres,[1] and he also planned the new fortifications of Bayonne.[2] He was in addition consulted about a project for a port near Bayonne,[3] but this seems to have come to nothing; it is unlikely that he ever worked at Sisteron, in spite of local legend. His fame spread outside France, so that in 1603 the duc de Bouillon advised the Elector Palatine to ask for his services – advice which was brusquely countermanded by Henri IV.[4] His later years were saddened by the death from an accident in Provence in 1607 of his son Maximilien, another engineer who 'knew almost as much about it as his father'.[5] Jean Errard died at Sedan in 1610, and his nephew Alexis became an *ingénieur du roi* after him.

Plate 5 is a good example of Jean's work, which is finely

---

[1] AM Langres, 920 and 1173.
[2] See the article of Élie Lambert, in *Congrès archéologique de France*, cii (1939), 507–22.
[3] See Claude Groulart, *Mémoires et voyages en Cour (1588–1600)*, ed. Michaud and Poujoulat (Paris, 1838), 589a.
[4] *Économies Royales*, i, 492b.
[5] *Économies Royales*, ii, 189b.

executed in a yellow and light blue wash. The endpapers show the style of his *conducteur des desseins,* Jean Martellier. The latter drew up a series of eighteen maps of the province, on a scale of about 1/130,000, and it is these which he used in producing the general map of Picardy. This was the most detailed coverage of the province which had until then been achieved and it corrected its predecessors in tracing the bed of the Somme more accurately, and in placing many towns more precisely. It was also very precocious in setting out France's frontier with her eastern neighbours.[1]

In Champagne the *ingénieur* was Claude de Chastillon; he was in the service of the king of Navarre about 1580, and was named *topographe du roi* about 1591, becoming an *ingénieur du roi* about 1595.[2] As we have seen, he carried out much work under Sully as *grand voyer,* completing the Tour de Cordouan, planning several canals, and designing the bridge at Rouen. Apart from these projects, and his work on the fortifications of his province, he probably designed several of the great new buildings at Paris, and also published his celebrated *Topographie française,* a splendid collection of engravings of notable sites in France. He died in 1616, leaving two sons, Hugues and Pierre, who also entered the fortifications-service, respectively as *topographe du roi et son ingénieur en Champagne* and as *intendant des fortifications de Picardie et de Champagne.*

His deputy was a certain 'Bartolomeo Ricardo' who had worked for the king of Navarre since at least 1577. He was probably the last of the long line of Italian engineers who worked for the kings of France, and it is interesting to notice that in June 1609 the Paris *chambre des comptes* confirmed the naturalization of 'Barthélemy Richard, ingénieur du roi, natif de Thurin'.[3] The work of these two in Champagne was extensive, for the annual expenditure there was about 75,000 *livres.* New bastions were constructed at Metz and Rocroi, and much work

[1] In *The seventeenth century* (Oxford, 1928), 144, for instance, Sir George Clark observes that the first cartographic boundaries of this kind that he knows date from the early eighteenth century.
[2] He is often confused with two mythical 'brothers'; I have tried to set this right in my article on 'Les *ingénieurs du roi*'.
[3] AN P 2669, fo. 54–5.

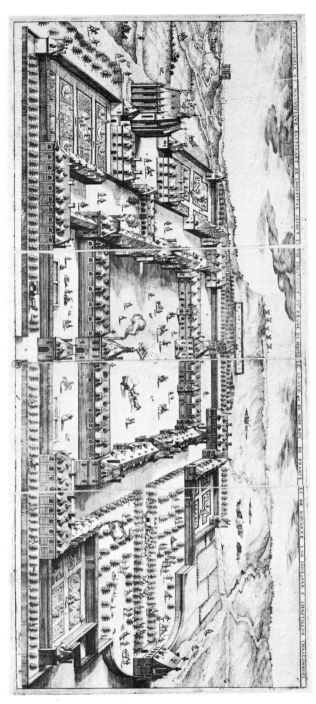

7. The Hôpital Saint-Louis at Paris, looking north towards the windmills of Montmartre. Engraving from the *Topographie française* of Claude de Chastillon (*BN Estampes*).

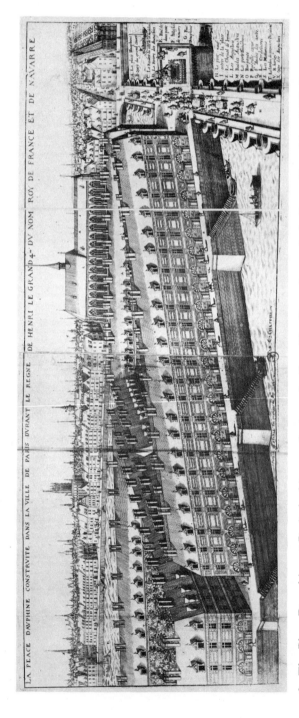

8. The Place Dauphine at Paris, looking south along the Pont Neuf into the newly-built rue Dauphine ('G'). Engraving from the *Topographie française* of Claude de Chastillon (*BN Estampes*).

was also done at Langres and Châlons-sur-Marne. But the
maps and plans for this province do not survive, which makes it
difficult to be more specific about what was done. Nevertheless
it is clear from map 3 that the defensive line running south
from Picardy was continued into Champagne.

Little work was done in Burgundy, where the defensive line
of the Saône running from Auxonne to Seurre and to Châlon-
sur-Saône seems to have been adequate. In Dauphiné on the
other hand Jean de Beins was very active, under the close
supervision of the duc de Lesdiguières; there the annual expenditure was about 100,000 *livres*. Jean Beins was the son of a
burgher ('notable bourgeois') of Paris, and served Henri IV
in all his campaigns between 1589 and 1594. When peace came,
as he had 'studied mathematics and mastered the science of
fortifications and of geography', he was sent to Dauphiné to
work under the *ingénieur* Raymond de Bonnefons whose own
region was Provence. After the death of Bonnefons in 1607 he
was appointed *géographe et ingénieur du roi* for Dauphiné, where
he worked on the sites marked on map 3. He was ennobled in
March 1610, and during the wars of Louis XIII played an
important part in the campaigns on the Italian front.[1]

The most important site in Dauphiné was Fort Barraux,
whose imposing mass still dominates the northern entrance to
the valley of the Isère, leading down to the provincial capital of
Grenoble. In that city too Beins was active, making considerable
additions to the citadel which still towers over the town. He
worked in close collaboration with the duc de Lesdiguières, and
the latter on occasion had to protect him from the town authorities who were jealous of the power of a man who nevertheless
had 'neither money nor goods in Grenoble or even in Dauphiné'.[2] Like that of Jean Errard, his fame spread outside his
province, and in 1612 he was consulted over the best route for
the canal which was to encompass Paris to the north. He is also
well known for the maps which he drew of Savoy, Dauphiné
and part of Languedoc; the British Museum volume has a great

---

[1] For the life of Jean de Beins, see AD Isère B 2920, fo. 210–39, and Bib.
Institut, fonds Godefroy, 191, fo. 22.
[2] AM Grenoble BB 80, fo. 119–20.

I

number of studies used in the preparation of the Dauphiné map, and they demonstrate his remarkable technical versatility. The region is extensive and very mountainous, but by using a great variety of orientations and scales he nevertheless managed to trace in its main features with greater accuracy than had hitherto been achieved.[1] Jean de Beins lived on until about 1645, still at work, and his son Laurent became *ingénieur et cartographe du roi* after him.

In Provence the *ingénieur* in 1600 was Raymond de Bonnefons, master of the young Jean de Beins. His life is obscure; we know only that he was killed in the accident in 1607 in which Maximilien Errard perished, and was succeeded by his son Jean, who had until then been his assistant. The maps and plans of Provence were drawn up by a certain François Martilleur, perhaps the son of Jean Martellier, *conducteur des desseins* to Jean Errard. François did not remain in Provence; in 1606 we find him making an urgent voyage to Holland, no doubt to consult with Dutch engineers, and in 1610 he became *ingénieur du roi* for Picardy on the death of Errard. The expenditure in Provence was about the same as that in Champagne, about 75,000 *livres* annually, spread over the sites shown in map 3. The two Bonnefons collaborated closely with Charles de Guise, governor of the province; he was also *amiral des mers de Levant*, and much time and money went on the construction of a new base at Toulon. At Saint-Tropez too, great works were completed and the citadel of Raymond de Bonnefons still dominates the old town. Another well-preserved example of his work may be seen farther to the west, the so-called 'fort Vauban' at the mouth of the Étang de Berre. The only inland site in Provence was at Sisteron, where Jean de Bonnefons worked in 1611 and perhaps before that. He was still alive in 1641, and twenty years later a certain Pierre de Bonnefons was active in the province as a cartographer. He must surely be a descendant of Raymond and Jean, member of yet another engineering dynasty, but one of which we know all too little.

[1] For illustrations of his skill as a topographer, see plates III and IV of my article on 'L'organisation défensive des frontières au temps de Henri IV', *Revue Historique de l'Armée* xx (4) (1964) 25–31. Father François de Dainville is about to publish a work on Jean de Beins.

In Guyenne on the south-western frontier expenditure was low, about 30,000 *livres* annually. The *ingénieur* there in 1600 was Louis de Foix, a Parisian by origin who had perhaps worked on the Escorial of Philip II, and who later undertook several civil and military engineering works in the south and west. We noticed in chapter VI that he began the reconstruction of the Tour de Cordouan; he also worked on the port of Bayonne, on the bastioned trace of Nantes, on a canal between Bordeaux and Carcassonne, and on a new bridge at Toulouse.[1] He died in 1606, and his successor as *ingénieur du roi* for Guyenne was probably Benedit de Vassallieu. The latter appears in the accounts as an engineer in 1585, 1595 and 1597, but his life is very obscure. He composed an interesting manual on the artillery and was a good topographer (plate 10). He also seems to have drawn up a map of the coasts of Normandy and Brittany, now lost, for in 1604 Sully, finding that he had no time himself to undertake a survey of this region, confided this task to Vassallieu and a certain 'Bois'.[2] Two years later we find Vassallieu being paid 1,200 *livres*

for himself and also for Estienne Boys, master mariner of Le Havre, for a voyage which they are about to make, by His Majesty's express command, from Paris along the coasts of Normandy and Brittany, to visit and reconnoitre the situation of the harbours and sea-ports in that region.[3]

The maps and plans of Brittany mentioned in a letter of October 1607 from the king to Sully[4] were probably the outcome of this trip; unfortunately no trace of them can be found. It is also difficult to say exactly what work Vassallieu accomplished on the fortifications of Guyenne, though he probably worked at Brouage, Blaye, the citadel of Saintes and the Château-Trompette in Bordeaux. But the work here was not extensive; in general the Atlantic and Channel coasts up to Picardy received little attention.

[1] See respectively, Bib. Institut, fonds Godefroy, 191, fo. 123; ibid., fo. 156; Poirson, *Histoire du Règne de Henri IV*, iv, 632; and Valois, n⁰ 4842.
[2] *Économies Royales*, i, 584a.
[3] AN 120 AP 5, fo. 102r⁰.
[4] *Économies Royales*, ii, 200a.

As well as the *ingénieurs* accredited to specific provinces, there were a few whom Sully used for occasional projects. Humphrey Bradley, as we have already noticed, was an expert on canals. Jacques Alleaume was a leading mathematician of the day, who had lectured at the Dutch military academy, perhaps teaching mathematics to Maurice of Nassau, and then returned in 1608 to be lodged at the Louvre as professor of mathematics.[1] Finally the well-known architect Salomon de Brosse was also on the artillery-rolls as *ingénieur du roi*.

Turning now to Sully's work as *surintendant des bâtiments*, it is natural to start with his building at Paris. The state of the Louvre there had astonished and frightened Marie de Medici on her arrival in February 1601; so dilapidated was it that at first she thought either that it could not be the royal palace, or that the French were making fun of her.[2] The restoration of the palace can be followed in great detail through various accounts, contracts and other documents.[3] Of the present *cour carrée*, only the south-western corner had been constructed under Henri II (the other quarters were to be added by Louis XIII and Louis XIV); between 1589 and 1610 this fragment was connected to the Tuileries by the completion of the *petite galerie* and the building of the *grande galerie*, otherwise known as the *galerie du bord de l'eau*. From 1606 onwards architects and craftsmen working on the palace and other projects were housed in the *grande galerie*; the work went on apace, partly because Henri IV, mindful of the embarrassments of his predecessor on the day of Barricades (1588), was anxious to have a means of quickly leaving the city in time of popular unrest.[4] Sully was formally responsible for the work after 1600, as the many contracts printed in the *Actes de Sully* show; the king would also seek his

[1] On Alleaume, see Gustave Cohen, *Écrivains français en Hollande dans la première moitié du XVIIe siècle* (Paris, 1920), 373, and J. J. Guiffrey, 'Logements d'artistes au Louvre', *Nouvelles archives de l'art français*, ii (1873), 21.
[2] According to the *Mémoires* of Ph. Hurault, ed. Michaud and Poujoulat (Paris, 1838), 608.
[3] For our period, the *Nouveaux documents sur le Louvre*, collected by Louis-Henri Collard and edited by Édouard-Jacques Ciprut (Paris, 1963), are particularly interesting; the standard work remains A. Berty, *Topographie historique du vieux Paris* (6 vols, Paris, 1885–97), i and ii.
[4] Berty, *Topographie historique du vieux Paris*, ii, 59–60.

opinion on technical matters. Thus in November 1603 Villeroy wrote to him that 'His Majesty wishes you to visit the Salle des Antiques to see if it is in danger as some have told him'; Sully wrote back to say that while Fourcy and Donon, respectively *intendant* and *contrôleur* of the buildings, thought that the vault would hold, for his part he was not so sure.[1] The decoration of the interior of the royal palaces had formerly been left to the discretion of the artists, normally Italians, but in 1600 the geographer Antoine de Laval presented a treatise to Sully, which suggested that for the future paintings should be commissioned to represent incidents from French history: royal victories, for instance. Sully seems to have agreed with his recommendations, for the *petite galerie* was decorated in this way, so that it became known as the *galerie des rois*.[2] The painter chiefly responsible for the work was the Protestant Jacob Bunel, whom Sully also employed at the Arsenal. Unfortunately little remains of all the interior work undertaken at this time both on the Louvre and on the Tuileries; Anne of Austria and Louis XIV extensively remodelled the former, whose *petite galerie* burnt down in 1661, and the latter was destroyed by the *communards* in 1871.

In the rest of Paris many of the great buildings of the reign survive, and their generally similar style suggests a common architect. The most impressive of them is the Place Royale (now 'Place des Vosges'). It was begun in 1605 as a centre for craftsmen who by the excellence of their work would 'threaten with ruin those foreigners who at present fleece us'.[3] Some craftsmen did establish themselves there for a time, but what stands out on the plan of tenants drawn up by Mallevoüe[4] is the number of Sully's officers who had lots on the square, so handy for his headquarters at the Arsenal (see plate 10). The engineer Claude de Chastillon, the *intendant des turcies et levées* Pierre Fougeu, Sully's secretaries Estienne de La Fond and Noël Regnouart,

---

[1] For these letters, see respectively, *Économies Royales*, ii, 519, and BN ms. fr. 15577, fo. 308.
[2] Berty, *Topographie historique du vieux Paris*, ii, 66.
[3] Isaac de Laffemas, quoted by E. Silberner, *La guerre et la pensée économique du XVIᵉ au XVIIᵉ siècle* (Paris, 1939), 117.
[4] *Actes de Sully*, facing p. 18.

Daniel de Massy, *lieutenant* at the Bastille, Jean de Fourcy, *intendant des bâtiments*; these and others too had their lots around the Place Royale. The buildings were completed in 1612, but the name of their architect is unknown. Some historians have contended that it was Claude de Chastillon, and this attribution is supported by an almost contemporary document in the Cabinet des Titres at the Bibliothèque Nationale.[1] But the best authorities are hesitant in giving him the credit for this work.[2] The same uncertainty surrounds the architect of the Hôpital Saint-Louis, a splendid but little-known structure which cost 795,000 *livres* to build between 1607 and 1612, and which survives intact about a quarter of a mile to the north of the Place de la République (plate 7).

Again, it is not known who designed the Place Dauphine, that remarkable triangular square on the western end of the Ile de la Cité which was probably begun in 1608, but whose delightful unity, evident in plate 8, has been lost by the monstrous additions of generations of greedy landlords. Between 1607 and 1608 the rue Dauphine was cut due southwards from the Left Bank end of the Pont Neuf to the city-walls; this too was probably lined with houses of uniform appearance.[3] The Pont Neuf itself had been completed in 1606; it was started in 1578, and was to have been built like the other bridges of Paris, with a street of houses running along both sides of it. However, as that would have blocked the view from the Louvre,[4] when work began again in 1599 Henri IV had it altered, perhaps by Claude de Chastillon, to its present form. This made it quite wide enough for the coaches which were just beginning to be used by town-dwellers. Claude de Chastillon was certainly associated with two other projects, the Collège de France, and the Place de France in the Marais. The first of these sites was reconnoitred in

[1] BN cabinet d'Hozier, 89.
[2] See for example, Henri Lavedan, *Histoire de l'urbanisme: Renaissance et temps modernes* (Paris, 1941), 282–3, or Émile Baudson, *Un urbaniste au XVIIᵉ siècle, Clément Métezeau* (Mézières, 1956).
[3] See the king's letter of 2 May 1607 to Sully, *Lettres Missives*, vii, 219. The rue Dauphine is also well shown on plate 8; for an accurate plan of the Place Dauphine, see Adolphe Berty, *La renaissance monumentale en France* (Paris, 1864).
[4] According to BN ms. fr. 21698, fo. 292.

December 1609, and the foundation-stone for it was laid by Louis XIII, assisted by Sully, in August 1610, but the work in its original form was never completed.[1] The same is true of the Place de France; this was to have been a very large monumental square, sited just to the north of the Place Royale and served in a fan-shaped pattern by eight major streets each bearing the name of one of the greater French provinces.[2] The 'rue de Normandie' and the 'rue de Bretagne' were cut before the project was abandoned, and allow the general outline to be traced still. While this royal activity had been going on the municipal authorities had not been idle, and particularly under François Miron had completed several important building schemes.[3] From this enumeration of all the projects on hand it is easy to see what Malherbe meant when he wrote to Peiresc in October 1608 that 'if you return to Paris in two years time you will no longer recognize it'.[4]

For all its fine buildings, however, Paris was a filthy city; according to the celebrated traveller Thomas Coryat, who had seen plenty of dirty towns, the streets were the most unkempt he had ever encountered.[5] Sully, who was *grand voyer* of Paris as well as of France, attempted to correct this by organizing a service to remove the rubbish, by paving certain areas and by ensuring a supply of water. Two contractors, one of whom was a captain at the Arsenal, were in 1608 appointed to collect the rubbish. In return for this they were entitled to levy certain fines and to receive annually 60,000 *livres*, levied at first directly on the inhabitants and then on wine entering the city.[6] However, the scheme met with considerable opposition – the contractors seem to have abused their powers – and after eighteen months had to be abandoned in favour of the time-honoured and

---

[1] *Le Mercure François*, 407.

[2] The plan is reproduced in Louis Martin's 'Sully architecte et bâtisseur des villes', *Urbanisme*, lxxv (1942), 72–80, and also in the article of Paul Lacroix, 'La porte et place de France sous le regne de Henri IV', *Gazette des Beaux-Arts* (1870), 561–6.

[3] Described by Marcel Poète, *Paris durant la grande époque classique* (Paris, 1911).

[4] *Œuvres de Malherbe*, ed. L. Lalanne, iii, 78–9.

[5] Coryat, *Crudities* (3 vols, London, 1776), i, 171.

[6] *Règlement* published at Paris in 1608 by R. Ruelle.

ineffectual method directed by the *lieutenant civil*, who relied on locally-appointed contractors for each *quartier*.[1] The laying of *pavé* went ahead much more smoothly and so has left fewer traces in the records.[2] At this time it was realized that more than the traditional *croisée* – the streets running from the Porte Saint-Antoine to the Porte Saint-Honoré, and from the Porte Saint-Denis to the Porte Saint-Jacques (see map 4) – needed to be paved, and work went ahead on many minor streets.

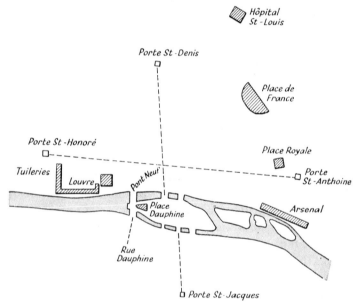

MAP 4 BUILDING WORK AT PARIS UNDER HENRI IV

The supply of water raised great problems, not least of which was that many private individuals had connected their pipes to the common conduit, so that public fountains often went short. There were repeated attempts to limit or licence private lines of this kind, and these attempts no doubt had some effect.[3] What

[1] On this development, see BN Cinq Cents de Colbert, 255, fo. 54.
[2] See S. Dupain, *Notice historique sur le pavé de Paris* (Paris, 1881).
[3] See the *Registres des délibérations du bureau de la ville de Paris*, xi, 121, and xii, 411.

was needed, however, was to increase the general supply of water. It was for this that Sully saw to the construction in 1604 of the four pumps on the Pont Neuf, which were the work of the Fleming Jean Lintlaer,[1] and which fed the conduits of Paris. Sully was not content merely to draw from the Seine; he also sought fresh sources of water outside Paris. The university quarter on the Left Bank had been short from the middle of the sixteenth century, which was no doubt why he concentrated on the area around Long-Boyau, between l'Hay and Arcueil. In 1609 he had preliminary trenches set out there, and in 1612 a general plan was drawn up after consultation with leading engineers: Louis Métezeau, Jacques Alleaume, Thomas Francini and Hugues Cosnier. The work was pressed ahead vigorously, and by 1623 the aqueduct of Arcueil, which was probably designed by Jacques Alleaume and Salomon de Brosse and which still stands, was delivering water to Paris.[2]

As well as cleaning up the city, Sully was concerned with embellishing it for special occasions, when the guns and fireworks of the Bastille and Arsenal would play freely. In July 1606 we find him writing to the king that the decorations of Notre Dame, the Louvre, and the Place Royale are not lightly to be undertaken, so that with the plague raging as it is in Paris it would be better to celebrate the baptism of the *dauphin* at Bourges. Or, he adds, better still at Sens, for there the king will find 'fine churches, splendid reception-rooms, good lodgings, an agreeable countryside and a river to bring up anything that may be necessary'.[3] The king agreed to forgo the festivities at Paris and in fact the baptism took place in September at Fontainebleau;[4] there Sully constructed a mock castle, which satyrs and savages besieged and took amidst a great display of fireworks.[5] The other occasion for which we have some record of

[1] An engraving of this installation may be found in Carré's *Sully*, facing p. 241.

[2] On this section, see Eugène Belgrand, *Les travaux souterrains de Paris* (5 vols, Paris, 1872–87), iii, 147–66.

[3] BM add. mss 19272, fo. 65, Paris, 22 July 1606. A contract had already been passed earlier that month for the work at Paris; see Mallevouë (ed.), *Actes de Sully*, 261.

[4] An engraving of it is reproduced by Carré, *Sully*, facing p. 225.

[5] *Le Mercure François*, 113.

the decoration of Paris is in February 1610. This time it was Claude de Chastillon who was chosen to dress up the main streets for the ceremonial entry of Marie de Medici after her coronation at Saint-Denis.[1] From all over France people came to admire the triumphal arches and decorative coats of arms, and to buy a place on one of the stands erected along the route of the procession.[2] Alas, the entry never took place, for the king was assassinated two days before the date fixed for the rejoicing.

Although the Parisian projects took most of the money spent by the treasurer of the buildings, about 700,000 *livres* annually (see table 4), some of the outlying châteaux also received attention. At Saint-Germain-en-Laye two wings were added to the original structure, and a remarkable series of garden-ramps of which one survives,[3] was constructed to lead down to the Seine; this work began in 1602.[4] Under the garden-ramps Thomas Francini, a Tuscan whom Henri IV called to France and who founded a dynasty of hydraulic engineers, built cunningly-contrived grottoes.[5] Some of these had figures of men and of animals from which occasional jets of water would shoot, drenching unwary spectators and delighting the king; nothing remains of these pleasing contrivances. Much work was also done after 1603 at Fontainebleau, and repairs were carried out at Villers-Cotterets and Saint-Léger; at the latter site the work included the building of a wall to protect the foals of the stud from wolves.[6] Finally the château of Montceaux-lès-Meaux was extended about this time, probably by Salomon de Brosse.[7] The importance of these works in the provinces does not compare with that of the buildings at Paris. The transformation of the medieval chief town into a modern capital was well begun,

[1] *Registres des délibérations du bureau de la ville de Paris*, xiv, 428, note 3.

[2] *Le Mercure François*, 422–3; for the contract for the work, see Mallevoüe (ed.), *Actes de Sully*, 264.

[3] A photograph of it is to be found in the remarkable *Châteaux de France disparus* (Paris, 1947) of Philippe de Cossé-Brissac.

[4] See L. de La Tourrasse, 'Le château-neuf de St-Germain-en-Laye', *Gazette des Beaux-Arts* (1924), 68–95.

[5] See Albert Mousset, 'Les Francine', *Mémoires de la société de l'histoire de Paris et de l'Ile-de-France*, li (1930), 1–53.

[6] *Actes de Sully*, 233.

[7] See Th. Lhuillier, *L'ancien château royal de Montceaux-en-Brie* (Paris, 1885).

not only in the piercing of wide streets and the erection of splendid buildings, as was being done in contemporary Rome, but also in the cleansing and paving of the streets, arts in which the Dutch excelled. Of the work of Henri IV and of Sully at Paris it might well be said, as it could formerly be said of Wren's work at London, 'if you seek their monument, look about you'.

For both the buildings and the fortifications Sully could call on his *ingénieurs*. We have seen them at work not only on the great defensive works of the eastern frontier, but also on a variety of other projects; Jacques Alleaume designed the aqueduct at Arcueil, Jean de Beins set out a plan for a new canal to circumscribe Paris, Humphrey Bradley constructed numerous other canals, Salomon de Brosse worked at Montceaux as well as on the aqueduct at Arcueil, Claude de Chastillon planned canals, worked on the buildings of Paris and decorated the city on occasion, while Louis de Foix undertook the construction of the Tour de Cordouan (see plate 9). This was the development of real importance for the future of French engineering; the establishment of a native school capable of the most extensive and varied works. Little was done to protect the frontier of the west, and even the great works on the eastern frontier were soon outdated. But the organization of a sound administrative system, and the founding of numerous engineering dynasties – one thinks of the Errards, the Chastillons, the Bonnefons, the Beins and the Martelliers to name only the greatest – meant that the reviving power of Louis XIII found a sturdy instrument to hand when it was needed against the renewed Spanish menace.

CHAPTER VIII

Grand maître de l'artillerie

During the civil wars, Rosny had shown himself to be a brave soldier and a skilful gunner. And so when it became clear to the king, late in 1599, that war with the duke of Savoy would soon be necessary, he persuaded the ineffectual Antoine d'Estrées to resign as *grand maître de l'artillerie*,[1] and appointed Rosny in his place. The letters-patent of 13 November 1599[2] contained the usual provisions for the grand master to control all artillery and ammunition on land and sea, and included clauses authorizing him to appoint *lieutenants* and to make inventories of all equipment coming under his jurisdiction. On 13 February 1601 the grand master's title was raised to the status of an *office de la couronne*, thus making its holder immune from dismissal. In December of that year Rosny drew up an edict defining his rights and regulating his functions,[3] and he retained the office until 30 April 1610, when in view of the forthcoming campaign he resigned in favour of his son Maximilien II de Béthune.[4] For he was then to have been appointed *maréchal de France*, a position which he could not hold concurrently with his grand mastership. As it was, the king's death interfered with this plan, and when his son died in 1634 it was in vain that the aged Sully tried to recover the office; he had to be content at that late date with his appointment as *maréchal de France*.

One interesting document emerged from this abortive

---

[1] Antoine is celebrated not only for being the father of the king's unfortunate mistress Gabrielle, but also for being the son of Jean d'Estrées, the famous grand master who organized the 'six calibres de France'.

[2] *Actes de Sully*, xl–xliii, and BN ms. fr. 16690, fo 41–3.

[3] *Actes de Sully*, xliv–xlviii.

[4] *Actes de Sully*, li–lii, and BN ms. fr. 16690, fo. 45–7.

exchange of offices: the 'Instruction de Sully à son fils relative à l'exercice de la charge de grand maître' written early in 1610.[1] In this memorandum the grand master outlined the procedure which he would recommend, and which he had himself presumably followed. First the new grand master was to familiarize himself with all the previous edicts, letters-patent and so forth concerning his charges, and then he was to control his department very closely. Thus he was to compile a general register of equipment at least every two years, using the inventories sent in by each of his *lieutenants*; he was to supervise the technical examination of all officers due for promotion, and he was to oblige all officers to report to him at least every two years. We shall see that this kind of close supervision was typical of Sully's method of work.

Annual expenditure on the artillery was controlled by the *état du roi*, following which the *trésorier de l'épargne* made payments to the various *trésoriers de l'artillerie* to be drawn on the provincial *recettes générales*. It was vital that these payments be made promptly, for otherwise the officers and men of the artillery tended to desert, and their commanders were then driven to anarchic financial expedients. Thus in 1590 the 'sieur de La Rochepot' was obliged to seize 150 *écus* from the Saumur *grenier à sel* to pay his artillery;[2] such cases were common in those years of constant war, and even the king wrote from Amiens in 1597 that his artillery officers would serve no longer without pay.[3] Another consequence of failure to honour the payments due might be, as in February 1595, that urgently-needed powder and bullets had to be left with the merchant who wished to sell them, for want of money to meet his demands.[4] Even apart from these dramatic crises, the functioning of the artillery was often dependent on the goodwill of the *trésoriers de France* who might, for example, be required to provide a house to serve as a magazine.[5]

The best way to free the artillery from undue reliance on its

[1] Printed by Pierre Clément, *Portraits historiques* (Paris, 1855), 503–9.
[2] Valois, n° 102.
[3] *Économies Royales*, i, 256b.
[4] Valois, n° 2114.
[5] Valois, n° 756.

uncertain colleagues in the financial system was, as Sully saw, to have a grand master who also controlled the finances.[1] For then he could not only make sure that the correct sums reached the artillery in normal times, but could also insist at times of crisis on priority being given to payments to the *trésorier de l'artillerie*. This Rosny did in the generalities of Poitiers and Caen in 1599 and 1600 respectively, as he claims in the *Économies Royales*.[2] Any tendency on the part of the *chambre des comptes* to dispute these priorities could be circumvented by ordering the officers of the artillery to account directly to the grand master; this happened in 1605 in the case of the *capitaines ordinaires du charroi*, officers in charge of the transport.[3] Table 4 shows the annual expenditure on the artillery. It rises sharply in 1600, 1606 and 1610 – years in which there were wars or preparations for war.

By the end of the sixteenth century the organization of the officers of the artillery was well defined. Below the grand master came the *lieutenant-général*, followed by the *contrôleurs, trésoriers* and *gardes généraux*, then by the *lieutenants et commissaires provinciaux*, and finally by the technicians; the *ingénieurs, canonniers, deschargeurs, armuriers, fondeurs, charpentiers*, and so on.[4] It is possible to trace fairly accurately the changes in the personnel of the artillery by means of the *états-généraux du paiement des officiers de l'artillerie*, which have survived for the years 1585, 1595, 1597 and 1611.[5] These lists include all the *officiers ordinaires*; during wars *officiers extraordinaires* might be called in, and by their 'bons et continuels services' might hope to join the permanent staff.[6]

The officers performed the duties implied by their titles. Thus the *lieutenant-général* was Sully's immediate deputy, the *contrôleurs* were responsible for the correct reception and maintenance of equipment, the *trésoriers* received the monies from the treasury,

[1] *Économies Royales*, i, 254a.
[2] Ibid., i, 331a.
[3] Valois, nº 9395.
[4] See Daniel Davelourt, *Briefve instruction sur le faict de l'artillerie de France* (Paris, n.d.), ch. xiv; Davelourt, who was of Scottish origin, appears as a *cannonier* on the lists of 1595 and 1597, and later became *commis du contrôleur-général*.
[5] BN ms. fr. 16692, fo. 6–15, 17–31, 32–45 and 50–7.
[6] Davelourt, *Briefve instruction*, chapter xiv.

and the *lieutenants* were the provincial representatives, one rank higher than the *commissaires*. After the signing of the treaty of Vervins in 1598, when most of the troops in other arms were being paid off, the artillery underwent a considerable expansion,[1] in the course of which these *lieutenants* played a capital part. The letters-patent of 1599, as we have seen, permitted the grand master to appoint such officers wherever he saw fit, and by the end of Henri IV's reign there were sixteen of them in the kingdom.[2] Their duties are well described in the commission for Claude Durant in Provence;[3] he is to control the arsenals at Aix and Marseilles, to see to the founding of guns and the making of powder, to survey all artillery on land and in ships, to send in regular reports of his financial dealings, and to punish all contraventions of the grand master's monopoly. He was, in short, to establish a provincial centre which, on a smaller scale, would carry out the same tasks as the Paris arsenal. The importance of the part played by him and his colleagues will become clear when we consider the routine operations of the artillery, as well as its organization in time of war.

Among the most skilled of the lesser officers were the *fondeurs*. They were highly regarded and were discouraged from leaving France. Thus in 1609 the *avocat-général* of the *parlement* of Provence wrote to chancellor Sillery to describe how

> we have in our prisons a royal founder captured while attempting secretly to carry metal to the Barbary States, where he intended to produce guns; this metal came from the royal arsenal at Marseilles.

Further letters tell us only the founder's name, Nicolas Reynier; we cannot tell what became of him.[4] Sully claims in the *Économies Royales*[5] that on becoming grand master he dismissed four

---

[1] See General L.-A.-V.-V. Susane, *Histoire de l'artillerie française* (Paris, 1874), 122.

[2] See appendix 3, whose list is a good deal more complete than that given in the *Actes de Sully*, xlviii.

[3] BN ms. fr. 4014, fo. 82; see also that for Jean Payon (Lyon), AD Rhône C 418, fo. 87–8.

[4] For these letters, see Arch. Aff. Étr., France 1700, fo. 135 and 145.

[5] Op. cit., i, 322b. His assertion has passed into legend; see for instance, Carré, *Sully*, 158.

or five hundred incapable officers. If this is true it is by no means obvious from the lists of officers which have survived, in which if anything it is the continuity of the personnel, particularly among the senior officers, which is striking. Thus from father to son it is the sieurs de Born who are *lieutenants-généraux* from 1585 to 1611, while two of the three *contrôleurs-généraux* of 1611, Zacharie de Perelles and Nicolas de Morely, had held important posts in 1597. Of the *lieutenants* at least four had been serving in the same capacity in 1597,[1] as had at least four of the *commissaires*; it is also noteworthy that most of the guns at Montmélian in 1600 were commanded by men who had been listed as *commissaires* in 1597. Rosny made considerable use of the former personnel, and the story of widespread dismissals is almost certainly incorrect.

He insisted upon a high standard of theoretical knowledge among his officers. We have noticed above that he advised his son to question the candidates for promotion carefully. He himself applied very rigorously the 'Instructions drawn up by the duc de Sully . . . concerning the artillery, its support and maintenance, on which the artillery officers are normally examined'.[2] These instructions took the form of a catechism, with questions like:

> Of what does the artillery consist?
> ANSWER: The whole material of the artillery may be divided into three headings: guns, powder and cannon-balls.

Sully, like many soldiers since his time, was probably pedantic in his insistence on the correct answer. Marbault has an interesting account of how a veteran gunner was failed because he could not define a 'gabion d'eminence'.[3]

It has been claimed that Sully instituted the system of monthly payments for the troops;[4] it is not easy to find evidence

---

[1] The senior, Robert Tiercelin, had been appointed by Philibert de La Guiche (grand master 1578–96) in 1594 (BN ms. fr. 20007, fo. 17), while the sieur de La Caillaudière was already a *lieutenant* in that year (BN ms. fr. 18159, fo. 113r⁰).
[2] Bib. Mazarine, Ms. 2117, fo. 25–30.
[3] *Remarques sur les mémoires de Sully*, 54b.
[4] E. Boutaric, *Institutions militaires de la France* (Paris, 1863), 381.

9. The Tour de Cordouan at the mouth of the Gironde. Engraving
from the *Topographie française* of Claude de Chastillon·(*B.N Estampes*).

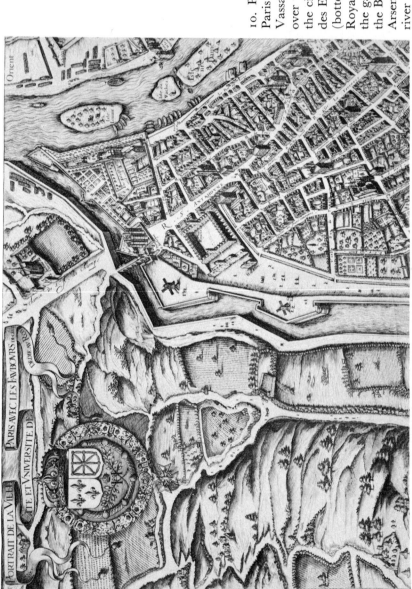

10. Part of a plan of Paris by Benedit de Vassallieu; looking east, over the eastern part of the city, we see the rue des Enfants Rouges (bottom right), the Place Royale, the Bastille and the garden separating the Bastille from the Arsenal, alongside the river (*BN Estampes*).

of this. Among the technical branches of the artillery, however, he did foster some remarkable developments. Chief among these was the expansion of the engineering arm, which in 1611 included the six *ingénieurs ordinaires* whose activities have been described in chapter VII. Their number had been steadily rising from the two of 1585 to the three of 1595 and the four of 1597. Sully also saw to it that armourers accompanied the royal forces in the field. This was an innovation; as Davelourt remarks in his *L'Artillier*,[1]

> Before the appointment of the duc de Sully . . . as grand master of the artillery, there was no question of having armourers with the troops.

As *surintendant des finances* Sully could bring pressure to bear on the *élus*, responsible for the recruiting of *pionniers*, who provided the labour for digging fortifications, manhandling artillery and so forth. At this time their dress and equipment were standardized; they wore hats of a colour decided by the *élus*, on their coats front and back the first and last letter of their *élection*, and a white cross on each arm.[2] This development of a rudimentary uniform probably derived from the Protestant soldiers of the civil wars, for they too were all dressed alike.[3] Eventually, uniforms would spread as well to the other arms, the cavalry and infantry, which still in 1600 preserved their feudal motley. The numbers of *pionniers* and their role in battle will become clear in the discussion of the Savoy and other campaigns.

The equipment of the artillery at this period was not very different from that of the 1550s, when the famous 'six belles fontes de l'artillerie' had been laid down, under the direction of grand master Jean d'Estrées.[4] Indeed, so primitive were some weapons that it was still possible to found them in private houses.[5] Most authors have accepted Sully's own word that

---

[1] Published at Paris in 1616; section 10 on the *armuriers*.
[2] BN ms. fr. 16694, fo. 101; see also Susane, *Histoire de l'artillerie française*, 112.
[3] See Agrippa d'Aubigné, *Histoire Universelle*, ed. A. de Ruble (10 vols, Paris, 1886–97), v, 353.
[4] E. Buat, *L'artillerie de campagne* (Paris, 1911), 18.
[5] *Lettres Missives*, i, 568; to the maréchal de Matignon, Bazas, 4 August 1583.

when he became grand master the Paris arsenal was denuded of guns,[1] as well as of powder, cannon-balls, and horses. In fact it seems unlikely that before 1599 the officers at the Arsenal were idle. At least four guns were founded in 1592,[2] and we read in the *Économies Royales*[3] of the founding of four cannon in 1597; it is not easy to believe that these were isolated instances, or that the forty-five pieces in use at the siege of Amiens in 1598 were all lost. As early as 1596 the *lieutenant-général* had submitted to the king a programme for the reform of the artillery which embodied many of the steps later taken by Sully;[4] in short, he probably took over a going concern.

Be that as it may, it is certain that after 1600 gun-founding went on apace and if, as Lecestre has pointed out,[5] it is impossible to calculate the yearly production of weapons, by 1610 at least a hundred cannon were available. It looks as though this was one of Sully's first cares in his new office, for Mallevoüe's contracts show considerable purchases of gun-metal in 1600 declining thereafter, with none later than 1605. By the latter date, too, Lyons and Bordeaux, two of the most important provincial centres, had received their full allocations of cannon, and would get no more during the rest of the reign.[6] By 1605, to give a figure, the cannon at the Lyons arsenal numbered twenty-five, as against the seven held in 1567.[7]

Most of the guns were produced in the arsenal at Paris,[8] where under Sully private contractors were replaced by the *forgeurs* of the establishment.[9] Cannon-balls, armour and small-arms continued to be ordered from contractors; however, the

---

[1] Throughout this chapter the term 'cannon' is used in its precise sense as meaning the greatest of the calibres of France.

[2] AM Rheims, Fonds Tarbé, dossier 45; quittance from the founder.

[3] Op. cit., i, 256b; in the same year the Paris *lieutenant* was authorized to cut a good many elms for *remontage* (Valois, n° 2641).

[4] BN ms. fr. 3447, fo. 54–5.

[5] Paul Lecestre, *Notice sur l'Arsenal royal de Paris* (Paris, 1916), 70.

[6] For these figures, see BN Cinq Cents de Colbert, 210.

[7] According to AN 120 AP 44; for the earlier figure, see M. Vilepelet, 'Inventaire de l'Arsenal de Lyon (septembre 1567)', *Bulletin Historique et Philologique* (1913), 388–408.

[8] Davelourt, *L'Arcenal et Magazin de l'Artillerie* (Paris, 1610), 38.

[9] According to Carré, *Sully*, 159.

prices were often lower than they had been in the past.[1] Sometimes, too, the supply of a certain number of small-arms would be the condition for the granting of a privilege,[2] and the Paris arsenal also received not a few consignments of contraband weapons.[3] As with the guns, the grand master quickly built up stocks to a satisfactory level. For the contracts mentioned by Mallevoüé[4] show about 80,000 balls *calibre de France* being bought in 1600, and 16,000 in 1601; thereafter such purchases were negligible. The acquisition of artillery-horses shows much the same pattern, with a great expansion in 1601, when nearly one thousand were bought, tailing off to an annual purchase of about fifty, no doubt as replacements for those which had died.

— The system of powder-supply involved the use of royal equipment by private contractors. Each half-year the *trésorier-général de l'artillerie* would advance money to the authorized collectors of saltpetre, who would then have to mix their powder, a combination of saltpetre, alder-charcoal and sulphur, in one of the *ateliers du roi*.[5] In Sully's time such *ateliers* were set up at Tours, Troyes, Châlons, Verdun and Marseilles, and the 1601 edict provided for the sale of powder to private individuals at three points in each province, apart from sales at the arsenal. The system seems to have worked quite well for the small wars of the reign, and Henri IV was able to make considerable shipments of powder to the Dutch, to aid them in their struggle against the Spaniards.[6]

In 1597 there were seventeen provincial *arsenaux et magasins ordinaires du roi*, each heading the district for which a *lieutenant*

---

[1] *Actes de Sully*, I.
[2] See for instance, Valois, n° 10105, in which a merchant of Lyons undertakes to supply 500 arquebuses in return for the right to mint certain coins.
[3] Like the Bayonne pikes; see above, pp. 66–7.
[4] We have noticed in the introduction that all the *actes* have not been published; enough have been, though, for generalizations of this kind.
[5] Davelourt, *Briefve instruction*, chapter vii.
[6] One hundred *milliers* in one shipment in 1604, for instance: *Économies Royales*, i, 579b. Other munitions had been shipped the previous year from Le Havre; see Bernard Barbiche (ed.), *Correspondance du nonce en France Innocenzo del Bufalo, évêque de Camerino (1601–1604)* (Rome/Paris, 1964), 563.

was to become responsible (see appendix 3). The Paris arsenal formed the eastern tip of the city on the north bank, as may be seen in the top right-hand corner of plate 10; it was thus well situated for supplying the eastern frontier towns by way of the Marne. The general plan of the Arsenal was the work of Philibert de L'Orme (1512/15–70), engineer-architect of the mid-sixteenth century; Sully merely completed his project.[1] From the 'porte de l'arcenal' by the Seine the main buildings ran alongside the river to the eastern bastion (called the 'bastion de l'eau'). The first court probably held the porters' lodge and perhaps quarters for the guard. Then came the vaulted passage leading to the second court, in which was the lodge of the *grand maître*, alongside the river; some guns may be seen here. After a smaller vaulted gateway came the third court, which had stables below and probably gun-lofts above; some riders are visible here. Finally in the fourth large court were the foundries and workshops; on the wall of one foundry Sully commissioned Jacob Bunel to paint a Vulcan fresco.[2] The small triangular court at the end was reserved for the chief founder; at the bottom of the gardens stretching away to the Bastille was the 'Petit Arsenal', where powder was made (the *salpêtrière*, across the river, was the work of Louis XIII). This was the scene of the terrible explosion of 1563, when thirty-three persons were killed; the building had been repaired and Sully merely saw to its up-keep.

In the grounds his work was extensive; he paved all the courts and approach-roads, and built a very strong wall at the end of the Celestines' garden, in order to retain the new raised roadway between the third gate of the Arsenal and the Petit Arsenal. He also extended the tree-lined walk, which formerly stretched only from the Bastille along the moat to the Arsenal, until it culminated in the 'bastion de l'eau'; this he built up as a terrace from which the king might enjoy the view up the river to Notre-Dame, during his frequent talks with the grand

[1] See Henri Clouzot, 'Philibert de L'Orme, grand architecte du roi mégiste', *Revue du seizième siècle*, viii (1921), 243–8; for what follows on the Paris arsenal, see Paul Lecestre, *Notice sur l'Arsenal royal de Paris*.

[2] Henri Sauval, *Histoire et recherches des antiquitez de la ville de Paris* (3 vols, Paris, 1724), ii, 331.

master.[1] Finally, on the river side of the Arsenal he constructed the long quay on which a line of elms, clearly visible in plate 10, was planted. This was the celebrated 'Palemail', on which fashionable persons came to play a croquet-like game with balls and mallets of box-wood; the ground must have been over five hundred yards long.[2] All this work converted the Arsenal-Bastille area into a self-contained royal enclave, and the municipality protested to the king in 1603 that there was no need for him to raise such a fortress against his loyal Parisians. Henri IV replied that alterations to fortifications were his business,[3] and meanwhile in the provincial arsenals Sully saw to similar repairs and extensions.

This was not a remarkable period for the development of gunnery; indeed, the years between the end of the Italian wars and Gribeauval's reforms in the late eighteenth century saw few major advances.[4] All the same, under Sully's guidance, and perhaps as a result of his experience in the Protestant armies, progress was made towards standardizing equipment and in making it lighter and more mobile.[5] These two characteristics come out very clearly from Benedit de Vassallieu's 'General regulations concerning the operation of artillery',[6] which contain many illustrations showing how powder-barrels, forges, field-hospitals and portable bridges were to be packed on the (standard-size) carts. Already in Davelourt's work details of the size and labelling of powder-barrels had been worked out; a barrel marked 'PM' would contain a hundred pounds of 'menüe grenée' (fine-corned powder) made at Paris (Paris-Menüe). By 1613 standardization was far advanced even for ancillary items; Vassallieu's work contains for instance views of weapons with scale drawings even of their smallest parts. Sully's remarkable enthusiasm for elm-planting, formerly attributed to

<hr/>

[1] See for instance, Économies Royales, i, 381b, 428b, 552b, etc.
[2] Louis Batiffol, 'Le mail de l'Arsenal au XVIIIᵉ siècle', Bulletin de la société de l'histoire de Paris et de l'Ile-de-France, lvi (1929), 5–22.
[3] Registres des délibérations du bureau de la ville de Paris, xii, 397–9.
[4] See for instance, Buat, L'artillerie de campagne, 20.
[5] On Huguenot artillery, see Jean de Pablo, 'Contribution à l'étude de l'histoire des institutions militaires huguenotes', Archiv für Reformationsgeschichte, xlviii (1957), 192–216.
[6] Written in 1613: BN nouv. acq. franç., 592.

his wish to shelter travellers,[1] is also eloquent of his desire to improve portability, for elm-wood was chiefly used in making the hubs of the great wheels on which the guns rode (see plate 12).

The only other technical development worthy of notice came in the fabrication of explosive charges and of fuses. Again, like the more mobile artillery, these seem to have been perfected in the Protestant armies. It was at the siege of Cahors in 1580 that an effective portable charge was first devised, by a Huguenot soldier,[2] and it was the Protestant 'capitaine Chansson', later *lieutenant* of the grand master in Poitou, who is credited with an early form of effective fuse.[3] Even if there was no major technical advance, we must visualize the Paris arsenal as a centre where constant experiments were going on to improve the various implements of war. We read for instance of new portable bridges[4] and new furnaces[5] being tried out, and plate 12 shows another kind of project; a winch for dragging guns out of mud or obstacles, designed by Jean Errard.[6]

One consequence of the greater uniformity of equipment was that more realistic inventories could be drawn up, allowing the grand master to know exactly where his strength lay. In a letter of uncertain date to the earl of Essex, Lord Willoughby described the best contemporary practice; the Venetians, he says, 'narrowly look into even the smallest matter, such as wood, nails, iron, boards for carriages and platforms; of which quarterly perfect examination is had throughout the seignory'.[7] Such

---

[1] The error of thinking either that Sully had travellers primarily in mind, or that his was an original idea, is pointed out by Jadart, 'Sully et les plantations d'arbres', *Revue Henri IV*, i (1905–6), 59–65.

[2] According to J.-A. de Thou, *Histoire Universelle* (16 vols, London, 1734) vii, 500.

[3] Aubigné, *Histoire Universelle*, vi, 9.

[4] Valois, n° 4723, and *Économies Royales*, i, 256b.

[5] Valois, n° 14576.

[6] This is taken from Errard's *Le premier livre des instruments mathématiques méchaniques* (Nancy, 1584); Claude de Chastillon made similar studies in his 'Recueil de géométrie et de machines', BN Estampes I a2, fo. 384–8. I am indebted to Dr Alex Keller, of the Department of the History of Science at the University of Leicester, for drawing my attention to this work by Errard.

[7] *Calendar of manuscripts of the marquis of Salisbury*, xiii, 606–7.

checks were becoming the rule in France; Davelourt points out that 'inventaires solemnels' are particularly necessary after wars, and mentions 1599 and 1611 as years in which such general stock-taking was carried out.[1] But Sully made some kind of check more often than that, if not biennially, as he advised his son to do. No copy of the 1599 inventory seems to have survived, which is unfortunate for those who would like to check Sully's account of his early labours. However, there was another inventory during 1604 and 1605, from which some interesting documents remain.[2]

On 30 March 1604, Rosny sent a general instruction, probably to all his *lieutenants*, that they were to make out not only an inventory of all fire-arms and ammunition in their districts, but also an account of the supply of elms suitable for gun-wheels, of the availability and price of various metals, powders, ropes and so forth, of relative costs by land and water-transport, and of the number of *pionniers* available in each parish. To this account they were to attach 'une carte bien exacte', on which the easy passages would be clearly marked. Jean Payon (Lyons) replied with a first-class summary, including a fine map and a good list of navigable rivers. The answers of Siphorien de Lezines (Amiens) and Jean de Mesmes (Bordeaux), although less complete, are also interesting as showing the considerable resources which they too had available in their areas; large numbers of boats and horses, for example, and stocks of wood, saltpetre and ferrous metals.

A further general survey was carried out in 1608 but of this, apart from the Lyons inventory,[3] we have as relics only the letters from Sully to his more laggard *lieutenants*. In 1609 he wrote to both Charles Hillaire (Metz) and Pierre de Bourdin

[1] Davelourt, *Recherches et considerations sur le faict de l'artillerie* (Paris, 1617), 12.
[2] AN 120 AP 44, 45, 46 and 47, 'enquêtes' and inventories from Lyon (1605), Amiens (1605), Bordeaux (1607) and Lyon (1608), respectively.
[3] There is an interesting cross-reference to this inventory in a *procès-verbal*, BN ms. fr. 16809, where on fo. 6r⁰ we read that the *échevins* of Clermont-Ferrand protested that the arms in the *hôtel de ville* belonged to the town and had recently been inventoried 'par ung nommé Payen' [Jean Payon, Lyons].

(Dijon) that they should hurry with the previous year's lists;[1] these had to be precise, as the sieur de Montmartin (Tours) was instructed in 1610.[2] From the major survey of 1610–11, following the transfer of office to Maximilien II de Béthune, we have both the working copy compiled directly from provincial returns, and the fair copy, which was probably sent to the young king.[3]

There is also at least one inventory commission, that for the Ile-de-France.[4] The *lieutenants* sometimes met with difficulty in carrying out these warrants, particularly in Protestant strongholds; in 1611, for example, the municipal officials of La Rochelle refused to allow their equipment to be checked, claiming that 'the king has always relied on them for the defence of the town, as their privileges demand'.[5] There was the same kind of disobedience at Toulouse and Villemur-sur-Tarn, and, more surprisingly, at Chartres, Châteaudun and Vendôme.[6]

The reason for it, apart from the general distaste for a statistically-minded administration, was that such surveys were often followed by the compulsory removal of guns from one area to another. Thus with the sieur de Servien's commission to make an inventory of the equipment of the town of Saint-Tropez came a letter from Sully ordering him to move the town's guns into the citadel there – in the course of which operation he would have to recover two pieces which had been hidden![7] Similarly in 1603 Jean de Mesmes (Bordeaux) visited all the Catholic strongholds in Guyenne to withdraw their weapons; the maréchal d'Ornano, governor of the province, assured the king that Mesmes would carry out his task 'with so much gentleness and prudence that Your Majesty will receive no complaints'.[8]

Often the motive for such changes was technical, for the better protection and maintenance of the weapons, or strategic; thus in 1602 the king announced his intention of equipping

[1] BN ms. fr. 16694, fo. 62.
[2] Ibid., fo. 62–3.
[3] BN Cinq Cents de Colbert, fo. 210 and 211, respectively.
[4] BN ms. fr. 16694, fo. 11–12.
[5] BN Cinq Cents de Colbert, 210, fo. 337r°.
[6] Ibid., fo. 479 and 711.
[7] BN ms. fr. 16694, fo. 6–7.
[8] BN ms, fr. 23197, fo. 306, letter of 8 May 1603 from Agen.

the frontier-towns of Picardy with the artillery necessary for their protection . . . by taking some guns from nearby towns which are not near the frontier and so no longer have any need of them.[1]

But often, too, the motive was political, part of the king's schemes for the reduction of internal centres of resistance. As he remarks in his letters-patent of 1605 for Sully, 'to us alone belongs the right to possess artillery'; he went on to direct that artillery officers be instructed to withdraw all such equipment from certain houses in Périgord, Quercy, Angoumois, Guyenne and Poitou, and in October 1605 the *lieutenant* received a commission from the grand master to get on with this.[2]

Sully himself would sometimes write to the noble concerned, in order to ease the tension. Thus in 1610 (?) he requested the comte de Chiverny 'at once to give up your four medium guns to the sieur de La Caillaudière (Orleans) – and without making any difficulties if you please'.[3] The kind of danger against which Sully and the king were forearming themselves is well shown by the way in which the maréchal d'Ancre used royal artillery to fortify his position in the château at Caen during his retreat into Normandy in August 1616.[4] After his death the pieces were removed, but the fact of their installation shows how easily a provincial stronghold could be built up, in the absence of effective supervision.

It was also the *lieutenants* who were responsible for the destruction of unauthorized private fortifications. As early as 1596 Rowland Whyte was writing to Sir Robert Sidney that 'out of France 'tis said that all the forts built within these 30 yeares shall be rased to the ground'[5], and after 1598 this work went on apace. Thus about 1604 Rosny wrote to the sieur Du Plessis-Prévost, a veteran of Montmélian, in these terms:

[1] BN ms. fr. 16694, fo. 13–14.
[2] Ibid., fo. 15–16.
[3] Ibid., fo. 17.
[4] See AD Calvados C 1680, both for the list of Ancre's weapons and for the list of small-arms authorized by Sully.
[5] *Calendar of manuscripts of Lord de L'Isle and Dudley at Penshurst Palace*, ii, 235, letter of 18 February 1596.

As the fortification of the château of Carlat in Auvergne is quite useless, being so far from this realm's frontiers . . .

it should be dismantled; at the same time, the local *élus* were requested to provide 1,200 *livres* to pay for this labour.[1] The fortification of Châlus in Auvergne was also dismantled,[2] as were those at Domfront (Orne)[3] and at numerous places in Brittany including Douarnenez and Craon.[4]

Political motives could lie behind what seemed routine administrative measures. The most innocuous-seeming operation by the grand master might conceal some deadly scheme; thus the rapidity of Biron's downfall in 1602 may, as Sully claims in the *Économies Royales*,[5] be partly attributed to the fact that most of the artillery at Dijon had been temporarily withdrawn, on some administrative pretext.

On occasion, too, the artillery organization played a more active part in the preservation of the internal order. Thus Charles de Goustemesnil (Rouen) was instructed to help the duc de Montpensier, governor of Normandy, in his attempts to evict the sieur de Saint-Denis Maillon from a house which the latter was occupying in defiance of a decision by the *parlement* of Rouen.[6] Again, Sully's guns were used in 1607 to reduce the castle of a noble who was holding captive a maiden whom he had ravished from her father, the sieur de Fontanges.[7] In rather different circumstances Jean Payon (Lyons) was ordered to provide equipment in 1605 for the expulsion of the Protestant Alexandre de Blacons from Orange. The evicting force was to be commanded by the duc de Lesdiguières, governor of Dauphiné,[8] and a letter survives in which Rosny advises his fellow-Protestant to give up his resistance, for he has already given proof of his courage, and in a battle the king would have as

---

[1] BN ms. fr. 16694, fo. 20–1.

[2] BN ms. fr. 24840, fo. 158r⁰.

[3] AD Seine-maritime C 1122, fo. 149v⁰.

[4] For a complete list, see BN ms. fr. 22315, fo. 29; see also *Économies Royales*, i, 591a and 615b.

[5] Op. cit., i, 397a.

[6] BN ms. fr. 16694, fo. 24–5.

[7] *Économies Royales*, ii, 191; see also *Lettres Missives*, vii, 339 note 1.

[8] *Économies Royales*, ii, 67–8; for details of the affair see *Dictionnaire de biographie française*, vi, col. 553–4.

many regiments as Blacons has soldiers, and as many batteries
as he has guns.[1] In another letter, to the king, written during the
imprisonment of the maréchal de Biron, Rosny inquires 'how
things are in Burgundy and if guns will be needed there', for, he
adds, the horses and men mobilized at Paris and Lyons in view
of a possible revolt are costing about 17,000 *livres* each month.[2]
At this time about twenty guns were also prepared for immediate use.[3] The grand master thus undertook considerable
operations 'in aid of the civil power'.

Apart from organizing these dramatic interventions, Sully
personally controlled every detail of the administration, down
to the movement of quite minor items of equipment. Thus the
installation of a pulley and rope at Orleans had to be passed by
him;[4] he was sharp in curbing all who infringed his monopoly,
and rigorous in all his contracts, as Mallevouë has shown.[5]
Subordinates who were disobedient or inefficient received curt
letters, as we have seen above, and on occasion he would go so
far as to suspend an officer's pay.

There was less trouble with the sovereign courts over affairs
concerning the artillery than over those connected with the
communications, no doubt because they needed the protection
of the grand master's guns. When the estates of Burgundy tried
to avoid paying the wages of Pierre de Bourdin, *lieutenant* at
Dijon, Rosny replied to their representatives that

> if the region was unwilling to maintain the artillery-officers
> then he would withdraw the guns and ammunition.[6]

There could be no question of further resistance.

The organization thus built up was tested by campaigns or
the threat of them in 1600, 1606 and 1610. Some authors have

---

[1] Bib. Salins, Ms. 37, fo. 46v°; this is the letter to which Sully refers in
his *Économies Royales*, ii, 68b.

[2] BN ms. fr. 15581, fo. 35; the letter is of 30 June 1602, and Biron was
executed on July 29. It is to this letter that Sully refers in his *Économies
Royales*, i, 399b.

[3] See Barbiche (ed.), *Correspondance du nonce en France*, 302–3, 310–11 and
314.

[4] BN ms. fr 16692, fo. 78.

[5] *Actes de Sully*, liv.

[6] AD Côte d'Or C 3075, fo. 273r°.

questioned the account in the *Économies Royales* of Rosny's part
in the Savoy campaign of 1600,[1] but two documents at the
Bibliothèque Nationale confirm it in some detail.[2] Sully
claimed to have directed the artillery at the sieges of Charbonnières and Montmélian,[3] and of these papers one, entirely in
his hand, is entitled 'Estat des batteries de Montmelian', while
on the other, a similar list of dispositions for Charbonnières, he
has inserted many names, even sometimes those of the humble
cannoniers.[4]

It was about the middle of June 1600 that the king decided
that war with the duke of Savoy could no longer be postponed,
as the latter would not restore to the French king, as he was
bound to do by treaty, the marquisate of Saluzzo. Rosny
arrived in Paris on 22 July and it is late in that month that we
find in Mallevouë's *Actes de Sully* the first of the numerous
contracts signed with various 'voituriers tant par eau que par
terre' for the transport of arms and ammunition to the campaign area. From Paris to Lyons took sixteen days for this
equipment, and about three for the grand master himself; by
9 September the cannon from the various arsenals were in
position above Charbonnières, and on the 10th the place fell,
after a sharp engagement well described in the *Économies
Royales*. This account rings true in several details; the difficulty
of the terrain is confirmed by the fact that each cannon had to be
served by twenty *pionniers* instead of the normal six, the sieur de
La Vallée is found in charge of the first battery as described, and
from the four batteries which first opened fire one *commissaire*
(the sieur de Chabannes) is thereafter missing, perhaps one of
the wounded mentioned in the *Économies Royales*.

At Charbonnières there were only nine cannon, but at
Montmélian thirty were sited in seven batteries. The nine from
Charbonnières were among these, with others which had just
served at Chambéry and Bourg-en-Bresse. As things turned out,
however, they were hardly needed except for a token bombard-

[1] Following Desclozeaux, 'Étude critique sur les *Économies Royales*',
Revue Historique, lii (1893), 316–22.
[2] BN ms. fr. 4561, fo. 4–11 and 28–32.
[3] *Économies Royales*, i, 335–7 and 339–43.
[4] *Lettres Missives*, v, 299 and 301.

ment, for the governor of the citadel came to terms on 8
October, and surrendered early in November.[1] Plate 11
reproduces Claude de Chastillon's engraving of the siege, which
clearly marks the 'logis de monsieur de Rosny . . .', and shows
the cannon in positions tallying closely with those given in the
autograph documents quoted above; map 5 brings out the
topography of the region and the towns involved.

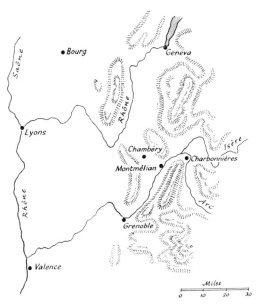

MAP 5   THE SAVOY CAMPAIGN OF 1600

The campaign, in which the artillery had played a prominent
part, was almost over. Rosny had put into the field fifty-seven
guns, forty-eight of them cannon, 500 *milliers* of powder and
30,000 balls.[2] Twenty of the cannon had come from Paris, with

[1] For the circumstances of the surrender, see Eugène Halphen, *Documents inédits concernant la prise de Montmélian* (Paris, 1885); see also the 'Apologie de Brandis, défenseur de Montmélian', ed. marquis d'Albon, *Documents d'histoire*, III (1912), 198–216.

[2] Daniel Davelourt, *Épitome ou abrégé sur le faict de l'artillerie* (Paris, 1619), 21. The figures given by Carré, *Sully*, 160, and by Mallevouë, *Actes de Sully*, li, are for material assembled at Paris only.

120 *milliers* of powder and 6,000 balls.[1] Of the others, eight had come from Grenoble, six from Lyons and five from Valence;[2] no doubt the rest were provided by the *lieutenants* and *commissaires* of the south-eastern provinces.[3] From these figures, for which it is not easy to give modern equivalents of measure, it is clear that the policy of the king and of Sully was to keep the bulk of the guns at Paris, relying in case of a campaign on the nearest arsenals to supply the greater part of the balls and powder. This system had the advantage of offering few tools for provincial malcontents; moreover, the Paris arsenal was near enough to the traditionally dangerous frontier of the north-east for delays in transport not to be serious.

At Montmélian there were at least 270 *pionniers*, and at Charbonnières at least 210, drawn mostly from the *élections* of Paris[4] and Chartres, but including forty from Orleans. Among them were the skilled carpenters who had perched the cannon on the inaccessible ridges of Charbonnières. *Pionniers* should also have been sent to Savoy by the estates of Languedoc and of Burgundy, but neither of these contingents seems to have joined the army.[5] Most of the officers who would later administer the artillery were to be found at Charbonnières and Montmélian; apart from the numerous *commissaires*, seven of the sixteen *lieutenants* of 1611 had served in the Savoy campaign. It is pleasant to notice that the officers and men of the artillery shared out 18,000 *livres* on their return, the sieur de Born receiving 3,000 and most of the future *lieutenants* 108 *livres*.[6]

Five years later it was against the duc de Bouillon, Henri de La Tour d'Auvergne, father of the great Turenne, that Sully had to mobilize his forces. Early in March 1606, the king decided to make a punitive expedition against the duke's stronghold at Sedan, and by April Fool's Day that year Bouillon was ready to surrender.[7] It is probable that during the latter

---

[1] *Économies Royales*, i, 331b; these figures are confirmed by the *Actes de Sully*.

[2] *Lettres Missives*, v, 276.

[3] *Économies Royales*, i, 331.

[4] See the royal summonses, AN Z 1 F 137, fo. 93v⁰.

[5] AD Tarn C55, fo. 26r⁰, and AD Côte d'Or C 3351, fo. 89r⁰ and 90r⁰.

[6] BN ms. fr. 16692, fo. 134.

[7] *Lettres Missives*, vi, 582–96.

part of March Sully had put into the field forty-five cannon, supplied with 52,360 balls and 800 *milliers* of powder.[1] As for the Savoy campaign the Paris arsenal supplied about half the guns; to be exact, Mallevouë records twenty-five cannon, 20,000 balls and 100 *milliers* of powder as having been transported from there to Châlons-sur-Marne by water.[2] Of the remaining twenty cannon, eight came from Metz, six from Mézières, and two each from Rocroi, Reims and Châlons. The hypothesis advanced above concerning the relative roles of the Paris and provincial arsenals is thus confirmed, the bulk of the balls and powder coming from the arsenals near Sedan.[3] The force included the seven *lieutenants* of the north-eastern provinces, and 1,130 *pionniers* from the *élections* of Paris, Soissons and Châlons. The unexpectedly easy capitulation of Sedan left them with little to do.

The organization of this relatively minor expedition posed problems of transport similar to those arising in 1610, when preparations were made for the great campaign which the death of the king made politically impossible. The sources do not permit any very accurate calculation of the forces mobilized, but it looks as though General Susane was right in claiming that about thirty-three cannon were put into the field.[4] Maximilien II de Béthune, freshly installed as grand master, led a force of twenty-six cannon and 1,275 horses from the Paris arsenal to Châlons,[5] where he found perhaps ten more cannon, assembled by the subordinates of the sieur de Viaspré (Troyes and Châlons). Of these guns six had come from Mézières, two from Rocroi, and two from Châlons itself. The *commissaire* responsible for the assembling of them had in addition to report on communications with the frontier towns, so that these could be repaired as necessary, and also to reconnoitre the routes from Mézières to Jülich. As his instruction says,

---

[1] BN ms. fr. 10311, fo. 90.
[2] *Actes de Sully*, articles 224 and 225.
[3] *Économies Royales*, ii, 134b.
[4] *Histoire de l'artillerie française*, 124.
[5] BN ms. fr. 16692, fo. 107–19; these figures for horses correspond with those cited in the *Actes de Sully*, articles 268 and 269.

he must find out about [the state of the roads] as secretly as he can and even visit possible routes if he can safely do it.[1]

All was ready by 21 May at Châlons, but by then the king had been dead a week.[2] The army went on to Jülich, joining the forces of Maurice of Nassau for the siege there in mid-August, thanks partly to the diligence of Charles Hillaire (Metz) and other officers of the artillery in bridging the Moselle in a day and and a half; the commander of the place came to terms early in September and then the French army returned.[3]

One of the most interesting aspects of this campaign is the attention given to food supplies. In the field, armies were fed either from *étapes* laid out in advance along their route, or from more permanent *magazins* stocked for the purpose; from these points the *généraux-surintendants* and their staff would then arrange for the troops' supply.[4] The great question was whether it was better to call upon the local financial organization to make levies to build up these centres, or to rely on specially-employed contractors, and impromptu purchases from merchants. In the preamble to the 'Règlement pour l'entretien de l'armée du Roi' of 1594[5] the king seems to have decided on the latter method:

The king, after consulting his council on the best means of supplying his army with food . . . and after interrogating certain contractors . . . has decided that [this latter method] is not only the most honest and certain but also the most practical, for it will ease his finances and take the burden off his subjects.

Two days later, on 17 January 1594, the 'Regulation . . . concerning the supply of food to the royal armies'[6] strictly forbade any governors or other officers to levy food for magazines, without the express permission of the king. Moreover, all accounting

---

[1] BN ms. fr. 16692, fo. 84-5.
[2] This account of the preparations is confirmed by that of de Crue, *Les derniers desseins de Henri IV*, who relies on diplomatic sources.
[3] BN ms. fr. 16627, numerous letters.
[4] Valois, n⁰ 369.
[5] Valois, n⁰ 371.
[6] BN Cangé 19 (Inventaire Réserve 177).

for *vivres* was to be done before the *surintendants*, without any intervention by the *trésoriers de France, chambres des comptes* or others.

Sully accepted, and may indeed have recommended, this system. Thus at Amiens, during the siege of 1597, it was the 'marchands-entrepreneurs' who ensured the bread supply, on contracts which Sully claims to have made.[1] Payments to them enjoyed a high priority; in January 1598, for example, Jacques Jacquelin, 'munitionnaire des vivres en l'armée de Bretagne' was to be paid by the *receveur-général* of Poitiers 'in preference to all other payments, even those destined for the treasury'.[2] They were also protected against the attacks of the provincial courts, as is shown by another *arrêt* ordering the grain of Christophe Bernard, 'munitionnaire', to be stored without hindrance at Rouen in spite of the *parlement's* opposition.[3]

No information survives concerning the commissariat arrangements for the campaigns of 1600 and 1606, but for that of 1610 we are better informed. Among the *Actes de Sully* is a contract of April 1610 for Philippe de Coulanges and Claude Barbin to supply 50,000 loaves a day to the army of the Meuse, using the *magazins* which were to be established along that river.[4] This was a considerable quantity of bread; the king's army at Amiens in 1597 had needed fewer than 30,000 loaves a day.[5] For the campaign Sully claims to have refused the *surintendance des vivres*,[6] but it was in any case he who made the preparations, relying as before on contractors. Although this was to be the method increasingly used during the seventeenth century, there were those even in 1630 who did not see the advantages of the method sponsored by Sully, and advised a return to the older method of living off the country.

The artillery had its own doctors and surgeons, whose equipment rode on special carts. It has often been claimed that Sully organized the model field-hospital at Longpré, near

[1] *Économies Royales*, i, 243a.
[2] Valois, n° 4351.
[3] Valois, n° 4016.
[4] *Actes de Sully*, article 6.
[5] BN ms. fr. 3447, fo. 41–2.
[6] *Économies Royales*, ii, 364–5.

L

Amiens, during the siege of 1597,[1] but Marbault's attack on this claim is fully substantiated by some surviving documents, which make it clear that the responsibility was Villeroy's.[2] His is the signature on each of the expenditure accounts, and he it is who regulates even such details as the storage of drugs and the feeding of the staff. Moreover, as we have already seen, during the siege Sully was at Paris looking after the finances.

Sully was concerned to build up not only the land forces, but also the French fleet.[3] As the former English ambassador to France, Sir George Carew, remarked, Sully was 'ever hammering for building a navy for the sea'.[4] When Henri IV came to the throne the royal navy was almost extinct on both 'seas' – the Atlantic and the Mediterranean.[5] The need to build up a naval force in the Mediterranean was the more urgent, for the king wished not only to protect the commerce of Marseilles from Turkish corsairs and English pirates, but also to be able to interrupt Spanish communications with Italy in time of war. For the time being, however, his naval weakness was painful; the new French ambassador for Rome in January 1600 had to take a borrowed Genoese galley, and when Marie de Medici crossed from Leghorn to Marseilles to join Henri IV in November 1600, galleys had to be hired from various places.[6]

The *amiral des mers de Levant* was Charles de Guise, who during the latter years of the civil wars maintained at his own expense a galley based on Marseilles, and whom we have already encountered working on the fortifications of the Mediterranean coast. Under his command was the *général des galères*, Philippe-Emmanuel de Gondi, responsible for day-to-day administration including such matters as food and discipline. The best of the galley-captains were knights of Malta, officers of the order of

[1] Following the *Économies Royales*, i, 250b.

[2] Marbault, *Remarques sur les mémoires de Sully*, 37b; the documents are found in BN Clairambault 359, used by Bonnault d'Houet in *La première ambulance sous Henri IV* (Paris, 1919).

[3] I have dealt with this in more detail in 'The French Mediterranean fleet under Henri IV', *The Mariner's Mirror*, 1 (1964), 297–306.

[4] Carew, *Relation of the state of France*, 487.

[5] See Paul Masson, *Les galères de France, 1481–1781* (Paris, 1938).

[6] Abel Desjardins (ed.), *Négociations de la France avec la Toscane* (6 vols, Paris, 1859–86), v, 424.

Saint John of Jerusalem which since 1530 had been based on Malta.[1] The leading captain was Jacques Vincheguerre; he had been awarded the 'croix d'or' of his order in 1594 for valorous conduct in the face of the Turk, and further distinguished himself after that against the Turks and against English pirates. In 1604 he put in to Marseilles and heard a proposition from Guillaume Du Vair, *premier président* of the Provence *parlement*, that he should henceforward serve the king of France. Two years later he went to see the king and was formally engaged, at the handsome salary of 6,000 *livres* for each year of full-time service. Other officers from the knights of Malta included Claude Douet, chevalier Des Maretz, Philibert de Foissy, *grand prieur de Champagne*, and also probably the Genoese captain Vassallo. From France the leading captains were Paul de Fortia, sieur de Pilles, member of an old Marseilles family and governor of the château d'If, and Julien de Montigny, sieur de La Hottière, who after fighting with the Spaniards in Brittany had changed his allegiance on their expulsion in 1598.

Table 4 shows how expenditure on the *marine de Levant* rose from about 200,000 *livres* in 1600 to about 400,000 in 1610. These figures include money spent on the fortifications of Provence as a whole, and most of the expenditure until 1605 went on the work described in chapter VII. By then, however, the fortifications were in reasonable order, and thereafter most of the money was spent on the navy. The chief cost was incurred in the construction of new galleys. In February 1603 a contract was passed with the Genoese Ambrogio Lomellini, a financier who had become *gentilhomme ordinaire* in 1597, for the building of six galleys at 180,000 *livres*. Each galley was to have two hundred oarsmen, forty-seven seamen and sixty soldiers; on the king's side his ministers promised to find for each ship one hundred and fifty convicts as oarsmen to start with – and fifteen each year 'to take the place of those who will have died' – and the artillery until Lomellini could provide his own. Voyages in December, January and February would be at the king's risk, while Lomellini could use each vessel for two months each year

---

[1] For a recent work, see Claire-Éliane Engel, *L'Ordre de Malte en Méditerranée* (Monaco, 1957).

for private trading.[1] The whole contract is an interesting mixture of private and public enterprise, designed to make the most of the royal purse. Lomellini probably fulfilled his part of the contract, for we find him receiving his agreed stipend of 3,000 *livres* until 1613.[2]

Other vessels were constructed by the officers themselves, under the supervision of Sully, who sent to Italy for details of building methods.[3] Philibert de Foissy's was the first to be completed, some time before 1601; it was named the *Saint-Louis* and handed over to the king in 1603. However, the terms of his contract are obscure and it is not certain that he was ever fully paid for it as this was still a matter for dispute in 1610. We are better informed about the galleys which Vincheguerre and Douet engaged themselves to build, in September 1606. They agreed that for 25,000 *livres* apiece they would each construct a galley, complete except for the artillery, and have it in the water by October 1607. In fact they kept their side of the bargain, but were only paid 12,000 *livres* apiece because of the obstruction of the *parlement* of Toulouse, so that in 1609 it was agreed that they could keep the vessels, for whose upkeep and crews they of course received an annual grant.[4] Finally we have the mention of a galley built and handed over to the king by the sieur de Pilles in 1610 for 18,000 *livres*.[5] It is probable that other officers, and notably Julien de Montigny, also constructed vessels, and others may in addition have been built by certain tax-farmers in return for their concessions. There would have been no trouble in finding builders at Marseilles, for timber was plentiful and craftsmen were available as galleys were often built there for the knights of Malta.

By 1600 the general form of Mediterranean galleys had been well established for some centuries, the most recent innovation having been the transition during the fifteenth century from two or more banks of oars, each pulled by one man, to a single

---

[1] *Actes de Sully*, 9.

[2] BN cabinet des titres, pièces originales, 1737.

[3] See the title in his hand – 'menu de la despance d'une galere' – to a list of materials necessary: AN 120 AP 48, fo. 86.

[4] For these transactions, see Valois, n° 10571 and 13815.

[5] AN 120 AP 48, fo. 96.

bank of oars on each of which up to five or six men might be stationed. About this time sailing-ships were just beginning to show their worth as war-vessels in the Mediterranean, having proved themselves in the Atlantic and other oceans; the Algerians had experimented with them during the sixteenth century, and the knights of Malta bought their first, the *Swan*, in 1601. But naval opinion was that these vessels needed galley support in the Mediterranean, often subject to calms. Thus Philibert de Foissy wrote to the king in 1602 to tell him that the galley which he had just built went well, adding that he did not think that the fleet which the Spaniards had assembled could be for use in the Mediterranean, as it contained too many 'vaisseaux ronds' for that.[1] Galleys long continued to prove useful in the Mediterranean (and in the Baltic) and the French galley service was only abolished in 1748.

The vessels constructed under Henri IV were of the type illustrated in plate 13, with a single bank of oars and two masts. Apart from the two command-galleys, the *Roialle* and the *Reine*, commanded by Gondi himself and by the sieur Vassallo respectively, which had twenty-eight benches each side and were 'quinquirèmes' – having five men to each oar – they had twenty-five or -six benches and four men to the oar. They were thus rather larger than the normal Italian or Barbary galley and sailed relatively well with their lateen rig;[2] this was important as captains liked to spare their oarsmen as much as they could, so as to have them fresh for a possible combat. The galleys were about sixty yards long, and so lightly constructed that one man in the wrong place could spoil their balance;[3] they could on occasion be rowed by fewer than the ideal number of men, by 170 for example instead of by 200. They had of course no broadside armament, and were terribly vulnerable to the broadside of a sailing-ship if it could sail alongside, but they carried a considerable weight of fire in the bows. This consisted of one 'canon de France', ten feet long and capable of reducing the strongest fortifications, and four to eight smaller weapons. They

[1] BN ms. fr. 23196, fo. 112.
[2] According to the Venetian ambassador; see Barozzi and Berchet, *Relazioni* . . ., serie II Francia, i (Venice, 1857), 458.
[3] Ithier Hobier, *De la construction d'une gallaire* (Paris, 1622), 48.

were all supplied to the galley-captains by the royal arsenal at
Marseilles, where some of them had been founded. This
armament lacked the sheer weight of a sailing-ship's broadside,
but it was in compensation more manœuvrable, even if in
general captains preferred not to fire while under way as it
upset the vessel's balance.[1] Powder and shot were also supplied
by the arsenal, which carried a large stock specially for
the galleys; it was in addition responsible for providing the
'flames de couleurs' – no doubt for signals – and the 'devises
de Sa Majesté', the pennants with which the galleys were be-
decked.

We know little of the fifty or so seamen and the sixty-odd
soldiers who served on each galley, but are well informed about
the oarsmen, chiefly because their recruitment gave rise to so
many problems. The *bonnevoiles*, or paid volunteers, were few
in the French fleet. Lomellini explains the difficulty of recruiting
them, in a letter of 1603 to the king's secretary;[2] he points out
that the chief source of oarsmen must be convicts, and urges
that the *parlements* of France be once more encouraged to
condemn their criminals to the galleys. In fact as early as 1600
the *parlement* of Brittany had received letters-patent to this
effect, and in the ensuing years the supply from this source was
adequate, even if there were difficulties about letting trained
men leave once their sentence had expired. Gondi seems to have
opposed the officials of the *parlement* of Provence who tried to
establish justice in this affair, but after 1609 he was compelled
by royal edict to keep a careful note of the convicts' time to be
served, and to release them once this had expired.[3] In the early
seventeenth century there was as yet no question of condemning
Protestants to the galleys, and the other chief source of oarsmen,
apart from a few Swiss convicts,[4] were Turkish captives. This
was one of the curious and distinctive elements of galley-war-
fare, that the soldiers and seamen of the defeated boat were apt
to find themselves in chains at the victors' oars, while the

[1] According to the knight of Malta Jacques de Fumée, in his *L'arsenac de
la milice françoise* (Paris, 1607), 86.
[2] BN ms. fr. 15578, fo. 176–9.
[3] Valois, nº 13482.
[4] See Rott, *Henri IV, les Suisses, et la Haute-Italie*, 9.

released oarsmen became soldiers and sailors in their turn.[1] The use of Turkish captives led to differences with the merchants of Marseilles, who felt that it made their relations with the Mohammedan states of the Mediterranean unduly difficult, besides exposing their ships and men to reprisals.[2] As Du Vair, *premier président* of the Provence *parlement*, put it, '. . . each one of these Turkish captives will cost the king thirty Christians'.[3] Gondi, however, would not give up his Turkish captives, and seems with them and French convicts – in all about two thousand – to have been able to man his boats.

The life of the *galériens* was obviously hard – as we saw in Lomellini's contract, a crew of 150 might need fifteen replacements a year – but at least they were fed and clothed, which was more than could often be said of the peasantry at this time. Gondi had the right to bring south annually a certain quantity of wheat, free from internal tariffs, and he used this concession to keep his men supplied. We find him writing in 1606, for example, to the mayor and corporation of Lyons to remind them of his right,[4] and two years later he was recovering the tolls unduly charged on a considerable quantity of wheat.[5] The convicts also received annually a sort of uniform, including a 'cloak to cover them from head to toe, and to protect them in cold weather or when they are asleep'.[6] It was in the captains' interest to keep their men reasonably fit, and their lot seems to have been preferable to that of many other prisoners both before and since, and especially to that of men in solitary confinement. The convicts' barracks, where they were allowed to carry on certain handicrafts, was at Marseilles. This, however, proved a very unsatisfactory base, not only because the merchants were often opposed to the attacks of the *général des galères* upon the Turks, but also because the port had to be shared with a mass of

---

[1] See the remarkable account of one such engagement in *Le Mercure François*, 40.

[2] See the letter of the *consuls* of Marseilles, Arch. Aff. Étr. France 1700, fo. 165; the same collection contains many of these complaints.

[3] Bib. Institut, fonds Godefroy, 264, fo. 155–6, letter to Villeroy, Aix, 8 April 1607.

[4] BM Lyon AA 78.

[5] Valois, nº 7696.

[6] Hobier, *De la construction d'une gallaire*, 55.

commercial vessels. About 1606 the king was considering
Hyères as an alternative base for his fleet, but the choice eventually fell on Toulon, which alone among Mediterranean ports
had remained loyal to Henri IV during the League. In chapter
VII we have described the work of Raymond de Bonnefons
there; the galleys were ordered to Toulon in November 1609
and that was the beginning of the great naval base.[1]

It remains to see what use Gondi made of his fleet. For the
early years three letters of his survive, to give us an idea of the
re-birth of French naval power.[2] In the first, written to the king
from Hyères on 4 August 1604, he describes how he has found
the five galleys 'fort lestes', and has rowed along the coast to
Antibes, where he dropped the duc de Guise, who no doubt
wanted to inspect the new fortifications. Then, he goes on, he
continued along the coast by Genoa, 'so that strangers may see
and admire the excellence of your galleys'. He chased two
Turkish galleys, but failed to catch them, and then sent two
boats back to Marseilles while he continued the patrol. A
second letter, written that August from Saint-Tropez, describes
how he had taken a Savoyard brigantine which had been
ravaging the coast. The next year we again find Gondi writing
from Saint-Tropez, to say that there have not been many
corsairs that year, either because of the plague in their country,
or for fear of the royal galleys. He goes on to say that he hopes to
sail next year with seven galleys, which he hopes will further
discourage the pirates and 'plusieurs voisins de Vostre Magesté'.
In August 1607 he provided a galley for the retiring papal
nuncio, Barberini; the fleet had made some progress since the
days when a French ambassador had to hire a Genoese vessel for
his passage to Rome.

Sully had been closely associated with this build-up of naval
strength, not only in sending to Italy for construction-details,
but also in supervising the various contracts made with the
officers. He was concerned too not only with the development of
bases in the Mediterranean, but also with the projects for the

[1] J. Cadis, 'Histoire de l'arsenal maritime de Toulon', *Mémorial de l'artillerie française*, xxvi (1952), 255–96.
[2] BN ms. fr. 23198, fo. 146, 151 and 528.

building of ports on the Atlantic seaboard, as we have noticed in chapter VII. The government of Henri IV is often criticized for neglecting the Atlantic and the 'vaisseaux ronds' which sailed upon it, and it is clear that funds for the *marine de Ponant* were kept very short. On the other hand, in the early seventeenth century it was probably correct to give the Mediterranean strategic priority, when the northern seas could if necessary be denied to the Spaniards by the Dutch and the English.

Sully, then, was involved in many aspects of military organization. If we could read his lost works, the *Traité de la Guerre*, the *Maréchal de Camp* and the *Instruction de Milice et de Police*,[1] we should be able to get a clearer notion of his views on the tactical problems and developments of the day. As it is we may be certain that, becoming grand master of the artillery at a time when this arm had become indispensable on the battle-field, but before the reforms of Louvois had subordinated its commander to the general military administration, Sully impressed on it his own brand of efficiency and uniformity.

No doubt he thoroughly approved of – and probably hired – the eulogist who spoke of his 'unbelievable speed in setting-up the war-machine';[2] we have seen that this praise was not unjust. In a sense, the artillery was his great love; he lived at the Arsenal when in Paris and often entertained the king there, he was known in the code of diplomatic dispatches as 'le cannonier'[3] and he had as his emblem the eagle, holding in its talons the divine bolts. For friends it was indeed the 'genereux oyseau', but for enemies of the realm the 'aigle courroucé'.[4]

[1] Mentioned in the *Économies Royales*, i, 286a.
[2] *L'Artillerie* (Paris, 1601), anon.
[3] BN ms. fr. 23026, fo. 209.
[4] Respectively, BN Dupuy 689, fo. 55v°, and BN Cinq Cents de Colbert 16, fo. 413v°.

CHAPTER IX

Sully's economic and political ideas

It is in vain that we search Sully's writings for his views on what now seem the great issues of his time; the causes and effects of the price-revolution, for example, or the use of provincial agents by the central government in France.[1] To discover what he thought about these and other questions we must have recourse to evidence scattered among his letters, and to the implications of his actions when he was in power.

The traditional interpretation of his economic position is that he was radically opposed to the 'protectionist' Barthélemy de Laffemas, being himself

more in favour of free-trade and above all more interested in finance and agriculture than in commerce and industry.[2]

This view will not stand up to close examination. It is true that in the *Économies Royales* Sully at one point speaks to the king with the tongue of Adam Smith:

Sire, Your Majesty must realize that just as there are many different climates and regions, so it seems that God has made them to abound in various goods and arts, each having its own speciality . . . so that by trade in these things (of which some have an abundance and others a scarcity) a lively

---

[1] The statements of his position in the *Économies Royales*, for example, i, 353–4, or ii, 442–50, are verbose and formalized.

[2] G. Mongrédien, 'Isaac de Laffemas d'après des documents inédits', *Revue des Questions historiques*, cviii–cix (1928), 11. See also H. Hauser, *Les débuts du capitalisme* (Paris, 1925), 170; E. Jung, *Henri IV écrivain* (Paris, 1855), 130; H. Pigeonneau, *Histoire du commerce de la France* (2 vols, Paris, 1885–9), ii, 317; C. Rupin, *Les idées économiques de Sully* (Rennes, 1907), 128; G. Zeller, 'L'industrie en France avant Colbert', *Revue d'histoire économique et sociale*, xxviii (1950), 15; and so on.

intercourse may be maintained between nations however far they are, the one from the other, as the great voyages to the East and West Indies show. In the second place you must consider if this realm has not a climate, a terrain and a natural inclination among its peoples contrary to Your Majesty's plans.[1]

The plans in question here were those for the silk-manufactures, and the passage has been taken to show Sully's opposition to the fostering of industries by the Crown. However, he was quite capable of preaching this divine interdependence and simultaneously calling for protectionist measures. His position in this respect was akin to that of Bodin, who, while writing on occasion in the same tenor as the passage cited above, nevertheless generally advocated the protection of industry and the regulation of trade by the monarch.[2] One of the earliest memoranda from Sully's hand in fact recommends

the prohibition of the wearing in France of any clothes made of foreign silk or wool, but only those made with native fabrics, so that the manufactures may be established to the great profit of the king and his whole realm.[3]

In practice he seems sometimes to have opposed the king's schemes for establishing exotic manufactures,[4] but this was on practical grounds and not from any formal adherence to the principles of 'free trade'.

Marbault claimed indeed that Sully had promoted 'manufactures',[5] and this also emerges from the record of his activity. It is true that he seems to have opposed their establishment in 1598, and that when in 1602 a project for establishing a silk-factory came before the council, he was careful to point out the financial difficulties which it would meet.[6] However, by 1603

[1] Économies Royales, i, 515.
[2] For a passage closely resembling that quoted above, see the one quoted by H. Hauser, 'Un précurseur: Jean Bodin, Angevin (1529 ou 1530–1596)', Annales iii (1931), 379–87. Bodin's political position was as unresolved and ambiguous as his economic position.
[3] BN ms. fr. 18510, fo. 105r°.
[4] Économies Royales, i, 534b, and Lettres Missives, v, 20–1.
[5] Remarques sur les mémoires de Sully, 69a.
[6] Documents historiques inédits (Documents inédits sur l'histoire de France), ed. M. Champollion-Figeac (4 vols, Paris, 1848), iv, 7–8, 41–2, 68, 74–7 and 110.

he had not only acquiesced in the scheme but had even arranged for the factory to be set up in his *gouvernement* at Mantes-la-Jolie.[1] The next year we find mulberry-trees for the silk-worms being planted in Poitou 'with the favour and wise permission of monseigneur de Rosny';[2] clearly if he had at first opposed these schemes his hostility had not lasted. Moreover, in the autumn of 1603 he was working with other members of the council for the general establishment of 'marchans et artisans estrangers' in France.[3]

The regulations concerning the corn-trade have often been held to demonstrate the 'free-trade' sympathies of Sully and Henri IV.[4] Here again a more attentive examination of the evidence shows that they did little more than apply the time-honoured principle of attempting to restrict exports in time of dearth, and of trying to open the customs after good harvests. Very often it was the provincial authorities themselves which appealed for grain-exports to be forbidden. In 1604, for instance, the harvest in the Mediterranean regions was unusually poor, and governors of those provinces wrote asking the king to close the customs so that corn from areas like Burgundy could be diverted southwards.[5] The government generally complied with this request, and when it did order the opening of the customs it was more concerned with the profit from the resultant customs revenue than with a matter of principle.

In the *Économies Royales* Sully describes how he refused the petition of the men of Tours who wished to have all imports of foreign textiles prohibited, so that their infant industries could flourish.[6] This, again, has been considered to show his hostility to protectionism. However, the city whose trade stood to lose

---

[1] Ibid., 112.

[2] *Archives curieuses de l'histoire de France*, ed. Cimber et Danjou (Paris, 1837), series I, xiv, 221–45.

[3] See the letters from Sillery to Bellièvre and to Villeroy, respectively, BN ms. fr. 15899, fo. 156, and Bib. Institut, fonds Godefroy, 264, fo. 52–3.

[4] For this section, see A. P. Usher, *The history of the grain trade in France, 1400–1710* (Cambridge, Mass., 1913).

[5] See the king's letter of 5 September 1604 to Bellièvre, *Lettres inédites du roi Henri IV à Bellièvre, 16 mars–28 octobre 1604*, ed. Eugène Halphen (Paris, 1883), and the letter from Du Vair, *premier président* of the Provence *parlement*, to the king, Aix, 4 September 1604, BN ms. fr. 23198, fo. 173.

[6] Op. cit., i, 317.

most from such a prohibition was Lyons, which Sully favoured as the leading Protestant stronghold in south-eastern France.[1] For the same reason he was hostile to the proposed tax on foreign merchants' and bankers' *lettres de change*,[2] although the advocates of this duty put forward compelling reasons for its adoption: that no merchant could afford to leave Lyons whatever the fiscal inconvenience of staying there, that a similar tax at Genoa had caused no decline, that the Spanish king could thus be prevented from drawing on French bankers, and so forth.[3] None of these arguments seems to have swayed Sully, who remained faithful to Lyons. Similarly, although we read in the *délibérations* of the *conseil de commerce*[4] that Sully was 'opposed to taxes on goods', this statement must be read within its context, which concerns the establishment of a monopoly. The 'daces' to which Sully was hostile were those in the hands of private monopolists; when the Crown stood to profit by duties they were retained, as in the case of the crippling *douane de Vienne*. In his early years, indeed, Sully seems to have been a crude 'provisionist', to use Hecksher's phrase; one of his proposals for raising money in 1598 was 'an increase in the tax on all goods leaving France, so as to avoid the great exportation which is going on.'[5]

Not only was Sully not opposed to Laffemas over royal regulation of trade and industry; many of their schemes and interests in fact coincided. One of the chief preoccupations of the *conseil de commerce*, over which Laffemas presided, was precisely that canalization of the rivers and development of the sea-ports which Sully directed as *grand voyer* and *surintendant des fortifications*. Like Laffemas, Sully tried to encourage inventors; John Nef went so far as to affirm that

> Numerous applicants came to Paris to demonstrate before
> Sully and his assistants, who then decided whether their

[1] Late in 1610, for instance, he quarrelled with Villeroy over Lyons, whose privileges he again wished to uphold: Zeller, *La minorité de Louis XIII*, 175.
[2] Permezel, *La politique financière de Sully*, 83.
[3] BN ms. fr. 18510, fo, 113–16.
[4] Champollion-Figeac (ed.), *Documents historiques inédits*, iv, 94.
[5] BN ms. fr. 18510, fo. 105.

methods were novel, successful and deserving of exclusive privileges.[1]

While one may doubt if things were quite as systematized as this, it is certain that in 1608 Sully examined and approved Christophe Marie's invention of a new kind of bridge, capable of bearing the heaviest loads, which could be built in four months on the widest rivers; Marie in fact constructed one of his bridges at Neuilly-sur-Seine, and later played a leading part in the development of the Ile-Saint-Louis.[2] Again, it was before Sully that the sieur Le Caire and Denis Thouyn demonstrated their new furnaces in 1609; Le Caire eventually received the monopoly, and was ordered to reappear before Sully so that his 'other inventions' could also be assessed.[3] Sully's colleagues knew of his interest in novel devices, and in 1608 for instance Jeannin sent him from Holland

> a soldier from Sedan, who serves in Maurice's company and who is very ingenious when it comes to warlike inventions; a few days ago he made a device, like the one invented by a lens-grinder of Middleburg [Johannes Lippershey],[4] for seeing a great distance. He will let you examine it and will make one for you.[5]

Laffemas also advocated that unification of the weights and measures which Sully tried to introduce into the administration of the fortifications.[6] Again, the English ambassador Neville wrote to Robert Cecil in 1599 concerning the exploitation of some silver-mines in Poitou and Auvergne that 'M de Rosni affects the matter much';[7] this too was one of Laffemas's preoccupations. Finally, both men were concerned to prevent the export of bullion from France, Laffemas for general 'mercantilist' reasons and Sully because he was intent on build-

[1] *Industry and government in France and England, 1540–1640* (Cornell, 1957), 64.
[2] See Maurice Dumolin, *Études de topographie parisienne* (3 vols, Paris, 1929–31), iii, 4–7.
[3] Valois, n° 14576 and n° 15288.
[4] See the description of this telescope in *Le Mercure François*, 339.
[5] *Négociations du président Jeannin*, 548.
[6] AN 120 AP 1, fo. 236.
[7] *Memorials of affairs of state*, i, 93.

ing up the treasure in the Bastille which gave his master the means of waging an effective war.[1]

So far, then, from being an opponent of Laffemas, a 'free-trader' and little concerned with trade and industry, Sully was in many respects sympathetic to Laffemas's aims and played a central role in the regulation of trade and manufactures. When he observed that 'labourage et pâturage' were the 'deux mamelles de la France' he did not mean to exclude or reduce the importance of all other economic activities, as has so often been understood. In speaking of the 'laboureurs et pasteurs' in the *Économies Royales* he always links them with those 'marchands et artisans' whom he regarded as the other useful working elements in society.[2] They were for him the last four of the eight classes, the first four being the ecclesiastics, nobles, officials and financiers. He took pains to point out that all the glory of these higher categories rested on the labour of the four others, using the traditional anatomical allegory to describe how each organ must play its part.[3]

He was much concerned at the declining influence of the old nobility, which he attributed largely to the negligence and stupidity of its members, who by

> their contempt of the various branches of knowledge and the little trouble they take to fit themselves for various posts[4]

no longer deserved to find employment. He may have encouraged nobles to enter various branches of commerce,[5] as Richelieu later did, but he concentrated chiefly on trying to persuade them to work with the royal administration in the higher councils.[6] In speaking of Sully's attempt to reinstate the old nobility it is important to emphasize that he had no sympathy

---

[1] I have avoided the use of the ambiguous term 'mercantilist', but my argument in fact is that Sully was more of a 'mercantilist' (in the sense of one favouring close royal control of economic affairs) than is usually allowed.

[2] *Économies Royales*, i, 513b; ii, 419a and 466a. This point is also made by Martin, *Sully-le-Grand*, 133, and by Grand and Delatouche, *Agriculture au Moyen Age* (Paris, 1941), 729.

[3] *Économies Royales*, ii, 463–8.

[4] BN ms. fr. 10307, fo. 98.

[5] Permezel, *La politique financière de Sully*, 48–9.

[6] *Économies Royales*, ii, 186.

with such complaints as that which the 'noblesse d'Anjou' presented in 1601,[1] to the effect that heavy taxes prevented them from maintaining their former forces for the king. In Sully's view nobles should enjoy all the privileges of their fighting function, but only within the royal administration and under strict control. His concept was thus similar to that of Louvois, and if he detested that proliferation of noble 'fainéants' at Paris which was a feature of the earlier, as well as of the later seventeenth century, he was equally opposed to the freebooting of, say, a Wallenstein.

His concern for the nobility expressed itself chiefly in a remarkable series of projects for councils, on which suitably-qualified nobles were to sit, with a number of *gens de robe*. There were to be the *'conseils' ordinaire, des affaires étrangères, des finances, de la guerre, d'État* and *des parties*.[2] The whole scheme was worked out in detail by Sully in 1609, and although it was never put into effect it reveals a rather unexpected side of him as a far-sighted cameralist who had no doubt learnt his lesson from the governmental organization of Phillip II of Spain. The *conseil ordinaire* ('ou secret, ou royal, ou de la personne, ou estroict, ou d'execution') would have been very similar to the small council with which Henri IV governed, and which consisted of Bellièvre while he lived, Sillery, Sully and Villeroy. We may take it that Sully approved of a directorate as restricted as this, the best instrument for an absolute monarch. The clearest statement of his views on the position of the monarch counsels obedience on the part of subjects as a divine precept,[3] a view which was in accordance with the contemporary trends of political theory.

The policy of Sully favoured the development of an authoritarian government and hence of an administration centred on Paris.[4] He was opposed to Bellièvre because the latter wished to establish a moderate monarchy relying to some extent on the *parlements* of Paris and the provinces; Sully despised the *gens de*

[1] BN Cinq Cents de Colbert, 41, fo. 111–13.
[2] The *règlements* for these are printed in Clément, *Portraits historiques*, 495–502, and in Valois, lv.
[3] *Économies Royales*, ii, 107–8.
[4] For much of what follows, see Mousnier, 'Sully et le conseil d'État', *Revue Historique*, cxcii (1941), 68–86.

Le portraict de la Ville & Chasteau de Mont-Mellian en Sauoye, assiegee par le Roy de France & de Nauarre. 1600.

Par Cl. Chastillon, Topographe du Roy.

A PARIS,
Chez Iean le Clerc, rue S. Iean de Latran, à la Salamandre.

11. Engraving by Claude de Chastillon of the siege of Montmélian, 1600; the 'fortification nouvelle' on top of the hill contrasts well both with the 'donjon' which it encloses, and with the wall surrounding the lower town. The 'logis de Monsieur de Rosny' is numbered '15', top right (*BN Estampes*).

12. Plan for a gun-winch by Jean Errard, taken from his *Le premier livre des instruments mathématiques méchaniques* (Nancy, 1584).

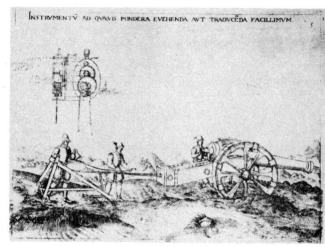

13. Plan of a galley; this one has five men to the oar and twenty-six benches, the size of the command-galleys of Henri IV (Ithier Hobier, *De la Construction d'une gallaire*).

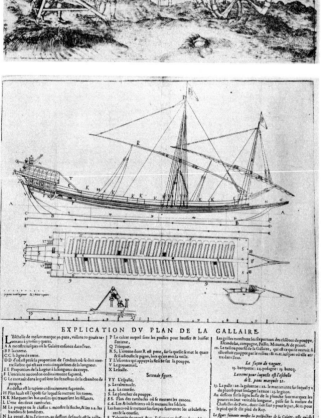

robe and wished to make use of the nobility in building up his strong centralized state. In troubled years like those of Henri IV's reign this was the policy which could hardly fail to be adopted. Hence the gradual decline of Bellièvre, who perhaps played the Marillac to Sully's Richelieu. We have noticed how in practice Sully did his best to encroach on the privileges of the provincial authorities. In theory, too, he was opposed to the exercise of power by a convention. Of the Rouen Assembly in 1596 he remarked that

> it is not only very difficult, but almost impossible in any large assembly of persons qualified and authorized to make laws . . . to ensure that all those present share the same ideas . . . so as to avoid all friction; this is why such assemblies never produce anything useful.[1]

He went on to indicate the even greater danger of a strong regional body, a point made again with reference to the Protestant Assembly of 1605. Writing from Châtellerault on this occasion, he insisted that

> we must in future be very careful in permitting such assemblies which scarcely ever do any good and can cause much harm, for when they speak in the name of so many provinces there are wild heads which imagine that the whole of France is committed to their resolutions.[2]

Seditious spirits were to be diverted by the traditional device of foreign war, or, as Sully is quoted as saying:

> the true means of setting the realm at rest is by keeping up a foreign war, towards which one can direct, like water in a gutter, all the turbulent humours of the kingdom.[3]

This was a truism, put forward among others by Bodin.[4] More original is the idea of engaging great numbers of the common people on public works, to provide employment.[5] Sully was

[1] *Économies Royales*, i, 236b.
[2] BN Clairambault, 360, fo. 271–2.
[3] Nouaillac, *Villeroy*, 390.
[4] *Les six livres de la République de Jean Bodin Angevin* (Paris, 1583), 525.
[5] According to Sir John Carew, this was one of the reasons for the building-programme: *A Relation of the state of France*, 461–2.

M

prejudiced against colonization, and seems to have opposed
the heroic enterprise of Pierre Du Guast, sieur de Monts, in
establishing the French colony at Quebec.[1] His reasons for this
were that such projects were

> disproportionate to the natural capacity and intelligence of
> the French people, whom I regretfully realize to have neither
> the foresight nor the perseverance which are necessary,[2]

and that 'great riches are never to be found in places below
forty degrees'.[3] He was equally reactionary in his attitude towards the formation of trading companies, partly because he
considered they were not suited to the French temperament
but partly, too, because of his sympathy for the Dutch, whose
own East India Company had been founded in 1602[4] and
whose agents probably bribed him.[5]

Sully's economic and political ideas have often been mis-
represented, for reasons which will emerge in the next chapter.
In fact he shared the enthusiasm of contemporaries like Laffemas
for the establishment of industries by the state, and showed
sympathy to 'free trade' only when it benefited the treasury. So
far from despising the merchants, he numbered them with the
agricultural and artisanal workers among those four classes
whose labours permitted the glories of the clergy, nobility and
other privileged groups in society. He was not content with the
status of the second class, which he wished to associate closely
with a powerful centralized government to which all lesser
corporations within the state would be subjected. This was
the political view of the future for, as we shall see, there were
close affinities between the ideas of Sully and those of Richelieu.

---

[1] M. Bishop, *Champlain, the life of fortitude* (London, 1949), 118.

[2] *Négociations du président Jeannin*, 281; letter from Sully to Jeannin, Paris,
26 February 1608.

[3] *Économies Royales*, i, 516b; presumably this curious maxim was intended
to apply only to the New World.

[4] On the circumstances of the foundation, see J. G. van Dillen, 'Isaac
Le Maire et le commerce des actions de la compagnie des Indes Orientales',
Revue d'histoire moderne, x (1935), 13.

[5] According to Charles de La Roncière, 'Les routes de l'Inde', *Revue des
questions historiques*, lxxvi (1904), 157–209.

CHAPTER X

Sully in Retirement
his fortune and the growth of his legend

Marie de Medici had had little reason to favour Sully during her husband's lifetime. After the death of Henri IV in May 1610 she tried for a while to make use of his services, realizing that

> he had much influence with the heretics, knew the finances better than anybody else, had a deep understanding of general affairs within the realm, and was himself committed to the maintenance of the government by reason of the many important posts he held.[1]

In July, however, she offended him by making it clear that in future she would authorize all expenditure, and in August, faced with the growing influence of Concini, he attempted to resign, and retired to his estate at Moret-sur-Loing. But he was persuaded to return to court in November, and the Florentine first secretary then wrote that

> Monsieur de Sully has begun to regain his former power because, quite apart from the fact that he is not dead as was rumoured, he has retained all his offices and is carrying out his duties as before, though less rigorously.[2]

This was, however, a false recovery; Marie de Medici could not keep the great nobles in order as Henri IV had done, and in January 1611, exasperated by their importunity, Sully again attempted to withdraw. Once more he was persuaded to stay on, but later that month he finally resigned his *surintendance des*

[1] Zeller, *La minorité de Louis XIII*, 69–70, quoting the Florentine ambassador.
[2] Ibid., 174.

finances and captaincy of the Bastille, after Villeroy had made his position untenable by uniting Condé, Soissons, Jeannin and Concini against him.

He left Paris that February, and went to Samur, where the Protestants were holding an assembly. There his attempts at mediation in the face of increasing discord were misunderstood by the queen and the Protestants alike.[1] He then spent most of 1612 and 1613 in his government of Poitou – composing the first draft of the *Économies Royales,* perhaps – while Marie de Medici ran into increasingly severe political and financial difficulties. In March 1614 he wrote to her to know whether or not he should act against certain seditious gentlemen of his province but received no clear instructions.[2] In October that year he returned to Paris, no doubt for the opening of the Estates-General. There the king and the queen-mother received him well and seemed ready to employ him again.[3] But the following December he received highly ambiguous replies to his requests to resume his offices,[4] and in April 1615 we find him writing in a very disillusioned tone to Pierre Fougeu, sieur d'Escures, describing how when he suggested measures to relieve flood-damage

> each person looks at the other and shrugs his shoulders; this comes I think not from a want of good will but from sheer necessity, for to judge from what the financial officers say things have never been worse.[5]

He left Paris in May for Saint-Maixent, whence he wrote to the royal ministers, Villeroy and Jeannin, in tones of rising indignation over the neglect of his services and the deterioration in the country's affairs.[6] In October he offered to mediate between the king and the prince de Condé, who had been declared a rebel the month before, but his efforts at reconciliation had

---

[1] Anquez, *Histoire des assemblées politiques,* 230–46.

[2] See the facsimile of his letter: Paris, *mairie du XVI*, Ms. 8, 118.

[3] According to Malherbe's letter to Peiresc, Paris, 17 October 1614: *Oeuvres de Malherbe,* iii, 466–7.

[4] BN Clairambault, 364, fo. 367–74.

[5] AN 120 AP 48, fo. 49.

[6] BN ms. fr. 3795, fo. 16, and Bib. Institut, fonds Godefroy, 268, fo. 49–50.

little success and in December he was obliged to admit Condé and his friends to Saint-Maixent and other towns within his government of Poitou.[1]

He did not give up his attempts to mediate, however, and the next spring (1616) played a notable part in the negotiations of the assembly at La Rochelle, at which a truce was agreed.[2] In August 1616 he had an audience with the queen-mother, at which he warned her of the renewed danger from the party of the princes, and pressed at least by implication for the arrest of Condé. After the latter had been taken into custody, however, Sully seems to have had second thoughts, perhaps because he ran some personal danger in being held partly responsible for the arrest. At all events, having expressed his doubts to Marie de Medici he was roundly rebuked by her for his volte-face;[3] after this he seems to have retired from high politics, expressing a wish to live quietly on his estates in future.[4]

His declining years were sadly filled with quarrels and mis-understandings with his children. In 1620 his eldest son, Maximilien II de Béthune, the child of Anne de Courtenay, became a Catholic in the fashion of the time, after an acri-monious open correspondence with his father.[5] One of Sully's letters to his son at this time reveals the rift between them; it begins: 'Sir, if abandoning yourself to voluptuous pleasures, neglecting your own wife, snatching the wife of another, and disobeying your father [are the marks of your conversion] . . .'[6]. Sully had done his best to establish Maximilien II in a favourable position; he had for instance had him appointed *surintendant des bâtiments* when he reached his majority in 1605, had ensured for him the *survivance* of his grand mastership of the artillery, and on the occasion of his marriage in 1609 to Françoise de Créqui, grand-daughter of the duc de Lesdiguières, had granted him

[1] H. Ouvré, 'Essai sur l'histoire de la ville de Poitiers', *Mémoires de la société des antiquaires de l'Ouest*, xxii (1855), 488–92.

[2] *Archives historiques de la Saintonge et de l'Aunis*, xv (1887), letter of 17 April 1616 to Duplessis-Mornay from La Rochelle.

[3] *Mémoires du cardinal de Richelieu*, ii, 89–90.

[4] Fichier Charavay, letter of 5 May 1617 to Villeroy from Figeac.

[5] See the *Lettre de M. le marquis de Rosny pour responce à celle de . . . son père* (Lyons, 1620).

[6] BN ms. fr. 3805, fo. 40, St-Amand-Montrond, 23 August 1620.

the duchy of Sully, reserving only the usufruct. Maximilien II, however, seems to have been a hopeless wastrel; as early as 1617 his debts were very extensive and in 1634, just before his early death, Sully, who had remained in community of goods with him, had a hard time with his creditors.[1] The relations of Maximilien II with his wife Françoise were equally unsatisfactory. She seems to have been a spendthrift and perhaps loose in her conduct,[2] and as he was much addicted to gaming and wenching the marriage broke up about 1620. Maximilien II and his wife had two children, of whom the elder, Maximilien de Henrichemont, married the daughter of Louis XIII's chancellor Séguier. This grandson, however, showed his father's spite towards Sully, entering into a legal action against him which he won, thanks partly to the intervention of Richelieu.[3] This blow to Sully, an old man now, seems to have precipitated his death in 1641. We may notice in passing that Richelieu went out of his way to be unpleasant to Sully, who had perhaps annoyed the great cardinal by refusing him a certain grant when he was still the young bishop of Luçon.[4]

With his other son, François, comte d'Orval, child of Rachel de Cochefilet, Sully's relations were more satisfactory. When François was eighteen he received his father's office of *grand voyer*, and on his marriage to Jacqueline de Caumont, daughter of the duc de La Force, in 1620, was endowed with a yearly income of 20,000 *livres* on the estate at Villebon. Although he caused his father some anxiety by dabbling in Protestant revolts he seems to have remained on good terms with his parents. They would sometimes stay with him when they visited Paris, before Sully bought his town-house on the rue Saint-Anthoine in 1634.[5] Sully's daughters Marguerite and Louise both gave him trouble. Marguerite had in 1605 married

---

[1] Mallevoüe (ed.), *Actes de Sully*, lxiii.

[2] AM Reims, fonds Tarbé xiii, dossier 54–5 has some details of shoes for which payment is due by Françoise to a certain 'Mme Massacre'.

[3] See AM Reims, fonds Tarbé xiii, dossier 161–2 for a 'Mémoire des prétensions que je puis avoir sur le bien de M. le duc de Sully' of Maximilien de Henrichemont.

[4] See G. d'Avenel (ed.), *Lettres, instructions diplomatiques et papiers d'État du cardinal de Richelieu* (8 vols, Paris, 1853–77), i, 90, note 4.

[5] See Jacques Houlet, *L'hôtel de Sully au Marais* (Paris, 1964).

Henri, duc de Rohan, who became involved in Protestant rebellions and conspiracies during Louis XIII's minority. By 1620 he was among the Huguenot leaders; in December that year the Protestant assembly at La Rochelle, to which Sully and the other moderates had refused to go, decided to establish a military government in the south. Slowly the rebellion grew; Rohan, pursued in his travels by letters from Sully counselling obedience, became its military leader.[1] The government of Marie de Medici was in the hands of the duc de Luynes, who in the summer of 1621 led an army south into the Huguenot region and laid siege to Montauban. Sully entered the besieged town with the king's permission in an attempt to bring the inhabitants to reason; here again he failed.[2] Rohan eventually came to terms with Marie de Medici, and lived on to serve France with great brilliance in North Italy, before being killed at Rheinfelden in 1638, fighting as a volunteer under Bernard of Saxe-Weimar. Louise, the second of Sully's daughters, was a poor creature who had to be married off with a dowry of 450,000 *livres* to Alexandre de Levis, marquis de Mirepoix; this union lasted only four years and after its dissolution Louise opened a legal case against her father to gain an even greater share of his estate.[3]

Sully's fortune at the end of his life was still immense, for assets exceeded liabilities by perhaps three million *livres*. According to Richelieu, he had entered the royal service with 6,000 *livres* of income, and left it with 150,000; clear evidence, he thought, of the *surintendant's* dishonesty.[4] The fortune of Sully – like that of Richelieu himself and of Colbert – has never been the subject of thorough study, and it is probably impossible fully to reconstitute its elements. All the same, certain documents in the 'Papiers de Sully', together with a new acquisition of the Bibliothéque Nationale and an unpublished manuscript of the British Museum,[5] now permit us at least to check on

[1] Auguste Laugel, *Henry de Rohan, son rôle politique et militaire sous Louis XIII (1579–1638)* (Paris, 1889).
[2] *Mémoires du cardinal de Richelieu*, iii, 155–6.
[3] See BM add. mss. 25593, fo. 48–65.
[4] *Mémoires du cardinal de Richelieu*, i, 139.
[5] BN nouv. acq. franç., 25116, fo. 210, and BM add. mss. 25593.

Sully's own estimates. Each year, according to the *Économies Royales*, he made out statements of his fortune, but all those which survive deal with the years of retirement only. The best account of the formation of his wealth is found in the *Économies Royales* itself and this will form the basis for our evaluation.[1]

The statement, which has been condensed for clarity's sake, runs as follows:

Annual income	from	offices	97,200 *livres*
		abbeys	45,000
		estates	60,000
			202,200
Capital gains	gifts from the king		480,000
	private acquisitions		530,000
	recompense for sales of office and land		1,300,000

The income from offices is easily checked with the *rôles de comptants et d'assignations;*[2] allowing for various 'gages, esmolumens et droits' over and above the salary of the post in question, the figures correspond well enough. It is hard accurately to check the income from abbeys, granted to Sully by the king and held by a 'prête-nom', but such grants were certainly numerous[3] and the resultant income may well have reached 45,000 *livres*. As for the income from Sully's own estates, for an income of 60,000 *livres* he would have needed about a million *livres'* worth of property; this was about what he possessed at the time of his retirement, though it had passed to two millions at the time of his death. A weakness of the statement is that it does not account for annual expenditure, but it seems reasonable to suppose that Sully was able to save some of his 200,000 *livres*, especially as he lived in the Arsenal at Paris and had his expenses paid when he went anywhere on the king's business.[4] Therefore the acquisition even of a million *livres'* worth of property seems quite possible on the figures given.

[1] Op cit., ii, 90–4.
[2] AN 120 AP 3–8; e.g. 120 AP 4, fo. 59v⁰ and 154r⁰.
[3] See for instance, *Lettres Missives*, v, 179 and Valois, n⁰ 12337; also *Économies Royales*, ii, 93b.
[4] For example, when he went to Châtellerault in 1605 he received 300 *livres*; AN 120 AP 3, fo. 236v⁰.

As for the figures of capital gains, those which can be checked are equally accurate. In the list of 'dons du roi' for 1605–9[1] the yearly gift to Sully is 60,000 *livres* (90,000 in 1609); assuming that it was smaller between 1598 and 1604,[2] the sum of such presents would just about have reached the figure quoted, 480,000 *livres*. The private acquisitions are less easily checked, but the individual entries seem credible. The next entry, the recompense for offices and land, can be verified in some detail;[3] Sully's figures are accurate. In the account printed in the *Économies Royales*, figures of expenditure follow those reproduced above. Most of them concern the acquisition of land, and in the introduction to his *Actes* Mallevoüe has said of these that 'all the elements of Sully's fortune which are described in the *Économies Royales* and which we have been able to check are confirmed by the notarial deeds'.[4] This may be our judgement on the statement as a whole; immense though Sully's gains were, they seem to have come to him legitimately. As Henri IV wrote to him on one occasion, 'you have given me so much help in running my affairs that I wish to help you in running yours.'[5]

Some of these gifts were to help Sully get on with his private building programme; as the king wrote in December 1607, he is sending a certain sum 'as the friend of those who build and as your good master'.[6] Sully began his private building at Rosny, near Mantes. About 1595 he decided that the old family house at Beurons was too small, and began building a new mansion. After the Brittany expedition of 1598, when he received his first large grant from the king, the construction went forward fast; by the next year the work was sufficiently advanced for visitors to be shown round the site, and in 1603

---

[1] Listed in AN 120 AP 2.
[2] In 1599, for instance, Sully received at least 25,000 *livres*; see the account for that year preserved in the library of the University of Ghent (Belgium).
[3] See for instance, BN Dupuy 90, fo. 203 et seq. containing the financial arrangements following Sully's resignation, and *Économies Royales*, ii, 410–11.
[4] Mallevoüe, lxxi.
[5] *Lettres Missives*, vii, 248, letter of 20 May 1607, Fontainebleau.
[6] Ibid., vii, 399.

the king visited Sully there.[1] The building was to have consisted
of a main block with two wings, forming three sides of a court,
but only the central part was finished in 1610, when Sully
stopped all work on the death of his master. It was not until
the early nineteenth century that the two wings, which have
since been destroyed, were completed, by the duchesse de
Berry. She was the widow of the duc de Berry, who had been
murdered in 1820; her years at Rosny were a peaceful inter-
lude before her romantic attempt to restore her dynasty in
1832–3. The duchess also altered the front of the château,
filling in the ditch and adding an ill-conceived conservatory
on the ground floor. All the same, the surviving main block is
a charming example of the 'style Sully', constructed like the
great contemporary buildings of Paris in brick with stone facings
to the windows and wall-corners.

It was in his houses to the south of Paris that Sully spent
more and more time in his later years. At Villebon, near
Chartres, he modified the towers of the existing château, so that
it came to look rather like the Bastille at Paris, and he also
built several terraces and a canal there. His life at Villebon is
described in the eighteenth-century edition of his memoirs,
following the description of an eye-witness;[2] getting up early as
was always his habit, Sully would say his prayers and then
spend the morning at work, probably composing the *Économies
Royales*. Sometimes he would decide to go for a walk before his
dinner, and then, after a great bell had been tolled, most of the
household would form up outside his room to line the way
to the garden. Returning to the house he would make his
way to his dining-room, where he and the duchess sat in
chairs at opposite ends of a very long table, with his family
on stools or folding chairs along the side. After the meal Sully
would spend the afternoon much as he had done the morning, working in his study and taking a ceremonious walk.
So the years of retirement passed, until his death at Ville-

---

[1] His supper was a catastrophe, as a great flood swept through the
kitchens and for a time endangered the royal party; see Thomas, *Rosny-
sur-Seine*, 218–19, and Barbiche (ed.) *Correspondance du nonce*, 537.

[2] *Mémoires de Sully*, iii, 413–17.

bon in December 1641; the property survives much as he left it.[1]

On the Loire he owned the estate of Sully, bought in 1602 from Claude de La Trimouille. The chateau there was in sad disrepair, and he put it to rights with his usual thoroughness, adding a great low tower from which artillery could play on the approaches to the building.[2] In the grounds he built a canal in 1607, and a great dyke after the floods of 1608, and constantly saw to the improvement and extension of the gardens, set out in the formal French manner.[3] His relations with the local canons of Saint-Ythier were excellent; he rebuilt their church for them and even appointed one of them, the canon Le Ber, his agent when he was away. The whole town of Sully-sur-Loire came under his care, so that in 1626, for instance, we find him giving instructions from Villebon about the measures to be taken in the town now that the epidemic of plague seems to have passed.[4]

The bulk of his property in 1610 lay to the south of Sully, in Berry. Here lay his estates of Baugy, Boisbelle-Henrichemont, La Chapelle-d'Angillon, Orval and Saint-Amand-Montrond (all in the *département du Cher*). Of his work at Baugy, La Chapelle-d'Angillon and Montrond little remains; the first was a fortress, the second a *Lust-Schloss* and the third a fortified residence. At Henrichemont he began in 1609 to construct a model town, laid out in a geometrical pattern rather like the plans to be found in the works of Errard.[5] It has recently been shown to have been designed by Salomon de Brosse; from a large central square there were to radiate diagonal streets to each corner of the enclosed rectangle, and streets

---

[1] See the photograph in Martin, *Sully-le-Grand*, facing p. 392.
[2] See the contract quoted by Martin, *Sully-le-Grand*, 344, note 1.
[3] See the contracts and the illustration in Louis Martin's *Histoire de la ville de Sully-sur-Loire en Orléanais* (Sully-sur-Loire, 1962), 35–6; and also E. de Barthélemy, 'Une page des comptes de Sully', *Bulletin du Bibliophile* (1865), 85–8.
[4] Louis Martin, *Histoire de la ville de Sully-sur-Loire*, 40.
[5] For what follows, see the article of Catherine Gauchéry-Grodecki, 'L'architecture en Berry sous le règne de Henri IV et au début du XVIIe siècle (1590–1620)', *Mémoires de l'union des sociétés savantes de Bourges*, iii (1951–2), 77–131.

at right angles to the main square serving four smaller squares:

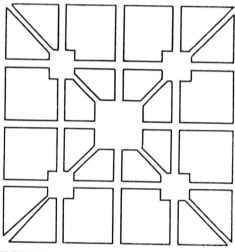

FIGURE 7   PLAN OF HENRICHEMONT

The project was interrupted by the death of the king and never completed in its original form, but the architect was able in 1612 to conduct a survey of what had been done which is of interest to us as showing the names of the owners of the uniform houses.[1] Sully's artillery *lieutenants,* the sieurs de La Vallée, Hillaire, Payon and Châteauvieux, occupy a prominent place, and many of the other tenants were concerned with the artillery or the finances. The estate was independent of the French crown; Sully was proud of this and insisted on his rights as a sovereign including, for instance, the exemption of his 'subjects' from the *taille* levied by the *bureau des finances* at Bourges.[2] There has been a difference of opinion over his motives for founding the town, whose primitive plan may still be distinguished among the houses which now threaten to obliterate it.[3] Some have claimed that it was designed as a refuge for Sully and his Protestant friends, but in fact it was probably built from *snobisme,* rather

[1] BM add. mss. 25593, fo. 11–16.
[2] AD Cher C 980, fo. 71–82.
[3] See the aerial photograph in Martin, *Sully-le-Grand,* 392–3.

as the town constructed by Richelieu would be.[1] For its defences could never have been very effective – there is for instance no bastioned trace on its perimeter – and Sully lost interest in it after 1610, just when as a refuge it would have been most useful to him. In all his work on his estates Sully was greatly helped by his wife Rachel, who had administered them almost alone during his years of power and who during his retirement continued to help him. Her portrait suggests a woman of parts, not afraid to sign a contract for the digging of a canal, or to check the accounts of one of Sully's abbeys.[2] When her husband died in December 1641 she commissioned a funerary statue of him from Barthélemy Boudin, son of the celebrated sculptor Thomas Boudin; this now stands in the chapel of the hospital of Nogent-le-Rotrou. Rachel followed her husband to the grave in 1659, and was buried with him at Nogent-le-Rotrou.[3]

Sully's death in 1641 passed unnoticed; the country was engaged in a life-and-death struggle with Spain, and the old minister had in any case done nothing to establish himself as a grand old man. When he came to Paris and wandered under the arcades of the Place Royale, dressed in an outmoded style and fingering the portrait of Henri IV which dangled from his neck, he was an object of pity and even ridicule rather than of respect. The historians agreed that he had been a hard and effective worker; even Marbault allowed that 'he was extremely hard-working and ran his offices very efficiently'.[4] Beyond that, however, they did not go, either because like Péréfixe, tutor of Louis XIV, they were chiefly concerned to glorify Henri IV, or, in the later years of the century, because it was becoming impolitic to mention the rather rustic origins of Bourbon splendour. Towards 1700 a new spirit is perceptible in the way writers looked at the reign of Henri IV, as the reaction against 'classical' philosophy and 'mercantilist' statesmanship aroused

[1] This is the argument of Gauchéry-Grodecki, op. cit., 89–90.
[2] See plate 14, and Philippe Des Forts, *Le château de Villebon* (Paris, 1914), 75–84.
[3] See Louis Martin, *Le tombeau de Sully au château de Sully-sur-Loire* (Sully-sur-Loire, 1935).
[4] *Remarques sur les mémoires de Sully*, 84. For what follows, see also my more detailed article, 'The legend of Sully', *The Historical Journal*, v (1962), 181–8.

a new enthusiasm for the land and those who work on it. When in 1707 Boisguillebert wanted to argue in favour of the free export of grain – and for the encouragement of agricultural production – he claimed that 'all Sully's efforts were concentrated on encouraging the export of grain, which we today nearly always try to stop'.[1] We have already noticed how inaccurate this notion is; equally false was the complementary idea that for Sully the earth was the prime and only essential source of wealth. This was developed by François Quesnay in his article on 'grains' in the *Encyclopédie* (1756–7), where he maintains that Sully 'wished, in order to ensure wealth for the king and the nation, to enlist the services only of ploughmen, vineyard-workers and shepherds'.[2] Similarly when Thomas won the *prix d'éloquence* of the Académie Française for 1763 by his *Éloge de Sully,* he claimed in the course of it that 'Athens and Rome made use of soldiers and men of learning; Sully, to bring prosperity to France, had need only of ploughmen and shepherds'.[3] Again, twenty years later we have the abbé Baudeau making Sully say

> I know that our land is the source of wealth, of population and of the state's strength, provided that it is well cultivated . . . I understand nothing of other things . . . these are merchants' business and no concern of mine.[4]

This distortion could be illustrated from many other eighteenth-century writers, were it not tedious to insist on the point.

Another aspect of the developing legend emerges from the idea that Sully had no concern with the affairs of soldiers, merchants and men of learning; this notion, false enough as we have constantly seen throughout this book, was developed into the theory that he was in fact merely an ignorant but honest gentleman who, like some noble savage of the administration, despised the tricks of the financial technicians, using his ancestral common sense to bring order to the administration.

[1] *Le détail de la France sous le règne present* (Paris, 1707).
[2] *Collection des principaux économistes,* ed. Eugène Daire (2 vols, Paris, 1843–6), ii, 264.
[3] *Éloge de Sully,* 39.
[4] *Principes économiques de Louis XIII et du cardinal d'Amboise* (Paris, 1785), 3.

Boisguillebert developed this idea[1] and so did the abbé Baudeau, making Sully say that

> the excessively simple principles followed by a sound gentleman in running his estates are those which should regulate the finances of a realm ... as for the details about which you make so much fuss, *foi de gentilhomme* I know nothing about them.[2]

In reality, though Sully had spent many years fighting in his king's battles, he had also sat in the royal councils, where financial questions were often discussed, and had thus acquired considerable knowledge of them. Moreover, once he came to power he showed as we have seen much zeal for collecting 'minces détails', or rather precise statistical data, and it is not easy to see how the principles of a 'bon gentilhomme père de famille' helped him in such essentially unfamilial operations as his monetary reorganization of 1609. The idea of Sully's happy ignorance is linked with another notion, that he was hostile to any intervention in the 'natural' course of trade. Or as Baudeau put it, 'Sully's plan was simple and uniform, like nature', demanding as little restriction of commerce as possible. We have seen how false this view is.

Finally the eighteenth century writers distorted Sully's role during the reign of Henri IV by falsifying his relationship with the king. In his prize-work Thomas as usual carried the falsification to its most extreme form; 'I shall add only one word', he says, 'which is that the very idea of Sully was for Henri IV what the thought of the Supreme Being is for the just man – a hindrance on his will to evil, and an encouragement to do good.'[3] In the end this distortion led to the idea that the king was a brave bungler who relied on Sully for all serious affairs; as d'Argenson wrote, 'it is clear that Henri IV was a good fellow and a brave soldier who made a mess of everything that he tried to do, but who had a good heart and could always fall back on his Sully'.[4] This idea that Sully was in some sense a

---

[1] *Le détail de la France*, 172–3.
[2] *Principes économiques*, 4–5.
[3] *Éloge de Sully*, 53.
[4] Quoted by L. Pingaud, 'Henri IV et Louis XIV', *Revue des Questions Historiques*, xlvi (1889), 183.

father-figure for the king is amusingly illustrated by eighteenth-century engravings of them both, which nearly always show Henri IV looking younger than the staid and elderly Sully – although in fact the king was six years older.

From the middle of the century onwards, ministers were regularly hailed as the new Sully, come to support the reincarnate king. As Lebrun put it,

> Worthy blood of Henri, how could I fail to recognize you? What am I saying? He lives on, and Sully will live again.[1]

L'Averdy (1736), Turgot (1774), Maurepas (1775) and Necker (1788) were all greeted in similar terms. But the enthusiasm waned, once it was clear that none was a new Sully – and that Louis XVI could never be a Henri IV. The Revolution, which saw the desecration of Sully's remains, saw also the decline of his reputation. Napoleon saw no reason to revive his legend, but with the Restoration Sully once again became the symbol of a certain type of minister of the *ancien régime*. Once again arguments which might be considered relevant to contemporary questions were extracted from his memoirs; most of these made great use of the pastoral distortion, which in our century has made Sully a figurehead for various Right-wing political groups. In fact he cannot be neatly encased in any of the categories provided for him by propagandists; his real action and his real attitudes were much more complex – and much more interesting.

[1] Pingaud, op. cit. 184.

14. Rachel de Cochefilet, second wife of Sully; the caption 'Anne de Courtenay' is incorrect (*Anon., BN Estampes*).

15. Sully with a classical background (*Anon., B.N Estampes*).

CHAPTER XI

Conclusion

Sully's work on the financial structure has some original features. Under his guidance a budgetary surplus was achieved which would be rare in the history of the French state, and which had few rivals in contemporary Europe. Progress was also made in subjecting provincial bodies of all kinds to the orders of Paris. But it is the establishment of his secretariat which is the most novel part of Sully's financial work; nothing like it had existed before. As in the case of his proposed councils, Sully may have got the idea from the Spain of Philip II, who constantly demanded statistical information and based his policy on its indications.[1] In France the first general surveys of population date from the 1630s, but the figures at the disposal of Sully represent a distinct advance on the figures of earlier authorities, which are generally far too high. Thus the traditional estimate of the number of parishes was 1,700,000; this was the figure accepted by the estates-general of 1593, but Sully reduced it to about 40,000, much nearer the correct figure.[2] We have noticed that he also extracted precise figures from artillery *lieutenants* and customs officials.

The significance of this increased accuracy becomes clear when we reflect on the part played in the development of modern government – and of modern civilization as a whole – by the growth of the habit of quantitive analysis.[3] By the turn

[1] For this paragraph, see *La Statistique (exposés et discussions)*, published by Presses Universitaires de France (Paris, 1944).

[2] A. Moreau de Jonnès, *État économique et sociale de la France, 1598–1715* (Paris, 1867), 17.

[3] On this, see particularly J. U. Nef, *Cultural foundations of industrial civilization* (Cambridge, 1958).

N

of the sixteenth century, mathematics figure prominently in a
nobleman's education; this was one of the subjects to be taught
at the 'académie pour la jeunesse noble' which Henri IV
planned to establish at Tours,[1] and Sully himself gave much
attention to this discipline, which certainly left its mark on his
methods. It is not easy to see how, in the light particularly of
his use of statistics, it is possible to claim that his working-
method was 'empirique et surannée', or that he was 'un homme
du passé'.[2]

All Sully's personal papers bear the imprint of a mind loving
order and uniformity. He kept up a book in which all regulations
concerning his various charges were inserted as they came into
force, and personally annotated this volume.[3] Twice yearly[4] he
made an inventory of all his papers, no doubt using numbers and
symbols keyed to a main list, as he did when preparing the
budget. His sense of order was also shown in his handling of
provincial officials, who took action only in accordance with
his instructions, conforming to the uniform *règlements* with which
they were all provided. In this respect Sully must be seen in
the great line of bureaucrats who enabled Colbert to carry the
policy of official supervision to its logical extreme. Whether this
type of government was advantageous or desirable is of course
another question.[5]

The officials of the *ponts et chaussées* and of the artillery were
among the foremost engineers of their age, and applied the
latest scientific principles to their work. Sully could deal with
them on equal terms, for he could not only direct the artillery
in person at sieges in difficult country, but was also capable of
setting out the ditches for a water-catchment scheme, of

[1] Valois, nᵒ 439; the academy was to teach young nobles to 'ride on
horseback, handle arms, dance, do gymnastics, read mathematics and
perform other virtuous and seemly exercises'.
[2] Quotations from G. Hanotaux, *Études historiques sur le XVIᵉ et le XVIIᵉ
siècle en France* (Paris, 1886), 154, and G. Hanotaux (ed.), *Un bon Français:
Sully*, 49.
[3] AN 120 AP 1; this is a magnificent volume, adorned with Sully's arms.
The working copy also survives; BN ms. fr. 10842.
[4] *Économies Royales*, i, 373a, or annually, i, 299a.
[5] The case against it is brilliantly set out in Bertrand de Jouvenel's
On power, its nature and the history of its growth (London, 1948).

inspecting a recently-completed building for its soundness, and of assessing the potentiality of inventions. Another aspect of his technical, statistical bent is the enthusiasm with which he commissioned maps of the whole realm, at a time when the estates of Languedoc, for example, had no map of their region and did not want one.[1] In short, Sully was abreast of the latest developments in the science of war and government, and it is totally mistaken to regard him as a kind of latter-day republican Roman, content to maintain the state by encouraging the simply bucolic values, and averse to any technical changes which might adulterate this primitive virtue.[2]

Nor is the image correct which sees him as indifferent to literature and art. Christian Pfister described his pride in his various literary works,[3] at a time when the fragment of his scabrous novel had not yet been discovered.[4] He also seems to have copied out in his own hand many of the poems of Malherbe and other contemporaries; as the author of the catalogue listing these works remarks, 'some of these poems are very loose in their moral tone, but that does not seem to have worried the great minister'.[5] One of his liveliest pleasures was the commissioning each year of a medallion commemorating the king's feats of the previous year. He put up 300 *livres* as the prize in a competition for the best design, which was usually won by the king's interpreter Robert III Estienne.[6] The medallions, along with small pouches of current money, were distributed among the royal household on New Year's Day. The *Économies Royales* has an amusing dialogue between the king and Sully on the occasion of one of these presentations to the maids of honour. 'What,' says the king to Sully, 'will you give them their New Year's presents without making them give you a kiss in return?' Sully answers that he has no need to ask them to kiss him, but the king persists in his joke; 'truly now, Rosny', he says, 'which

[1] AN H 748/20. fo. 42v°.
[2] For this view, see particularly Charles Turgeon, 'Les idées économiques de Sully', *Revue d'histoire économique et sociale*, xi (1923), 249–69.
[3] 'Les *Économies Royales* de Sully', *Revue Historique*, liv (1894), 301–3.
[4] And published by P. de La Raudière; *Les Estranges Amours de la Reine Myrrha* (Paris, 1930).
[5] Catalogue of the Musée Condé, Chantilly, Ms. 534.
[6] See Marbault, *Remarques sur les mémoires de Sully*, 55–6.

of them would it give you most pleasure to kiss – which do you find most beautiful?' Sully's answer is a good example of his sardonic humour; playing on the king's Catholicism, he replies, 'I cannot tell you, sire. For I have no time to think of love, and I imagine that they think as little about my feelings as I about theirs. For my part I should kiss them as though they were relics to which I was making an offering.'

In his houses Sully was personally responsible for many alterations and improvements; there survives for instance an autograph 'devis pour la peinture des singes' which he drew up.[1] This was to have shown three scenes in which the actors were monkeys; the first was a market-place, the second a law-court and the third a wedding with a dance going on. It is unlikely that the project was in fact carried out. As *surintendant des bâtiments* Sully was responsible for the decoration of the Louvre, and we have noticed that he also commissioned Bunel to execute a work at the Paris arsenal. His extensive use of military engineers for civil architecture probably accounts for the development of the 'style sévère', and it is even possible that, having used a distinctive blend of brick and stone for his house at Rosny, he was responsible for the fact that most of the great buildings of Paris were later constructed in this fashion, the so-called 'style Sully'.

Another aspect of Sully's activity which has usually been neglected is his role as a strategist in the councils of Henry IV. We have noticed in chapter VIII that he was much concerned to build up the Mediterranean fleet; his grasp of Atlantic strategy is shown not only by his investigations for ports on the west coast of France, but also by his advice to Jeannin in 1608. ['I have always considered,'] he says, 'that we ought to attack Spain in her heart and belly, that is to say at this time in the East and West Indies which, as they have been the main cause of her greatness, may also become the chief agent of her downfall.'[2] Here speaks the authentic Sully, the implacable enemy of Spain. There is nothing in his writings or action before 1611 to

[1] AD Caen, acquisition Prévost 1905, fo. 82; for his work at Villebon, see the work of Philippe Des Forts.

[2] *Négociations du président Jeannin*, 281; letter to Jeannin, Paris, 26 February 1608.

suggest that either he or the king was concerned with the so-called Grand Design for setting up in Europe fifteen roughly equal states, balancing each other off and so giving peace to the continent.[1] What they were interested in was penning the Spaniards into their peninsula and extending the power of France. The Grand Design owes most of its fame to the eighteenth century edition of the memoirs, where what had been a self-contradictory mass of different schemes was welded into a relatively neat whole by the abbé de l'Écluse des Loges, and caught the attention of Europe at a time when Sully was popular for other equally misconceived reasons. Many schemes for a new political organization in Europe were in the air on the eve of the Thirty Years' War; his ideas on this were neither coherent nor original. More interesting, and more revealing about his political standpoint, is his use of the word *patrie*. This Latinism was only slowly winning acceptance in French during the sixteenth century,[2] but Sully repeatedly uses it in contexts like 'voyant perdre à ma patrie son bon roy',[3] or 'loyal et fidel à vostre Roy vostre maistre, et à vostre patrie'.[4] Intensely loyal as he was to Henri IV, Sully was all the same beginning to visualize France as a political entity independent of the monarchy; she was becoming a 'fatherland' as well as a realm.

Spain was of course for Sully the religious as well as the political enemy. His religious position was often criticized by contemporaries, who accused him of insincerity and maintained that the king's attempts to convert him to Catholicism were part of a 'jargon' or 'comedie' which the two were playing out.[5] Certainly he always maintained good relations with high

[1] Much has been written about the Grand Design; Pfister gives a good analysis of its development in Sully's writings ('Les *Économies Royales* de Sully', *Revue Historique*, lvi (1894) 304–39), and Hinsley explores its later implications in *Power and the pursuit of peace* (Cambridge, 1963).

[2] See R. R. Palmer, 'The national idea in France before the revolution', *Journal of the history of ideas*, i (1940), 95–111, and Sainte-Beuve, *Vues sur l'histoire de France* (*Cahiers de l'unité française*, Paris, 1946), 30–1, 'Sully et l'idée de la patrie'.

[3] BN nouv. acq. franç., 1095, fo. 37, letter of 30 May 1610 from Paris to the *trésoriers de France* at Caen.

[4] *Économies Royales*, ii, 409b.

[5] See my article written in collaboration with Bernard Barbiche, 'Les convictions religieuses de Sully', *Bibliothèque de l'École des Chartes*, cxxi (1963), 223–30, for what follows.

Catholic personalities, and particularly with cardinal Du Perron, bishop of Évreux. He was also on amicable terms with the papal nuncios, Innocenzo Del Bufalo and Maffeo Barberini who succeeded him; after they had returned to Rome he continued to correspond with these prelates. But it would not be correct to suppose that the efforts of these friends to convert Sully were not sincere. The king himself often took Sully with him to hear celebrated Catholic preachers like the père Cotton or the père Fenouillet,[1] and Du Perron made a protracted attempt to bring him into his church. Thus he wrote to Sully on the occasion of the latter's appointment in 1599 as *grand maître de l'artillerie* that 'the joy which I have in seeing you command the cannons of France will be consummated when I see you obey the canons of the church'; he returned to the attack in 1604 and again in 1605. In the latter year Du Perron went so far as to obtain a letter from the new pope, Paul V, reminding Sully of the faith of his illustrious ancestors and pressing him to return to it. Sully, pleased to be able to demonstrate his literary talents, replied with a long autograph letter which greatly pleased the pope, even though it contained a courteous refusal. Again in 1607 the pope sent Sully a letter urging his conversion; this was timed to coincide with more material offers from the king, who promised Sully his appointment as *connétable de France* and the hand of his illegitimate daughter Mlle de Vendôme for his son Maximilien II, if both father and son would come over to Catholicism. This time the general opinion was that Sully would give way, and the English ambassador wrote on 4 November that he was about to be converted by the offer of the *connétablie* and 'the stringes of a cardinal's hatt' [Du Perron's]. Once again Sully stood firm; he wrote another long autograph letter to the pope setting out his position, and replied to the king that while his son might choose his own faith for his part he would never abjure.

It is hard to believe with some writers that Sully's firmness in this matter was due to his desire to supplant Duplessis-Mornay at the head of the Protestants. In fact by 1607 'les conversions étoient à la mode'; it was clear that on political

[1] See for instance, Desjardins (ed.), *Négociations diplomatiques*, v, 410.

grounds Sully would have done better to accept the king's offer. His reasons for refusal were theological ones, which he explained in an interview of 1608 with Du Perron; he could never accept the Catholic doctrines of transubstantiation, communion in one kind and the supposed cult of images. He was ready, moreover, to support his theological standpoint; he had read Calvin's *Institution de la religion chrétienne* with great care, and was in general well briefed for controversy. As Sir George Carew remarked,

> de Sully is not void of learning, both of knowledge of Latin, and other studies of humanity; but chiefly in arguing points of religion, whereof he is very ready and confident.

And so he was often found in controversy with leading Catholic theologians; in 1600, for example, it was with André Duval of the Sorbonne that he had a discussion over dinner at the Celestine abbey outside the Arsenal's gates, and in 1608 he was deep in controversy with Fenouillet.

These firm personal convictions went along with great objectivity and a readiness to concede that the other side had made some good points. Thus after the famous debate at Fontainebleau in May 1600, when Duplessis-Mornay was convincingly controverted by Du Perron, Sully conceded that the Protestant champion had committed several mistakes. Again, in 1605 he reported to the king after a certain Catholic sermon that he had never heard a preacher 'set out his argument better, or argue more clearly and intelligibly'. His absence of fanaticism also emerges from the way in which he agreed to take up the case of the English Catholics when he visited James I in 1603; he had assured Del Bufalo before he left that he would do this, and the promise was not in vain. We have noticed above how he enjoyed excellent relations with the canons of Saint-Ythier at Sully; at Poitiers in 1604 he went so far as to overcome the opposition of the *trésoriers de France* there to the establishment of a Jesuit college in the town.[1] In short, while he held to his own reasoned opinions with great firmness, he was

[1] See the article of Bélisaire Ledain, 'Les maires de Poitiers', *Mémoires de la société des antiquaires de l'Ouest,* xx (1897), 215–774.

always ready to maintain a dialogue with those of a contrary persuasion – who remained his friends.

It is easier to chart out Sully's religious opinions than it is to give an idea of his general moral position. As we have seen above, he cannot be accused of financial peculation; Motley put it well when he remarked that Sully 'filled his own coffers without dishonesty'.[1] By some standards it was rather blatant for him to press for a French campaign in Flanders largely to further a private interest, and as *grand voyer* he spent an excessive amount on the roads and bridges near his own and his relatives' houses. But these were peccadilloes; what are both more serious and more mysterious are the accusations levelled against his private conduct. Marbault, always his most severe critic but often an accurate one, describes how each evening at the Arsenal Sully would put on a 'bonnet extravagant' and dance by himself to the music of a lute, with two cronies and several women of ill-repute as spectators.[2] Similarly Jean Héroard, physician to the young *dauphin,* the future Louis XIII, relates that each evening at the Arsenal after supper Sully would amuse himself by listening to the 'mauvais contes' told by one of these cronies, La Clavelle, and others.[3] These references could be multiplied; Sir George Carew, for example, found Sully's private life as blameworthy as the king's.[4] We have also noticed the curious novel which he composed; it is clear that there is an element in the nature of Sully which does not chime with the usual image of him as the grave and austere Huguenot, though it is not easy to seize on this aspect of his character.

When we come to consider the life and work of Sully in its seventeenth-century context, he seems much more similar to Richelieu both in his origins and in his aims than is normally allowed. Like Richelieu, Sully was a member of the *noblesse d'épée* who owed his fame to the war; just as Richelieu came

---

[1] Motley, *The life and death of John of Barneveld,* i, 151.

[2] *Remarques sur les mémoires de Sully,* 36a.

[3] *Journal de Jean Héroard,* ed. E. Soulié and E. de Barthélemy (2 vols, Paris, 1868), i, 416. Sully also acted as master of ceremonies when ballets were danced at the Arsenal; it is possible that plate 15 shows him dressed for this.

[4] *Relation of the state of France,* 472.

into his own after the fateful decision of 1630, so Sully first
demonstrated his gifts as a money-raiser during a foreign
emergency, and remained indispensable because of his role in
time of war. The two men thought alike on the great political
issue of the day, the place of the old nobility in the emergent
centralized state,[1] and used the same means – recruitment into
the royal service on the one hand, and destruction of unauthorized strongholds on the other – to accomplish their ends.
Richelieu's concept of the monarchy was scarcely more
absolutist than Sully's, and, as Henri Hauser has shown,[2]
the minister of Louis XIII was by no means concerned only
with the grand political projects of conventional historiography.
He set on foot a great campaign for mineral-prospecting in France,
just as Sully and Henri IV had done, showed a keen interest in
the communications (completing the Briare canal in 1638),
and encouraged numerous manufactures. Like Sully, he was
much concerned to build up the galley-fleet, for the sake of
French influence in the Mediterranean, and with increased
resources was able to begin building up the Atlantic fleet as
well. Both men gave much attention to the army as well as to
the navy. In short, if it is false to see Richelieu as preoccupied
with political affairs, so it is equally mistaken to see in Sully a
narrow financial minister, for he was in all these ways the
precursor of Richelieu.

There is a sense in which Sully's career was highly paradoxical.
As a noble, he contributed greatly to the subjection of his class
by the renascent absolutism of Henri IV; as a Protestant, he
co-operated in the building-up of a church which was to
persecute Huguenots mercilessly. The unifying element in his
life was his patriotism, his devotion to the France which was
emerging as a 'modern' state. His part in this development is
most obvious in the history of the great administrative institutions on which the achievements of the 'splendid century'
would rest; it was he who restored the finances, he who set up
a directorate for the communications, the artillery and the

---

[1] See V. L. Tapié, *La France de Louis XIII et de Richelieu* (Paris, 1952),
210, for a succinct account of Richelieu's attitude to the nobles.
[2] *La pensée et l'action économiques du cardinal de Richelieu* (Paris, 1944).

fortifications with in each case a strongly-centralized provincial structure, and he who decisively influenced the growth of Paris as a great capital city.

But his part is also reflected in a score of lesser details, symptoms of the developing power of the French state. Political hegemony within an area leads to the need for a unified system of weights and measures; Sully had attempted to provide for this. It is reflected in the need to know the 'national' boundaries exactly; Sully was active in the delineation of France's frontier. Again, to take only one more example, it reflects itself in the need to have accurate figures of national resources in men and materials; this too was one of Sully's preoccupations. Henri IV, speaking of the *dauphin,* once remarked that the latter was 'the principal foundation of the state and that to him as the centre all the lines of power within the realm should lead'.[1] Sully, working at his king's side, did much to realize this ambition; truly he was a great servant of the French Leviathan.

[1] Arch. Aff. Étr., France, 767, fo. 120-7.

MAP 6 FRANCE, TO SHOW ALL PLACES MENTIONED IN
THE TEXT

APPENDICES

The Re-establishment of the Budgets

It is simple to show that the figures for income given by the newly-available *états au vrai* correspond with those of Mallet. In the *états au vrai* they are grouped under seven main headings:

1. *Recettes générales* (for the generalities described in chapter III)
2. *Ventes de bois* (sales of wood on royal domain)
3. *Parties casuelles* (income from offices)
4. *Gabelles*
5. *Fermes*
6. *Comptables extraordinaires* (various minor treasurers)
7. *Recettes extraordinaires* (miscellaneous fines, rebates, and so on)

Mallet sets the figures out in the same categories and so a direct comparison is possible; for example:

	1605	1606	1607
Ventes de bois:			
état au vrai	159,317	162,600	447,955, etc.
Mallet	160,117	162,600	447,955, etc.
Parties casuelles:			
état au vrai	2,489,169	1,918,067	1,842,628, etc.
Mallet	2,324,394	1,918,067	1,842,628, etc.

Clearly, Mallet's figures of income correspond well enough with those of the *états au vrai*. It is more difficult to check his figures for expenditure. In the *états au vrai* expenditure is listed under the following headings:

1. *Despence par rolles*
2. *Dons*
3. *Deniers en acquit*
4. *Deniers par ordonnance par acquit*
5. *Comptants és mains du roy*
6. *Comptants par certiffication du conseil*
7. *Gaiges, deniers rendeuz et non receuz, voyages,* etc.

Mallet, on the other hand, makes use of a more informative set of headings, those which the *état au vrai* would have had when it was eventually submitted to the *chambre des comptes*. This set of headings ran as follows:

1. *Offrandes et aumônes* (. . . household)
2. *Cent gentilshommes* (. . . guards)
3. *Ordinaire des guerres* (. . . guerres)
4. *Marine* (*de Ponant,* and *de Levant*)
5. *Deniers payés par ordonnance par rolles* . . .
6. *Dons par acquits patents*
7. *Deniers payés par ordonnance et acquit patent*
8. *Deniers comptants*

Headings 1–5 in this list comprise payments made *par rolles,* and so correspond to section 1 in the *état au vrai* list. The two sets of headings correspond as follows:

État au vrai	Mallet
1. *Despence par rolles*	1. *Offrandes et aumônes* . . . to
	5. *Deniers payés par ordonnance et par rolles*
	[the first twelve headings in table 4]
2. *Dons*	6. *Dons par acquits patents*
3 and 4. *Deniers en acquit* and *deniers par ordonnance par acquit*	7. *Deniers payés par ordonnance et acquit patent*
5 and 6. *Comptants és mains du roy* and *comptants par certiffication du conseil*	6. *Comptants par certiffication*

When we come to compare the two sets of figures, having set out the corresponding sections in this way, they are found to agree fairly closely. If we take the *despence par rolles* for 1608, for instance, we can by analysing the breakdown of the *état au vrai*[1] extract the following sums for *marine de Levant* and *artillerie*:

marine de Levant	artillerie
274,450	280,000
77,520	6,000
30,000	400
299	
382,269	286,400

This corresponds almost exactly with Mallet's figures (see table 4). If we compare the figures from the other corresponding headings the same result is obtained. For instance, the *dons* run as follows:

	1605	1606	1607	1608
État au vrai	1,339,770	1,539,032	995,260	1,206,181, etc.
Mallet	1,339,470	1,539,032	995,210	1,205,981, etc.

[1] Contained in AN 120 AP 6.

In each case Mallet's figures agree well enough with those of the *état au vrai* for us to accept them as accurate.

This conclusion is reinforced by the comparison of Mallet's figures with two other contemporary documents, the *état méthodique des comptes de l'épargne pour 1601*,[1] and the *comptes rendus par le trésorier Puget pour l'année 1610*.[2] These again coincide almost exactly, and are the final vindication of Mallet's figures.[3]

[1] BN ms. fr. 18489.
[2] BN ms. fr. 4518.
[3] In his 'État-Général des finances de France', *Revue Henri IV*, iii (1909–12), 210–15, Louis Batiffol tried to obtain a check on Mallet's figures. But the documents Batiffol used were not appropriate for this purpose.

The *lieutenants du grand voyer*

Generality	
Paris	François de Donon
	Laurent de Gaumont
	Henri Godefroy
	François Hotman
	oJacques Le Conte
	François Le Fèvre
	Simon Le Gras
	François Valée
Amiens	oNicolas Delan
Bourges	oFrançois Le Mareschal, s^r de Corbet
Bordeaux	— de Causse
	— de Geneste
	Jean de Martin
	oÉtienne de Pontac
	Pierre de Prugues
Caen	Thomas Morant
	Guillaume Novynce, s^r d'Aubigny
Châlons	Jean de Lon, s^r de Lorme
Limoges	Martial Benoist
Lyons	Jean Payon, s^r de La Brosse[1]
Moulins	Pierre Fougeu, s^r d'Escures[2]
Orleans	„ „ „ „
Poitiers	René Androuet Du Cerceau
	— de La Parisière
	oScévole de Sainte-Marthe
Rouen	— de La Barre
	Thomas Morant
Riom	o— Fauve
	— Gallois
	— Ribeyre
Soissons	Isaac Payon

Tours	Jean Le Blanc, s^r de La Vallière
	Galliot Mandat
	— Melloy
	— Parochel

....

| Brittany | — de La Vallée[1] |
| Languedoc | Miles Marion, s^r de Nevers |

---

[0] Represented the treasurers at Rouen in 1596.
[1] Also *lieutenant du grand maître de l'artillerie.*
[2] Also *intendant des turcies et levées sur les rivières de Loire et Cher.*

The list is compiled from AN 120 AP 38-42, supplemented by reference to BN ms. fr. 10884, fo. 1–10 for the treasurers at the Rouen Assembly, and by the *arrêts* concerning *voirie* matters in Valois.

APPENDIX 3

The *lieutenants du grand maître de l'artillerie*

Arsenal	
Paris (Ile-de-France)	Robert Tiercelin, s[r] de La Chevalerie
Aix (Provence)[1]	Georges Dupuy, s[r] de Servien
	Claude Durant
Amiens (Picardie)	Siphorien de Lezines, s[r] de Mortefontaine
Bordeaux (Guyenne)	Jean de Mesmes, s[r] de Paiemen
	Abraham de Vienne
Bourg (Bresse)	Bernard de Vienne
Dijon (Burgundy)	Pierre Bourdin, s[r] de Montmansois
Grenoble (Dauphiné)	André Perrinel, s[r] de Châteauvieux
Lyon (Lyonnais)	Jean Payon, s[r] de La Brosse
Metz (Messin)	Charles Hillaire
	— de Feugère
Nantes (Brittany)	— de Maignan[2]
	— de La Vallée
Narbonne (Languedoc)	Pierre Duparc, s[r] de La Salle
Niort (Poitou)	François de Chansson
Orleans (Orléannais)	Mathias Tricquoys, s[r] de La Caillaudière
Rouen (Normandy)	Charles de Goustemesnil, s[r] de Boisrozé[3]
Tours (Touraine)	Michel Moussart, s[r] de Montmartin
Troyes and Châlons	
(Champagne)	Nicolas Corberon
	Richard Petrenol, s[r] de Viaspré

---

[1] Transferred from Marseilles about 1605.
[2] This is the 'fidèle Maignan' of legend; *Économies Royales*, i, 223.
[3] See the anecdote about Boisrozé, *Économies Royales*, i, 145.

The list is compiled from BN ms. fr. 24840 and BN ms. fr. 16692, fo. 50–7. There were not many changes in personnel between 1600 and 1611, but where these did take place the second of the names is the successor.

List of sources

A. GUIDES TO MANUSCRIPTS

C. V. Langlois and H. Stein, *Les archives de l'histoire de France* (2 vols, Paris, 1891–2)
[concerns material found in manuscript sources of all kinds].

État sommaire par séries des documents conservés aux Archives Nationales (Paris, 1891)
[a general guide to the more detailed inventories found for each letter; still satisfactory except for series 'F'].

État général par fonds des Archives Départementales (ancien régime et période révolutionnaire) (Paris, 1903)
[a general guide to the more detailed lists found under the headings of the *départements*].

État des inventaires des Archives Nationales, Départementales, Communales et Hospitalières (Paris, 1937, to be completed by the *supplément*, 1937–54, Paris, 1955)
[these are lists of the inventories available].

L. Delisle, *Le cabinet des manuscrits de la Bibliothèque Impériale* [= BN] (3 vols, Paris, 1868–81)
[gives the provenance of BN manuscripts; see also the detailed catalogues for each *fonds*].

Catalogue général des manuscrits des Bibliothèques Publiques de France
(i) Paris [special series for each of the great libraries; e.g. Archives de la Guerre, 3 vols, Paris, 1912–20];
(ii) the provinces [about 50 volumes; Paris, 1886–1954].

Répertoire des sources manuscrites de l'histoire de Paris, ed. M. Poète (3 vols, Paris, 1915–16).
'La documentation historique militaire en France', *Revue de Défense Nationale* (numéro hors série, décembre 1952).

B. MANUSCRIPTS

1. *Bibliothèque Nationale, Paris*

Cabinet d'Hozier 89, a document from the genealogical collection acquired by the Crown in 1717 from Charles d'Hozier.

Manuscrits français 592, an artillery manual by Benedit de Vassallieu (de Mesmes, acquired by the royal library in 1731).

Manuscrits français 663, a *traité de fortifications* by Jean Errard (old royal library).

Manuscrits français 2408, a collection of financial papers of the early seventeenth century (old royal library).

Manuscrits français 3447, a collection of original documents and copies concerning the reign of Henri IV (old royal library).

Manuscrits français 3548, a collection of original letters and copies, 1590–9 (old royal library).

Manuscrits français 3795, a collection of original letters and copies, 1610–22 (old royal library).

Manuscrits français 3982, a collection of original documents and copies concerning the year 1592 (de Mesmes, acquired by the royal library in 1731).

Manuscrits français 4014, a collection of copies of documents concerning the period 1483–1615 (de Mesmes).

Manuscrits français 4518, the balance-sheet for 1610 of Étienne Puget, *trésorier de l'épargne.*

Manuscrits français 4559, a collection of *rôles de comptants* for the years 1599–1610.

Manuscrits français 4561, various original documents concerning the artillery, 1600–33 (Le Tellier-Louvois, acquired by the royal library in 1718).

Manuscrits français 4680, a collection of original documents and copies concerning military history, 1562–1624.

Manuscrits français 4740, the first of ten volumes concerning French relations with Spain and Italy during the sixteenth and seventeenth centuries (de Mesmes).

Manuscrits français 4827, copies of documents concerning the reign of Henri IV (Baluze, acquired by the royal library in 1719).

Manuscrits français 5319, copy of the register of the *trésoriers de France* at Poitiers for 1599.

Manuscrits français 6604–21, collection of original letters of the sixteenth and seventeenth centuries.

Manuscrits français 10305–14, manuscript memoirs of Sully.

Manuscrits français 10842, extracts from the registers of the *conseil d'État*, 1598–1610 (Petits-Pères, acquired by the BN at the time of the Revolution).

Manuscrits français 10884, journal of the assembly of Notables, Rouen, 1596–7 (Lancelot, acquired by the royal library about 1732).

Manuscrits français 11165, collection of financial documents, 1575–1613.

Manuscrits français 14727, manual of an engineer-architect, first half of the seventeenth century.

Manuscrits français 15540–84, collection of original letters and other documents concerning French history, 1477–1657.

Manuscrits français 15890–911, papers and correspondence of Pomponne de Bellièvre (Harlay, Saint-Germain, acquired by the BN at the time of the Revolution).

Manuscrits français 15987–9, original dispatches addressed to the French court, mostly from England (Harlay, Saint-Germain).

Manuscrits français 16626, collection of documents concerning the French finances, 1570–1616 (Harlay, Saint-Germain).

Manuscrits français 16649–58, collection of documents, mostly drawn from the *trésor des chartes*, concerning the French provinces (Harlay, Saint-Germain).

Manuscrits français 16690–5, collection of documents of the sixteenth and seventeenth centuries concerning the artillery (Harlay, Saint-Germain).

Manuscrits français 16697–729, registers of the *trésoriers-généraux de l'extraordinaire des guerres*, 1599–1623 (Séguier-Coislin, Saint Germain, acquired by the BN at the time of the Revolution).

Manuscrits français 16738–40, collection of documents concerning trade and communications in the early seventeenth century (Harlay, Saint-Germain).

Manuscrits français 16809, *procès-verbal* concerning the *comté* of Auvergne, etc. (Séguier-Coislin, Saint-Germain).

Manuscrits français 16910, collection of documents concerning the Comtat-Venaissin and Orange, thirteenth to seventeenth centuries (Séguier-Coislin, Saint-Germain).

Manuscrits français 17291, varied collection of documents, thirteenth to seventeenth centuries (Séguier-Coislin, Saint-Germain).

Manuscrits français 17919, collection of diplomatic documents, 1596–1620, formerly belonging to Villeroy (Harlay, Saint-Germain).

Manuscrits français 18159, copies of the *arrêts du conseil d'État* for 1594 (Séguier-Coislin, Saint-Germain).

Manuscrits français 18489, income and expenditure of the *épargne* for 1601 (Séguier-Coislin, Saint-Germain).

Manuscrits français 18510, collection of documents concerning the finances, 1554–1654 (Séguier-Coislin, Saint-Germain).

Manuscrits français 20007, various documents concerning the artillery and general French history of the early seventeenth century (Séguier-Coislin, Saint-Germain).

Manuscrits français 20051, letters of Nevers, Condé, etc. (Séguier-Coislin, Saint-Germain).

Manuscrits français 21545–808, collection of N. Delamare on the administration of Paris and of France (acquired by the royal library in 1788).

Manuscrits français 22314–15, registers of the *greffe* of the estates of Brittany (Blancs-Manteaux, acquired by the BN at the time of the Revolution).

Manuscrits français 23026, copies of documents concerning the reign of Henri IV (Saint-Victor, acquired by the BN at the time of the Revolution).

Manuscrits français 23042, collection of documents concerning the reign of Louis XIII (Minimes, acquired by the BN at the time of the Revolution).

Manuscrits français 23054, letters and documents concerning the history of Spain, France, Italy and Malta, 1589–1626 (Missions-Étrangères, acquired by the BN at the time of the Revolution).

Manuscrits français 23194–8, letters and documents concerning French internal affairs during the reign of Henri IV (Missions-Étrangères).

Manuscrits français 24917, collection of documents concerning the reign of Louis XIII (Missions-Étrangères).

Nouvelles acquisitions françaises 238–40, original letters concerning the history of Normandy, 1585–1659 (collected by the antiquary Lechaudé d'Anisy and acquired by the BN in 1865).

Nouvelles acquisitions françaises 728–39, copies of the registers of the *parlement* of Brittany, 1557–1669.

Nouvelles acquisitions françaises 999, accounts of the *marine de Ponant* for 1610.

Nouvelles acquisitions françaises 1095, original letters of the early seventeenth century, mostly coming from the archives of the *bureau des finances* at Caen.

Nouvelles acquisitions françaises 23798, financial documents, including some accounts for Bayonne annotated by Sully.

Nouvelles acquisitions françaises 25116, documents concerning Sully, his family and his various public offences.

Cinq cents de Colbert 16–20, collection of original documents and copies concerning French affairs between 1458 and 1635 (the *Collection des Cinq Cents de Colbert* was acquired by the royal library in 1732).

Cinq cents de Colbert 41, financial documents of the late sixteenth and early seventeenth centuries, from the library of J.-A. de Thou.

Cinq cents de Colbert 210–11, inventories of the French artillery and its equipment, 1611–12.

Cinq cents de Colbert 254–5, collection of documents concerning the administration of Paris.

Collection Dupuy 90–4, a collection of original documents and copies concerning the end of Henri IV's reign and the reign of Louis XIII (many of the copies are in the writing of Pierre Dupuy; it was in 1754 that the royal library acquired the collection of the brothers Dupuy).

Collection Dupuy 154, documents concerning Provence, 1239–1630.

Collection Dupuy 240, documents concerning political affairs in France, 1593–1619.

Collection Dupuy 407, letters mostly written by members of the French royal family, 1582–1604.

Collection Dupuy 562, documents concerning the sovereign courts, 1447–1639.

Collection Dupuy 689, documents concerning French financial, religious and political history, 1549–1633.

Collection Clairambault 312–458, a collection of original documents and copies concerning the history of France in the sixteenth and seventeenth centuries, drawn from many sources for the education of the *dauphin* under Bossuet (the collection of Pierre de Clairambault was acquired by the BN at the time of the Revolution).

Collection de Périgord 6–8, a collection of copies of letters to the lords of Caumont-La Force (from the papers of Prunis, Leydet and the abbé Lespine, acquired by the BN in the first half of the nineteenth century).

2. *Archives Nationales, Paris*

E 1–26, *arrêts du conseil* from 1593 to 1610.

H 748/20, register of the proceedings of the estates of Languedoc, 1604–12.

K 99–108, 'monuments historiques', 1574–1610 (part of the collection on French history formed in 1794 from a variety of sources).

KK 147–56, accounts of the *argenterie*, of the *maison du roi* and of the *écurie*, during the reign of Henri IV.

O^1 2387, payment of officials of the *bâtiments*, 1605.

P 2665–70, copy of the register of the *chambre des comptes*, 1596–1610.

Z^1 A 158–9, copy of the register of the *cour des aides*, 1582–1629.

Z^1 F 135, register of the Paris *bureau des finances*, 1599.

120 AP 1–50, the *papiers de Sully*, comprising:

1 regulations made by the royal council, 1598–1610

2–11 general accounts, 1593–1610

12 royal gifts

13 provincial finances, 1598–1610

14–15 domain

16-18 *tailles*

19–20 *fermes*

21–4 royal debts

25–8 calculations for the budgets of 1610 and 1611

29–32 miscellaneous papers

33–4 royal debts

35–7 *rentes*, officers and monetary problems

38–43 *ponts et chaussées*

44–7 artillery
48 miscellaneous and personal papers

3. *Other libraries and archives in Paris*

(a) *Archives du Ministère des Affaires Étrangères*
Mémoires et documents, 766–7, internal affairs, 1604–26.
Mémoires et documents, 1700, a collection of documents concerning Provence, 1416–1626.

(b) *Bibliothèque de l'Institut de France*
[The Godefroy collection was the work of Théodore (1580–1649) and Denis II (1615–81) Godefroy, father and son who were both *historiographes royaux*; it was acquired by the Institut de France at the time of the Revolution.]
Godefroy 144, a collection of original documents and copies concerning the finances, 1491–1679 (from the papers of Villeroy).
Godefroy 191, original documents and copies concerning the French towns and provinces, 1225–1700.
Godefroy 262–72, original letters concerning the reigns of Henri IV and of Louis XIII (some of these volumes formerly belonged to Sillery).
Godefroy 284, a collection of original letters, mostly undated (from the papers of Puisieux, Villeroy's son-in-law and secretary of state after him).
Godefroy 375, copies of documents concerning Provence, 1480–1650.

4. *Libraries and archives in the French provinces*

Agen, Archives Communales, CC 123, letters of M. de Selves, *député en cour*, to the municipality.
Albi, Archives Départementales du Tarn, C 55, register of proceedings of the estates of Languedoc, 1599–1607.
Avignon, Archives Communales, AA 46, letters to the municipality.
Bordeaux, Archives Départementales de la Gironde, C 3873–5, registers of the *bureau des finances* at Bordeaux, 1601–10.
Bordeaux, Archives Départementales de la Gironde, 1B 18, register of edicts approved by the *parlement* of Bordeaux, 1603–7.
Bordeaux, Bibliothèque Municipale, Ms. 371, copy of the proceedings of the *parlement* of Bordeaux, 1584–1620.
Bourges, Archives Départementales du Cher, C 973–80, register of correspondence of the *bureau des finances* at Bourges, 1598–1608.
Caen, Archives Départementales du Calvados, C 1680, documents concerning the armaments of the castle of Caen.
Caen, Archives Départementales du Calvados C (not yet inventoried), proceedings of the *bureau des finances* at Caen, 1600–8
Châlons-sur-Marne, Archives Départementales de la Marne, C 2490–1, register of the *bureau des finances* at Châlons, 1597–1610.
Châlons-sur-Marne, Archives Communales, AA 8, letters to the municipality, 1593–1609.

Chantilly, Musée Condé, Ms. 534, book of poems formerly belonging to Sully and including some in his hand.

Chantilly, Musée Condé, Ms. 1325, a collection of maps and plans of north-eastern France, 1602–3 (acquired at the Beckford sale).

Chantilly, Musée Condé, Ms. 1326, a similar collection of maps, 1602–3 (given to the duc d'Aumale by 'M. de Molènes').

Dijon, Archives Départementales de la Côte d'Or, C 3419, register of correspondence of the *parlement* of Dijon, 1598–1607.

Dijon, Archives Départementales de la Côte d'Or, C 3075–6, register of the proceedings of the estates of Burgundy, 1602–13.

Dijon, Archives Départementales de la Côte d'Or, C 3351, correspondence of the estates of Burgundy.

Dijon, Archives Départementales de la Côte d'Or, C 2082 bis, register of royal enactments concerning the *bureau des finances* at Dijon, 1605–10.

Dijon, Archives Départementales de la Côte d'Or, C 2090–9, register of correspondence of the *bureau des finances* at Dijon, 1599–1623.

Dijon, Bibliothèque Municipale, fonds Saverot, 1496–1501, extracts from the registers of the *parlement* of Dijon, 1515–1693.

Grenoble, Archives Départementales de l'Isère, B 2920, letters-patent of Louis XIII 1618–27.

Grenoble, Archives Municipales, BB 80, consular deliberations for 1613.

Langres, Archives Municipales, Ms. 920, accounts of the Langres treasurer, 1607–12.

Langres, Archives Municipales, Ms. 1173, documents concerning the fortifications of Langres.

Lyon, Archives Départementales du Rhône, C 418, royal legislation, 1605–6.

Lyon, Bibliothèque Municipale, AA 49, 54 and 78, original letters to the municipality.

Mâcon, Archives Communales, CC 103, account of the town's use of revenues, sent to Sully in 1607.

Marseille, Archives Départementales des Bouches-du-Rhône, C 9–11, deliberations of the estates of Provence, 1602–10.

Marseille, Archives Départementales des Bouches-du-Rhône, C 468, documents concerning *ponts et chaussées*, 1611–97.

Mende, Archives Départementales de la Lozère, C 536–8, copies of the register of the estates of Languedoc, 1599–1610.

Poitiers, Bibliothèque Municipale, Ms. 298, memoirs and correspondence of the sr Du Maurier (1566–1636).

Reims, Bibliothèque Municipale, fonds Tarbé, carton xii, n⁰ 176, marriage contract of Maximilien II de Béthune (1609).

Reims, Bibliothèque Municipale, fonds Tarbé, carton xiii, n⁰ 33–4, documents concerning Sully's private property.

Reims, Bibliothèque Municipale, fonds Tarbé, carton xiii, n⁰ 45 and 53–5, papers concerning Françoise de Créquy.

Rouen, Archives Départementales de la Seine maritime, C 1119–22, register of the *bureau des finances* at Rouen, 1600–8.

Salins, Bibliothèque Municipale, Ms. 37, collection of letters and other documents, apparently formed by Étienne Puget.

5. *British Museum, London*

Cotton manuscripts, Caligula E X–XI, original letters and copies concerning Anglo-French relations during the reign of Henri IV (collected by Sir Robert Cotton and acquired by the royal library in 1700).

Stowe manuscripts, 166–7, the papers of Sir Thomas Edmondes (1592–1633) (this collection was purchased by the British Museum from the earl of Ashburnham in 1883).

Additional manuscripts 15726, an artillery-manual, probably drawn up during the grand-mastership of Maximilien II de Béthune.

Additional manuscripts 19272, 'autograph letters of foreign princes and distinguished persons'.

Additional manuscripts 21117, maps and plans of fortresses in France, executed for Sully.

Additional manuscripts 21512, original letters written by eminent Frenchmen, 1452–1852.

Additional manuscripts 25593, a collection of documents concerning Sully's fortune.

C. CONTEMPORARY PRINTED BOOKS

Aubigné, Théodore-Agrippa d', *Histoire Universelle*, ed. A. de Ruble (10 vols, Paris, 1886–97).

Bassompierre, François, maréchal de, *Mémoires*, ed. marquis de Chantérac (4 vols, Paris, 1870–7).

Benoist, Élie, *Histoire de l'édit de Nantes* (5 vols, Delft, 1693–5).

Bodin, Jean, *Les six livres de la République* (Paris, 1583).

Chastillon, Claude de, *Topographie française* (Paris, 1648).

Coryat, Thomas, *Crudities* (3 vols, London, 1776).

Dallington, Robert, *The view of Fraunce* (London, 1604).

Davelourt, Daniel, *L'Arcenal et magazin de l'artillerie* (Paris, 1610).

Davelourt, Daniel, *L'Artillier* (Paris, 1606).

Davelourt, Daniel, *Briefve instruction sur le faict de l'artillerie de France* (Paris, 1597).

Davelourt, Daniel, *Épitome ou abregé sur le faict de l'artillerie* (Paris, 1619).

Davelourt, Daniel, *Recherches et considerations sur le faict de l'artillerie* (Paris, 1617).

Duchesne, André, *Histoire généalogique de la maison de Béthune* (Paris, 1639).

Errard, Jean, *Le premier livre des instruments mathématiques méchaniques* (Nancy, 1584).

Errard, Jean, *La fortification reduicte en art et demonstrée* (Paris, 1604).

Expilly, Claude, *Plaidoyez* (Paris, 1612).
Fumée, Jacques de, *L'arsenac de la milice françoise* (Paris, 1607).
Groulart, Claude, *Mémoires et voyages en Cour* (1588–1600) (ed. Michaud and Poujoulat, Paris, 1838).
Hennequin, Jean, *Guidon general des financiers* (Paris, 1585).
Hobier, Ithier, *De la construction d'une gallaire* (Paris, 1622).
Hurault, Philippe, *Mémoires*, ed. J. A. Buchon (Paris, 1838).
Jeannin, Pierre, *Négociations*, ed. J. A. Buchon (Paris, 1838).
Le Mercure François (Paris, 1611).
L'Estoile, Pierre de, *Journal*, ed. L.-R. Lefèvre (3 vols, Paris, 1948–60).
Palma-Cayet, Pierre-Victor, *Chronologie septenaire* (Paris, 1607).
Richelieu, Armand Jean Du Plessis, cardinal de, *Mémoires*, ed. Courcel, Delavaud and Lacour-Gayet (10 vols, Paris, 1908–31).
Sauval, Henri, *Histoire et recherches des antiquités de la ville de Paris* (3 vols, Paris, 1724).
Tavernier, Melchior, *Carte géographique des postes* (Paris, 1632).
Thou, Jacques-Auguste de, *Histoire Universelle* (16 vols, London, 1734).
Turenne, Henri de La Tour d'Auvergne, vicomte de, *Mémoires*, ed. G. Baguenault de Puchesse (Paris, 1901).

D. COLLECTIONS OF DOCUMENTS

M. le marquis d'Albon (ed.), 'Apologie de Brandis, défenseur de Montmélian: *Documents d'Histoire*, iii (1912), 198–216.
Archives curieuses de l'histoire de France, ed. M. L. Cimber and F. Danjou (27 vols, Paris, 1837).
G. d'Avenel (ed.), *Lettres, instructions diplomatiques et papiers d'État du cardinal de Richelieu* (8 vols, Paris, 1853–77).
B. Barbiche (ed.), *Correspondance du nonce en France Innocenzo del Bufalo, évêque de Camerino (1601–1604)* (Rome/Paris, 1964).
N. Barozzi and G. Berchet (ed.), *Relazioni degli stati europei, lette al senato degli ambasciatori veneti nel secolo decimosettimo* (10 vols, Venice, 1856–8).
E. de Barthélemy (ed.), 'Un page des comptes de Sully', *Bulletin du Bibliophile* (1865), 85–8.
R. de Beaurepaire (ed.), *Cahiers des états de Normandie sous le règne de Henri IV* (2 vols, Rouen 1880–2).
Berger de Xivrey. See Xivrey.
T. Birch (ed.), *An historical view of the negotiations between the courts of England, France and Brussels, 1592–1617* (London, 1740).
A. M. de Boislisle (ed.), *Correspondance des contrôleurs-généraux des finances* (3 vols, Paris, 1874–9).
G. Boussinesq (ed.), 'Règlement des finances du 19 janvier 1599', *Revue Henri IV*, i (1905), 189–90.
D. J. Buisseret (ed.), 'Lettres inédites de Sully aux trésoriers-généraux de France à Caen (1599–1610)', *Annales de Normandie*, xiii (1963), 269–304.

G. G. Butler (ed.), *Edmondes Papers* (London, 1913).

Calendar of manuscripts of the marquis of Salisbury at Hatfield House (15 vols, London, 1883, etc.).

Sir George Carew, *A Relation of the state of France*. See Birch.

P. Champion (ed.), *Sommaire mémorial de Jules Gassot* (Paris, 1934).

M. Champollion-Figeac (ed.), *Documents historiques inédits (Documents inédits sur l'histoire de France)* (4 vols, Paris, 1848).

M. L. Cimber et F. Danjou. See *Archives curieuses*.

P. Clément, *Portraits historiques* (Paris, 1855).

L.-H. Collard and E.-J. Ciprut (ed.), *Nouveaux documents sur le Louvre* (Paris, 1963).

A. Desjardins (ed.), *Négociations diplomatiques de la France avec la Toscane* (6 vols, Paris, 1859–86).

A. Galitzin (ed.), *Lettres inédites de Henri IV* (Paris, 1860).

J. Garnier (ed.), *Correspondance de la mairie de Dijon* (3 vols, Dijon, 1870).

E. Halphen (ed.), *Documents inédits concernant la prise de Montmélian* (Paris, 1885).

Henri IV. See Galitzin, Lajeunie and Xivrey.

F. A. Isambert (ed.), *Recueil général des anciennes lois françaises* (29 vols, Paris, 1821–33).

A. Isnard (ed.), *Actes Royaux*, vol. i [origins–1610] (Paris, 1910).

J. E. M. Lajeunie (ed.), 'Correspondance entre Henri IV et Béthune . . . 1602–1604', *Mémoires et documents publiés par la société d'histoire et d'archéologie de Genève*, xxxviii (1952), 189–474.

L. Lalanne (ed.), *Oeuvres de Malherbe* (4 vols, Paris, 1862).

P. de La Raudière (ed.), *Les Estranges amours de la reine Myrrha* (Paris, 1930).

Lettres Missives. See Xivrey.

J. R. Mallet, *Comptes rendus de l'administration des finances du royaume de France* (London, 1789).

F. de Mallevoüe (ed.), *Les Actes de Sully . . .* (Paris, 1911).

Memorials of affairs of state in the reigns of queen Elizabeth and king James I . . . (3 vols, London, 1725).

J. Nouaillac (ed.), 'Dix lettres inédites de Sully', *Revue des Questions Historiques*, li (1914), 136–45.

J. Nouaillac (ed.), *Un envoyé hollandais à la cour de Henri IV: lettres inédites de François Aerssen à Jacques Valcke (1599–1603)* (Paris, 1908).

A. Péricaud (ed.), *Notes et documents pour servir à l'histoire de Lyon . . . (1594–1610)* (Lyons, 1845).

A. Poirson (ed.), *Mémoires de Sancy et de Villeroy, documents divers . . .* (Paris, 1868).

Registres des délibérations du bureau de la ville de Paris, ed. Bonnardot, Tuetey, Guérin, etc, (15 vols, Paris, 1883, etc.).

Report on the manuscripts of lord de L'Isle and Dudley preserved at Penhurst Place (5 vols, London, 1925–62).

R. Ritter (ed.), *Lettres du cardinal du Florence sur Henri IV et sur la France, 1596–1598* (Paris, 1955).

Robillard de Beaurepaire. See Beaurepaire.

L. Romier (ed.), *Lettres et chevauchées du bureau des finances de Caen sous Henri IV* (Paris, 1910).

L. Romier (ed.), 'Lettres inédites de Sully aux trésoriers-généraux de France à Caen, 1599–1610', *Bulletin Historique et Philologique* (1910), 569–70.

E. Soulié and E. de Barthélemy (ed.), *Journal de Jean Héroard* . . . (2 vols, Paris, 1868).

J. de Sturler, 'Documents diplomatiques et administratifs relatifs aux différends commerciaux et maritimes survenus entre les Pays-Bas et la France, 1599–1607', *Bulletin de la commission royale d'histoire de Belgique* (1939).

E. Thoison (ed.), 'Un traité inconnu entre Henri IV et Mayenne', *Bulletin Historique et Philologique* (1894) 452–63.

N. Valois (ed.), *Inventaire des arrêts du conseil d'État (règne de Henri IV)* (2 vols, Paris, 1886 and 1893).

M. Vilepelet (ed.), 'Inventaire de l'Arsenal de Lyon (septembre 1567)', *Bulletin Historique et Philologique* (1913), 388–408.

B. de Xivrey and J. Guadet (eds), *Lettres Missives de Henri IV* . . . (9 vols, Paris, 1843–76).

E. SECONDARY WORKS

L. Anquez, *Henri IV et l'Allemagne* (Paris, 1887).

Histoire des assemblées politiques des Réformés de France (1573–1622) (Paris, 1859).

R. Ashton, *The Crown and the money-market, 1603–1640* (Oxford, 1960).

G. d'Avenel, *Richelieu et la monarchie absolue* (4 vols, Paris, 1884–90).

G. E. Aylmer, *The King's Servants: the civil service of Charles I, 1625–1642* (London, 1961).

G. Bapst, *Histoire des joyaux des la Couronne de France* (Paris, 1889).

B. Barbiche, *Étude sur l'œuvre de restauration financière de Sully (1596–1610)*, summarized in *Positions des Thèses* . . . [of the École des Chartes], 1960.

B. Barbiche, 'Une tentative de réforme monétaire à la fin du règne d'Henri IV', *XVIIe siècle*, lxi (1963), 3–17.

B. Barbiche and D. J. Buisseret, 'Les convictions religieuses de Sully', *Bibliothèque de l'École des Chartes*, cxxi (1963), 223–30.

B. Barbiche and D. J. Buisseret, 'Sully et la surintendance des finances', *Bibliothèque de l'École des Chartes*, cxxiii (1965), 538–43.

L. Batiffol, *La vie intime d'une reine de France au XVIIe siècle; Marie de Médicis* (2 vols, Paris, 1931).

L. Batiffol, 'Le mail de l'Arsenal au XVIIIe siècle', *Bulletin de la société de l'histoire de Paris et de l'Ile-de-France*, lvi (1929), 5–22.

L. Batiffol, 'Le trésor de la Bastille de 1605 à 1611', *Revue Henri IV*, iii (1909–12), 200–9.

E. Baudson, *Un urbaniste au XVIIe siècle: Clément Métezeau* (Mézières, 1956).

E. Belgrand, *Les travaux souterrains de Paris* (5 vols, Paris, 1872–87).

A. Berty, *La Renaissance monumentale en France* (Paris, 1864).

A. Berty, *Topographie historique du vieux Paris* (8 vols, Paris, 1885–97).

M. Bishop, *Champlain, the life of fortitude* (London, 1949).

A. M. de Boislisle, *Chambre des comptes de Paris* (Nogent-le-Rotrou, 1873).

P. Boissonade, 'L'essai de restauration des ports et de la vie maritime en Languedoc de 1593 à 1661 et son échec', *Annales du Midi*, xlvi (1934), 98–121.

P. Boissonade, 'Les voies de communications terrestres et fluviales en Poitou sous le règne de Henri IV', *Revue Henri IV*, ii (1907–8), 193–228 and 295–311; and iii (1909), 65–102.

G. Bonnault d'Houet, *La première ambulance sous Henri IV* (Paris, 1919).

H. Boone, 'Le protestantisme à Saint-Hilaire-sur-Autise,' *Bulletin philologique et historique* (1926–7), 33–93.

E. Buat, *L'artillerie de campagne* (Paris, 1911).

D. J. Buisseret, 'The communications of France during the reconstruction of Henri IV', *Economic History Review*, second series, xviii (1965), 43–53.

D. J. Buisseret, 'The French Mediterranean fleet under Henri IV', *The Mariner's Mirror*, 1 (1964), 297–306.

D. J. Buisseret, 'Les *ingénieurs du roi* de Henri IV', *Bulletin de Géographie*, lxxvii (1964), 13–84.

D. J. Buisseret, 'The legend of Sully', *The Historical Journal*, v (1962), 181–8.

D. J. Buisseret, 'L'organisation défensive des frontières au temps de Henri IV', *Revue Historique de l'Armée*, xx (4) (1964), 25–31.

D. J. Buisseret, 'A stage in the development of the *intendants*; the reign of Henri IV', *The Historical Journal*, ix (1966), 27–38.

D. J. Buisseret and B. Barbiche. See Barbiche.

J. Cadis, 'Histoire de l'arsenal maritime de Toulon', *Mémorial de l'artillerie française*, xxvi (1952), 255–96.

A. Callery, *Histoire des institutions financières de l'ancienne France* (Fontainebleau, 1878).

L.-J.-M. de Carné, *Les états de Bretagne* (Paris, 1868).

H. Carré, *Sully, sa vie et son oeuvre* (Paris, 1932).

A. Chamberland, 'Le budget de la généralité de Châlons en 1602', *Revue Henri IV*, iii (1909–12), 151–65.

A. Chamberland, 'Le conseil des finances en 1596 et 1597 et les *Économies Royales*', *Revue Henri IV*, i (1905–6).

A. Chamberland, 'Jean Chandon et le conflit entre la cour des aides et le conseil du roi', *Revue Henri IV*, ii (1907–8), 113–25.

A. Chamberland, 'Recherches critiques sur les réformes financières en Champagne à l'époque de Henri IV et de Sully', *Travaux de l'Académie de Reims*, cxi (1901), 243–71.

A. Chamberland, 'La tournée de Sully et de Rybault dans les généralités en 1596', supplement to the *Revue Henri IV*, iii (1909).

R. Charlier-Meniolle, *L'assemblée des Notables tenue à Rouen en 1596* (Paris, 1911).

J.-P. Charmeil, *Les trésoriers de France à l'époque de la Fronde* (Paris, 1964).

J.-J. Clamageran, *Histoire de l'impôt en France* (3 vols, Paris, 1867–76).

Sir George Clark, *The seventeenth century* (Oxford, 1928).

H. Clouzot, 'Philibert de L'Orme, grand architecte du roi mégiste', *Revue du seizième siècle*, viii (1921), 243–8.

G. Cohen, *Écrivains français en Hollande dans la première moitié du XVIIᵉ siècle* (Paris, 1920).

P. de Cossé-Brissac, *Châteaux de France disparus* (Paris, 1947).

R. Couzard, *Une ambassade à Rome sous Henri IV* (Paris, 1901).

F. de Crue, *Les derniers desseins de Henri IV* (Paris, 1902).

F. de Crue, *Henri IV et les députés de Genève* (Geneva/Paris, 1901).

A. Des Cilleuls, *Henri IV et la chambre de justice de 1606* (Nancy, n.d.).

A. Desclozeaux, 'Étude critique sur les *Économies Royales*', *Revue Historique*, lii (1893), 316–22.

P. Des Forts, *Le château de Villebon* (Paris, 1914).

F. C. Dietz, *English public finance, 1558–1641* (New York, 1932).

J. G. van Dillen, 'Isaac Le Maire et le commerce des actions de la compagnie des Indes Orientales', *Revue d'histoire moderne*, x (1935).

R. Doucet, *Les institutions de la France au XVIᵉ siècle* (Paris, 1948).

R. Doucet, 'Les finances de la France en 1614', *Revue d'histoire économique et sociale*, xviii (1930), 133–63.

R. Doucet, 'Le grand parti de Lyon au XVIᵉ siècle', *Revue Historique*, clxxi (1933), 473–513; and clxxii (1933), 1–41.

P. Du Colombier, *Le style Henri IV-Louis XIII* (Paris, 1941).

C. Dufayard, *Le connétable de Lesdiguières* (Paris, 1892).

M. Dumolin, *Études de topographie parisienne* (3 vols, Paris, 1929–31).

S. Dupain, *Notice historique sur le pavé de Paris* (Paris, 1881).

L. Dussieux, *Étude biographique sur Sully* (Paris, 1887).

C.-E. Engel, *L'Ordre de Malte en Méditerranée* (Monaco, 1957).

É. Éverat, *Le bureau des finances de Riom, 1551–1790* (Riom, 1900).

G. Fagniez, *Économie sociale de la France au temps de Henri IV* (Paris, 1897).

L. Febvre, 'Aspects méconnus d'un renouveau religieux en France entre 1590 et 1620', *Annales* xiii, (1958), 639–50.

R. Forster, *The nobility of Toulouse in the 18th century; a social and economic study* (Baltimore, 1960).

O. Fox, 'Notice sur Isaac Casaubon', *Bulletin de la Société de l'histoire du Protestantisme français*, xiv (1865), 185–95 and 262–80.

R. Fromilhague, *La vie de Malherbe* (Paris, n.d.).

C. Gauchéry-Grodecki, 'L'architecture en Berry sous le règne de Henri IV et au début du XVIIᵉ siècle (1590–1620)', *Mémoires de l'union des sociétés savantes de Bourges*, iii (1951–2), 77–131.

G. Gaufrès, *Philippe Mornay de Bauves, ou l'éducation d'un gentilhomme protestant au XVIᵉ siècle* (Paris, 1868).

P. Gaxotte, *Le siècle de Louis XV* (2 vols, Paris, 1935).

P

J. J. Guiffrey, 'Logements d'artistes au Louvre', *Nouvelles archives de l'art français*, ii (1873).

G. Hanotaux, *Études historiques sur le XVIe et le XVIIe siècle en France* (Paris, 1886).

G. Hanotaux, *Sur les chemins de l'histoire* (2 vols, Paris, 1924).

G. Hanotaux (ed.), *Un bon Français, Sully* (Paris, 1941).

H. Hauser, *Les débuts du capitalisme* (Paris, 1925).

H. Hauser, *La pensée et l'action économiques du cardinal de Richelieu* (Paris, 1944).

H. Hauser, 'Un précurseur: Jean Bodin, Angevin (1529 ou 1530–1596)', *Annales*, iii (1931), 379–87.

P. Henrard, *Henri IV et la princesse de Condé, 1609–1610* (Brussels, 1870).

J. H. Hexter, 'The education of the aristocracy in the Renaissance', *Journal of Modern History*, xxii (1950), 1–20.

F. H. Hinsley, *Power and the pursuit of peace* (Cambridge, 1963).

J. Houlet, *L'hôtel de Sully au Marais* (Paris, 1964).

H. Jadart, 'Sully et les plantations d'arbres', *Revue Henri IV*, i (1905–6), 59–65.

B. de Jouvenel, *On power; its nature and the history of its growth* (London, 1948).

E. Jung, *Henri IV écrivain* (Paris, 1855).

J. E. King, *Science and rationalism in the government of Louis XIV* (Baltimore, 1949).

J. Koren, *The history of statistics* (New York, 1918).

Abbé L. Lacroix, 'Richelieu à Luçon', *Mémoires de la société des antiquaires de l'Ouest*, 2nd series, xii (1899), 79–376.

P. Lacroix, 'La porte et place de France sous le règne de Henri IV', *Gazette des Beaux-Arts* (1870), 561–6.

P. P. Laffleur de Kermaingnant, 'Sommes dûes par Henri IV à l'Angleterre', *Revue Henri IV*, i (1905–6), 66–8.

E. Lambert, 'Bayonne', *Congrès archéologique de France*, cii (1939), 507–22.

C. de La Roncière, 'Les routes de l'Inde', *Revue des Questions Historiques*, lxxvi (1904), 157–209.

B. de La Tourrasse, 'Le château-neuf de St-Germain-en-Laye', *Gazette des Beaux-Arts* (1924), 68–95.

A. Laugel, *Henry de Rohan, son rôle politique et militaire sous Louis XIII (1579–1638)* (Paris, 1889).

H. Lavedan, *Histoire de l'urbanisme; Renaissance et temps modernes* (Paris, 1941).

P. Lecestre, *Notice sur l'Arsenal royal de Paris* (Paris, 1916).

B. Ledain, 'Les maires de Poitiers', *Mémoires de la société des antiquaires de l'Ouest*, 2nd series, xx (1897), 215–774.

E. G. Léonard, *Le protestant français*, (Paris, 1953).

T. Lhuillier, *L'ancien château royal de Montceaux-en-Brie* (Paris, 1885).

A. C. Littleton and B. S. Yamey, *Studies in the history of accounting* (London, 1956).

C. Loriquet, *Catalogue historique et descriptive du musée de Reims* (Reims, 1881).

F. de Mallevouë, 'Les devises de Sully', *Bulletin de la société d'histoire de Paris et de l'Ile-de-France*, xl (1913) 172–82.

J.-H. Mariéjol, *Henri IV et Louis XIII* (vol. vi of the *Histoire de France*, ed. E. Lavisse, Paris, 1905).

L. Martin, *Histoire de la ville de Sully-sur-Loire en Orléanais* (Sully-sur-Loire, 1962).

L. Martin, *Le tombeau de Sully au château de Sully-sur-Loire* (Sully-sur-Loire, 1935).

L. Martin, 'Sully architecte et bâtisseur des villes', *Urbanisme*, lxxv (1942), 72–80.

M.-M. Martin, *Sully-le-Grand* (Paris, 1959).

P. Masson, *Les galères de France, 1481–1781* (Paris, 1938).

A. Miron de L'Espinay, *François Miron et l'administration municipale de Paris sous Henri IV de 1604 à 1606* (Paris, 1885).

A. Moreau de Jonnès, *État économique et sociale de la France, 1598–1715* (Paris, 1867).

J. L. Motley, *The life and death of John of Barneveldt, advocate of Holland* (2 vols, London, 1874).

R. Mousnier, 'L'assassinat de Henri IV, 16 mai 1610' (Paris, 1964). *La vénalité des offices sous Henri IV et Louis XIII* (Rouen, 1945).

R. Mousnier, 'État et commissaire . . .', chapter in *Forschungen zu Staat und Verfassung: Festgabe für Fritz Hartung* (Berlin, 1958).

R. Mousnier, 'L'évolution des finances publiques en France et en Angleterre', *Revue Historique*, ccv (1951), 1–23.

R. Mousnier, 'L'opposition politique bourgeoise à la fin du XVIe siècle et au début du XVIIe siècle, *Revue Historique*, ccxiii (1955), 1–20.

R. Mousnier, 'Sully et le conseil d'État et des finances', *Revue Historique*, cxcii (1947), 68–86.

A. Mousset, 'Les Francine', *Mémoires de la société d'histoire de Paris et de l'Ile-de-France*, li (1930), 1–53.

J. U. Nef, *Cultural foundations of industrial civilization* (Cambridge, 1958).

J. U. Nef, *Industry and government in France and England, 1540–1640* (Cornell, 1957).

J. U. Nef, 'Comparison of industrial growth in France and England, 1540–1640', *Journal of political economy*, xliv (1936), 289–317, 505–33 and 643–66.

J. Nouaillac, *Villeroy, secrétaire d'État et ministre de Charles IX, Henri III et Henri IV, 1543–1610* (Paris, 1909).

J. Nouaillac, 'Henri IV et les Croquants du Limousin', *Bulletin historique et philologique* (1912), 321–50.

H. Ouvré, *Aubery Du Maurier* (Paris, 1853).

H. Ouvré 'Essai sur l'histoire de la ville de Poitiers', *Mémoires de la société des antiquaires de l'Ouest*, xxii (1855), 488–92.

J. de Pablo, 'Contribution à l'étude de l'histoire des institutions militaires huguenotes', *Archiv für Reformationsgeschichte*, xlviii (1957), 192–216.

G. Pagès, 'Essai sur l'évolution des institutions administratives en France', *Revue d'histoire moderne*, vii (1932), 8–57 and 113–37.

R. R. Palmer, 'The national idea in France before the revolution', *Journal of the history of ideas*, i (1940), 95–111.

J. Pannier, *L'Église réformée de Paris sous Henri IV* (Paris, 1911).

C. Pfister, 'Les *Économies Royales* de Sully . . .', *Revue Historique*, liv (1894), 300–24; lv (1894), 67–82 and 291–302; and lvi (1894), 39–48 and 304–39.

L. Pingaud, 'Henri IV et Louis XIV', *Revue des Questions Historiques*, xlvi (1889), 169–204.

J. Permezel, *La politique financière de Sully dans la généralité de Lyon* (Lyons, 1935).

H. Pigeonneau, *Histoire du commerce de la France* (2 vols, Paris, 1885–97).

H. Pinsseau, *Le canal Henri IV ou canal de Briare* (Paris/Orléans, 1943).

M. Poète, *Paris durant la grande époque classique* (Paris, 1911).

A. Poirson, *Histoire du règne de Henri IV* (4 vols, Paris, 1865).

A Rébillon, *Les sources de l'histoire des états de Bretagne* (Rennes, 1932).

F. Robiou, 'La politique de Henri IV en Italie', *Revue des Questions Historiques*, xxi (1877), 5–34.

P. Robiquet, *Histoire municipale de Paris* (3 vols, Paris, 1880–1904).

E. Rott, *Henri IV, les Suisses, et la Haute-Italie* (Paris, 1882).

C.-A. Sainte-Beuve, *Vues sur l'histoire de France* (*Cahiers de l'unité française*, Paris, 1946).

B. Schnapper, *Les rentes au XVIᵉ siècle: histoire d'un instrument de crédit* (Paris, 1957).

E. Silberner, *La guerre et la pensée économique du XVIᵉ au XVIIᵉ siècle* (Paris, 1939).

F. C. Spooner, *L'économie mondiale et les frappes monétaires en France* (1493–1680).

M. Steichen, *Mémoire sur la vie et les travaux de Simon Stevin* (Brussels, 1846).

General L. Susane, *Histoire de l'artillerie française* (Paris, 1874).

N. M. Sutherland, *The French secretaries of State in the age of Catherine de Medici* (London, 1962).

V. L. Tapié, *La France de Louis XIII et de Richelieu* (Paris, 1952).

H. Thomas, *Rosny-sur-Seine* (Paris, 1889).

E. Trocmé and M. Delafosse, *Le commerce rochelais de la fin du XVᵉ siècle au début du XVIIIᵉ siècle* (Paris, 1952).

C. Turgeon, 'Les idées économiques de Sully', *Revue d'histoire économique et sociale*, xi (1923), 249–69.

A. P. Usher, *The history of the grain trade in France, 1400–1710* (Cambridge, Mass., 1913).

P. de Vaissière, *Henri IV* (Paris, 1925).

J. Viénot, *Histoire de la Réforme française* (2 vols, Paris, 1934).

E. J. M. Vignon, *Études historiques sur l'administration des voies publiques en France* (3 vols, Paris, 1862).

P. Viollet, *Le roi et ses ministres* (Paris, 1912).

B. Zeller, *La minorité de Louis XIII: Marie de Médicis et Sully* (Paris, 1892).

B. Zeller, *Louis XIII: Marie de Médicis, chef du conseil* (Paris, 1898).

B. Zeller, *Louis XIII: Marie de Médicis, Richelieu ministre* (Paris, 1899).

G. Zeller, *Les institutions de la France au XVIᵉ siècle* (Paris, 1948).

G. Zeller, *L'organisation défensive des frontières du nord et de l'est au XVIIᵉ siècle* (Paris, 1928).

G. Zeller, 'L'administration monarchique avant les intendants', *Revue Historique*, cxcvii (1947), 180–215.

G. Zeller, 'L'industrie en France avant Colbert', *Revue d'histoire économique et sociale*, xxviii (1950), 3–20.

Index

Brouage (Charente-Maritime), 123, 131
Brûlart, Nicolas, sieur de Sillery. *See* Sillery
Bueil, Jacqueline de, comtesse de Moret. *See* Moret
Bugey (region), 50
Bunel, Jacob (painter), 133, 148, 196
Bureaux des finances, 31, 59, 61, 62, 67, 72, 88; Bordeaux, 22, 61, 62, 64, 65; Bourges, 22, 61, 88; budget analyses, 75–8, (table 3) 77; Caen, 22, 61, 62, 63, 64–5, 88; Châlons-sur-Marne, 22, 61, 62, 63, 64; *élections*, 31, 57, 59, 76; English debts, 83; *épargne*, 59–60, 74, 80, 86; expenditure, 79, 80, (table 4) 81, 107; farms, *fermes*, 60, 88, 103; financial cycle, 59–61, 74 *et seq.*, (table) 61, 75; generalities, 58, 60, 63, (table 2) 58; hierarchy (table), 58 *et seq.*; Lyons, 61; *pays d'élections*, 58–60, 107, 108, 110, 112, 114, 119; *pays d'états*, 31, 58–60, 107, 114; Paris, 22, 57, 61, 62; Poitiers, 22, 61, 64; Rouen, 22, 61; subsidy to United Provinces (table), 82; taxes (graph), 78
Burgundy (province), 58, 88, 98, 100, 102, 127, 129, 155, 172; estates, 22, 31, 112, 155, 158; governor of, 51. *See also Parlements*

Cabeljau, Abraham (financier), 85
Caen (Calvados), 20, 22, 56, 61, 62, 63, 64–5, 88, 142, 153; *receveur* at, 68; *trésoriers de France* at, 107, 110. *See also Bureaux des finances*
Cahors (Lot), siege of, 150
Calais (Pas-de-Calais), 25; fortifications, 127
Canal-works, 107–8, 117–19, 128, 131, 132; expenditure, 107–8, 117, 118. *See* Aisne, Bordeaux, Briare, Carcassonne, Cher, Clain, Loire, Maine, Marseilles, Meuse, Netherlands, Seine, Vesle
Capelle-en-Thiérache, La (Aisne), fortifications, 123
Carcassonne (Aude), 113, 121, 131
—, bishop of, 90
Carew, Sir George (English ambassador), 46, 47, 70–1, 91, 162, 199, 200
Carlat (Cantal), château, 154
Casaubon, Isaac (scholar), 86

Cateau-Cambrésis, treaty of, 25
Catelet, Le (Nord), fortifications, 123
Catholic groups, 27, 33, 34, 40, 47, 70, 71, 152, 198–9; battles, 27–8, 83; Holy League (*Sainte Ligue*), 27, 33, 38, 42, 56, 83, 168
Caumont, Jacqueline de, 182
Cecil, Sir Robert, 48, 52, 53, 174
Cecil, William, Baron Burghley, 41
Chabannes, N., sieur de, *commissaire de l'artillerie*, 156
Chahu, Philippe (*trésorier*), 69
Châlons-sur-Marne (Marne), 22, 61, 62, 63, 67, 119, 129, 147, 159–60; bridge at, 65; *lieutenant* of, 111. *See also Bureaux des finances*
Chalon-sur-Saône (Saône-et-Loire), 129
Châlus (Haute-Vienne), 154
Chamberland, Albert (historian), 42, 61, 63, 79
Chambéry (Savoie), 156
Chambord, treaty of, 36
Champagne (province), 116, 124, 128, 129, 130
Channel coast, 131
Chappelle-d'Angillon, La (Cher), 187
Chansson, François de, *lieutenant du grand maître de l'artillerie*, 150, 212
Charbonnières-les-Bains (Rhône), siege of, 156, 158
Charles V (Holy Roman Emperor), 123
Charles IX of France, 27, 28, 38
Charles-Emmanuel of Savoy, duke. *See* Savoy
Charleville-Mézières (Ardennes), 159
Chartres (Eure-et-Loir), 152, 158, 186; siege of, 41
Chastillon, Claude de (engineer), 80, 108, 109, 116, 118, 128, 133–4, 138, 139, 157; his *Topographie française*, 128
Chastillon, Hugues (engineer), 128
Chastillon, Pierre, *intendant des fortifications*, 128
Châteaudun (Eure-et-Loir), 152
Châteauvieux, sieur de, André Perinnel. *See* Perrinel
Châtellerault (Vienne), 50, 52, 98; Protestant assembly at, 52–3, 177
Cher canal (Saint-Amand), 118
Cheverny, Philippe Hurault de, chancellor, 30
Chiverny, N., comte de, 153
Chronique bordelaise, quoted, 117

Montmartin, sieur de, Michel Moussart, *lieutenant du grand maître de l'artillerie*, 152, 212

Montmélian (Savoie), 153; fortifications, 121; siege of, 121, 156–7, 158

Montpellier (Hérault), *chambre des comptes* at, 94–5. *See also Parlements*

Montpensier, Henri de Bourbon, duc de, 65, 154

Monts, sieur de, Pierre Du Guast (Canadian pioneer), 70, 178

Morely, Nicolas de, *contrôleur-général de l'artillerie*, 144

Moret, Jacqueline de Bueil, comtesse de, 84, 98

Moret-sur-Loing (Seine-et-Marne), 42, 179

Mornay, Philippe de, sieur de Duplessis-Mornay. *See* Duplessis-Mornay.

Mortefontaine, sieur de, Siphorien de Lezines. *See* Lezines

Moselle river, 160

Motley, John Lothrop (writer), 200

Moulins (Allier), 110

Mousnier, Roland (historian), 103

Moussart, Michel. *See* Montmartin

Musée des Plans-Reliefs (Invalides), 121

Nantes (Loire-Atlantique), 94, bastions, 131; bridge, 116; edict of, 33, 45, 50, 83. *See also Parlements*

Napoleon Bonaparte, 192

Narbonne (Aude), 113

Naunton, Robert (later Sir), 44

Necker (German river), 192

Nef, John (historian), 173–4

Neuilly-sur-Seine (Hauts-de-Seine), 174

Nemours, duchy of, 56

Netherlands (Dutch), United Provinces, Holland, 35, 36, 53, 82–3, 85, 130, 147, 169; ambassador to, 70; conveyance of goods from, by canal, 117; 'Dutch finance', 103; pirates, 37; subsidy to (table), 82; truce with Spain, 53, 82

— (Spanish), 28, 34, 53, 66; fortifications, 123. *See also* Flanders

Neufville, Charles, marquis de Villeroy. *See* Alincourt

Neufville, Nicolas, sieur de Villeroy. *See* Villeroy

Nevers, sieur de, Miles Marion. *See* Marion

Neville, Sir Henry (English ambassador), 174

Nogaret, Jean-Louis de, duc d'Épernon. *See* Épernon

Nogent-le-Rotrou (Eure-et-Loir), 189

Normandy (province), 63, 131, 153, 154; estates, 31, 67, 96, 99, 108; *gens des comptes de*, 93; governor, 65

Novynce, Guillaume, sieur d'Aubigny, 63, 210

Noyons (Oise), siege of, 41

Nürnberg, 45

O, François, marquis d', sieur de Fresnes et de Maillebois (financier), 56, 71

Obigny, sieur d'. *See* Novynce

Orange, principality, 116, 154; bridge, 116

Orleans (Loiret), 43, 50, 153, 155, 158; bridge, 116, 117; floods at, 107; *lieutenant* for, 110; roads, 116, 117

Orme, Philibert de L' (architect), 148

Ornano, Alphonse duc d', 32, 97–8, 102, 152

Orval (Cher), 187

Orval, comte d', 107

Paiemen, sieur de. *See* Mesmes

Palatine, Elector, 127

Paris, 25–6, 44, 50, 51, 53, 61, 62, 63, 66, 67, 88, 92, 110, 111–12, 129, 131, 132–9, 143, 146–7, 148–9, 155, 156, 157, 158, 159, 162, 169, 176, 180, 182, 196, 202; Arsenal, site of, 118; bridges, 107, 117, 134; Châtelet, 25; Collège de France, 134–5; *conseil des finances*, 57, 60, 61; generality, 58; Hôpital Saint-Louis, 134; Ile de la Cité, 134; League stronghold, 28; Louvre, 25, 35, 132–3, 134, 137, 196; Notre Dame, 25, 137, 148; Place Dauphine, 134; Place de la République, 134; Place de France (Marais), 134–5; Place Royale (Place des Vosges), 42, 133–4, 135, 137, 189; Pont Neuf, 134, 137; *rentes*, 89; roads, 105, 116, 117, paving of, 135–6; Sainte Chapelle, 25; siege of, 28, 41; Tuileries, 132–3. *See also Bureaux des finances*

Parlements, 29, 31, 87–8, 90–100 *passim*, 103, 109–10, 166; Aix, 30, 94;

ANGLETERRE

DOVRE

LE PAS DE CALAIS

CALAIS

GRAVELINGHE

DVNCKERCK

CASSEL

BOVLONGNE

AIRE

MONTREVIL

BZTVNE

STAPLE

S. POL

MONSTREVIL

CROTOY

ABLEVILE

DOVRIANS

DIEPE

NORMANDIE

PICQVIGNI

AMIEN

BEAVES

OCCIDENT